THE NEW ELIZABETHANS

1952 – 1977

John Colville

COLLINS
St James's Place, London
1977

William Collins Sons and Co Ltd
London · Glasgow · Sydney · Auckland
Toronto · Johannesburg

First published in 1977
© John Colville 1977
ISBN 0 00 216241 5
Set in Monotype Bembo
Made and Printed in Great Britain by
William Collins Sons and Co Ltd, Glasgow

For Meg

Contents

Preface

This book attempts to describe some of the changes that have taken place in Britain between the Accession of Queen Elizabeth II on 6th February, 1952 and her Silver Jubilee twenty five years later. It makes no pretence to paint a detailed picture of events which dominated those years, for that would require volumes, both of words and statistics. It is rather an account of developments in the way of life of a generation, in the movement of power within society, in the morals and habits of the people, in the arts, industry, the economy, communications and the environment. Such an account cannot be anything but generalised, for there are many facets of every development, and many developments I have not attempted to describe.

This has been a transitional period in the history of civilisation, a transition from a society we can identify, because we were part of it, to a new one which is in the process of being radically altered, and the shape of which we can now dimly begin to foresee. In these twenty five revolutionary years men have walked on the Moon, ingenious machines have scooped and analysed the soil of Mars, cosmonauts have circled the world in space-ships; and on Earth itself sleeping giants have stretched their muscles in China, Africa and the Middle East, while the countries of Western Europe have taken the first halting steps towards unity. Communications have become at once so rapid and so distinct that far-away lands are found to be close neighbours, in time and vision if not in distance. For officials and businessmen, travel is a common episode, no longer an adventure; and at home the quarantine, which the English Channel long provided against foreign influence as effectively as against enemy armies and rabies, has vanished for ever. The beliefs and prejudices of a previous generation are scarcely discernible in their children.

In Britain the historic institutions have changed but little. New, and in some ways, more powerful ones have grown up alongside them. The United Kingdom, sorely tried by recurring troubles in the economy, and by a long and irrational civil war in Northern Ireland, has nevertheless retained much of its traditional stability. A great deal of the credit for that is due to the most ancient of all the institutions, the Monarchy. In an age of melting convictions and questionable creeds, the Queen's unassuming virtues and faultless example have stood out like a rock in a sea of troubles, lashed but unmoved by angry waves and changing tides. Neither she nor the Duke of Edinburgh nor their children have fought against change. They have adapted themselves to it with dignity and without rejecting the values that, whatever else changes, remain constant. It is therefore fitting that much of this book, published in the year of the Silver Jubilee, should be written against the background of the Monarchy.

I hope I shall not be judged too fanciful in relating some of the trends which have been noticeable in these years to the symbolism of the Coronation. At the end of that magnificent service and ceremony in 1953 there was a special benediction. It included the words:

'The Lord give you faithful Parliaments and quiet realms; sure defence against all enemies; fruitful lands and upright Magistrates; leaders of integrity in learning and labour; a devout, learned and useful clergy; honest, peaceable and dutiful citizens.'

The Lord has seen fit to grant some of these requests but not, as yet, quite enough of them.

I am indebted to a long list of distinguished men and to one no less distinguished woman (a discrepancy that puts me in deep fear of that expensively over-personned Equal Opportunities Commission in Manchester) for ideas and information without which I could not have written this book. Not one of them bears an ounce or, as I shall shortly be obliged to say, a gramme of responsibility for the opinions I have expressed. For these I accept all the blame, but for many suggestions and for painstaking advice and correction I owe them a great deal. Thus, had not Lord Wavell already used the title, I might aptly have called this book *Other Men's Flowers*. The weeds are my own.

Those whose flowers I gratefully acknowledge are: Lord Adeane, Lord Aldington, Mr Julian Amery, Lord Annan, Lord Armstrong of Sanderstead, Field Marshal Sir Geoffrey Baker, the Hon. Mark Bonham-Carter, Mr Robin Campbell, Lord Carr of Hadley, Lord Carrington, Mr Frank Chapple, Sir Martin Charteris, Sir Robert Clark, Mr W. M. Clarke, the Hon. L. H. Cohen, Mr Reginald Crabbe, Mr John Denison, Sir Richard Dobson, Lord Drogheda, Lord Duncan Sandys, the Rt Rev. Gerald Ellison, Bishop of London, the late Lord Feather, Sir Edward Ford, Lord Garner, Mr Maurice Green, Lord Hailsham, Sir William Hawthorne, Mr Alfred Hecht, Sir Nicholas Henderson, Sir Conrad Heron, Professor Michael Howard, Sir Robert Mark, Mr H. R. Moore, Lord O'Neill of the Maine, Mr Derek Palmar, Sir Anthony Part, Mr W. D. Pattinson, Sir Francis Pemberton, Lord Porchester, Sir George Porter, Sir Richard Powell, Lord Redcliffe Maud, Lord Rothschild, Mr Leopold de Rothschild, Lord Selwyn Lloyd, Sir Christopher Soames, the Hon. Maxwell Stamp, Mr Howard Thomas, Mr John Thompson, Lord Trend, Dame Ninette de Valois, Sir Arnold Weinstock and Lord Zuckerman.

Lastly, I thank Mr Adrian House of William Collins, whose help in moulding the framework of this book has been invaluable, Miss Josephine Butler who, without one murmur of protest, has typed and retyped most of these chapters, and Mrs Symonds and Mrs Old for considerable assistance.

November, 1976

Prologue

February the 5th, 1952, was the pleasantest of winter days, with a cloudless pale blue sky and a sharp nip in the air which foretold a hard frost. King George VI, recovering from two grave afflictions, an embolism in the leg and an operation for lung cancer, had spent a healthy day out of doors at Sandringham, and went cheerfully to bed after a peaceful family dinner party.

The Heiress to the throne, Princess Elizabeth, had flown away to Kenya with the Duke of Edinburgh less than a week before, the King standing bare-headed on the tarmac at Heathrow to wave good-bye. It was the first leg of a long journey to Australia where the Princess and the Duke were to make an extensive tour; and after performing a number of functions in the Colonial Capital of Nairobi, Princess Elizabeth was spending the night in a house on the slopes of the Aberdare Mountains, where she had gone to watch the wild animals.

It was less peaceful in London, at any rate in the vicinity of the House of Commons. The first day of a Foreign Affairs debate ended at 10.00 p.m. after vehement attacks by the Labour Opposition on the Prime Minister, Mr Churchill. He was accused of conniving with President Truman and the American administration at the preparation of atomic warfare against the Chinese and the North Koreans in the event of their crossing the Yalu river during the war which was raging in Korea. Mr Churchill had not, in fact, done anything of the sort, although he had agreed to support the Americans with all the strength he could muster in resisting further Chinese aggression. He spent the last hours of February the 5th and the first of the 6th in composing a violent retort to Mr Attlee and Mr Herbert Morrison which was by no means one of his finest speeches, though it made up in vigour what it lacked in finesse. He went to bed in a politically belligerent mood.

During the night King George VI died in his sleep. He was only

56 years of age. The public announcement was delayed until the new Queen, four and a half thousand miles away from her native land, could be told. Then the news was broken to a stunned and deeply distressed nation. Just as King George V had been surprised, at the time of his Silver Jubilee in 1935, to discover how widely he was loved, so his son, whose innate modesty was one of his most endearing characteristics, might have been astonished by the warmth of affection which his peoples displayed.

Nobody's emotions were more stirred than those of the 77 year old Prime Minister, once the champion of King Edward VIII but long since the trusted friend and truly loyal servant of King George VI, from whom he withheld no secrets, and to whose simple common sense he invariably gave his earnest attention. When, early in the morning, he was told of the King's death, he sat in bed, gazing at the wall of his room, tears in his eyes and scarcely able to speak. The Korean War, the Yalu river, Mr Herbert Morrison and the debate in the House of Commons were forgotten. 'I really did love him,' he said. 'His advice was so good and I could always count on his support in times of difficulty. I hardly know Princess Elizabeth; and she is only a child.' With an effort he pulled himself together; he summoned the Cabinet; the whole dignified procedure relating to a Demise of the Crown was followed with sorrowful exactitude; and the following evening Mr Churchill broadcast to the nation and to the world. Memories of distant days came back to him and he finished his tribute to the late King by saying: 'I, whose youth was passed in the august, unchallenged and tranquil glories of the Victorian Era, may well feel a thrill in invoking once more the prayer and the anthem, "God Save The Queen".'

It was scarcely surprising that once the initial shock was over, and the long, constantly replenished queue of the mourning public had filed past the King's coffin in Westminster Hall, people began to speak and write of a new Elizabethan Age. Here was a young and romantically attractive Queen, her beauty magnified by her simple black mourning as she was photographed stepping from the aircraft on her return from Kenya to greet the entire Cabinet and the leaders of the Opposition waiting at London Airport to receive their new Sovereign. Her first, unconscious act had been to change the title of her namesake and distant predecessor, enshrined for nearly four hundred years in the national heritage, to Queen Elizabeth I. Britain had never been more glorious than under her Queens, Elizabeth, Anne and Victoria. Youth was now at the helm and an era of enterprise and adventure was about to dawn.

The first gleams of the neo-Elizabethan dawn were a little hard to discern. Rationing was still in force, the gaps in the London streets were vivid reminders of the Luftwaffe and the V-bombs, paint for the houses was still in short supply, Stock Exchange prices were unexcitingly low, taxes were unacceptably high, and the country was suffering from one of its more serious balance of payments crises.

The dawn did, however, break earlier than it seemed reasonable to expect, as if in homage to a new and delectable Sovereign. The Korean war ended, the problems with Mr Mossadeq in Persia which had threatened Britain's oil supplies were resolved, and before the Coronation of Queen Elizabeth II on June the 2nd, 1953, the Prime Minister insisted, against the strong advice of the Ministry of Food, that the last rationed commodity, sugar, be offered freely for sale. By the autumn there was a glut of sugar and shortly afterwards the Ministry of Food was abolished.

The Coronation was not the apotheosis of Great Britain and her Empire; indeed, as far as the Empire was concerned it was the Grand Finale. But it was an occasion of universal rejoicing, which centred the attention of the whole world on the British Isles. It was the duty of the Archbishop of Canterbury to present the new Sovereign to the people before he placed Edward the Confessor's Crown on her head. So, while the Queen stood by St Edward's Chair, turning and showing herself to the people 'at every of the four sides' of Westminster Abbey (and also, on this occasion, to the millions watching on television), the Archbishop moved to all four points of the compass, proclaiming in each direction:

'I here present unto you Queen Elizabeth, your undoubted Queen.'

The people in the Abbey, as was expected of them, signified 'their willingness and joy by loud and repeated acclamations, all with one voice crying out: God Save Queen Elizabeth'.

'Then,' said the instructions for the Service, 'the trumpets shall sound.'

Sound they did: love and loyalty to the Throne poured forth

from every corner of the British Commonwealth and Empire, still comprising a high proportion of the world's population and territory; and on the very morning of the Coronation it was announced that, for the first time in history, Mount Everest had been conquered by an intrepid New Zealander and a Nepalese Sherpa who were members of a British expedition.

The scene, twenty five years later, is hard to recognise. A revolution, slow and by comparison with most of the better-known revolutions, comparatively painless, has changed not only Britain but the world. During this quarter of a century, the British have swum with the revolutionary tide, breasting the waves for the most part evenly, facing the storm with bewilderment, with alternating hope and despondency, but on the whole with equanimity. This is in part due to their temperament, but also in part to the national stability, which the Queen, her husband and her family have done much to sustain.

The optimistic prophecies of a splendid new Elizabethan age, made with such facility in 1952, have not been fulfilled. There have been no Francis Drakes (although there has been a Francis Chichester), and as yet there is no hint of a Shakespeare or a Burleigh. But if the anxieties which beset Queen Elizabeth I early in her reign have been repeated, in an entirely different context, during the first twenty five years of Queen Elizabeth II's, it is worth considering that a book such as this, written in 1583, would have been dismal reading, and that it was in the last twenty years of the first Elizabethan Era that fame, glory and prosperity came to the British Isles.

Part I

BRITAIN AND THE WORLD

CHAPTER I

Britain's Place in the World

On February the 6th, 1952, the war had been over for less than seven years. Memories of it were vivid and much of the world was still dominated by the towering figures whom wars create. In Britain Churchill was Prime Minister once again, Anthony Eden was Foreign Secretary and others whose names had become household words between 1939 and 1945, such as Woolton and R. A. Butler, held important Portfolios. The War time Joint Secretaries to the Cabinet, Sir Edward Bridges and General Ismay, were much to the fore in yet more exalted positions. Mr Attlee was Leader of the Opposition, supported by Mr Herbert Morrison; Field Marshal Slim had recently succeeded Field Marshal Montgomery as Chief of the Imperial General Staff; and Field Marshal Alexander, Governor General of Canada, had agreed to join the Government as Minister of Defence. Lord Mountbatten had exchanged the Viceroyalty of India for high naval command and was about to become Commander in Chief, Mediterranean; nor should it be overlooked that the British Admiral in charge of that armada of warships based on Malta was not held to command just the Mediterranean Fleet, but the Mediterranean itself.

For the next ten years all the members of the War Cabinet Defence Committee, which had been the body charged with the effective control of the British war effort, were still alive and could have reassembled in London. If most of them had retired from public life, their renown was still remembered and acclaimed. Only two, Lord Avon and Lord Mountbatten, were to survive from the Queen's Accession until the year of her Silver Jubilee. It was a romantic coincidence, less probable in the 20th century than in the 17th or 18th, that the Queen's cousin by birth and uncle by marriage should be the last of the Supreme Allied Commanders, having also been Chief of Combined Operations in war, Chief of the Defence Staff in peace and the last Viceroy of India.

It was not only in Britain that the war leaders continued in authority. In Washington President Truman occupied the White House while General Eisenhower, commanding the Allied Forces in Europe, was soon to be drafted as Republican candidate in the forthcoming Presidential Election. In Moscow Stalin tyrannised from the Kremlin with the inhuman and inscrutable Molotov at his side. Western Germany, divided into Allied Zones of Occupation, was receiving unstinted aid from all the victors except Russia, and her citizens were indefatigably rebuilding their bomb-blasted towns and factories without consideration of working hours, holidays with pay or any of the luxurious grumbles to which all classes of every community consider themselves entitled in days of affluence.

Italy, too, was the recipient of lavish American aid, laying the foundations of a scintillating, if comparatively short-lived, economic miracle; and Japan was helped to her feet by General MacArthur and an American generosity even more munificent than that bestowed on Germany and Italy. The former Axis Powers were thus provided with the means of recovery, of which they took full, hardworking advantage; and American beneficence was also extended to the shattered European victors, to Britain and France, to Holland, Belgium, Greece and Yugoslavia.

Four years before her accession, the Queen and her newly-married husband had paid the first post-war royal visit to France, to the unaffected joy of vast Parisian crowds whose royalist enthusiasm for foreign princes is only surpassed by their unswerving republican sentiments at home. The French were struggling to recover from the prostration, moral rather than physical, to which the crushing disasters of 1940 had reduced them. The Fourth Republic, risen from the ashes of occupation and beset by squabbling factions of the former Resistance Movement, was a phoenix with tattered feathers, obliged to keep one bleary eye on rebellion in the restored Colony of Indo-China and the other on stirrings of discontent in Algiers. Inconstancy of Government and parliamentary instability were apparently endemic French diseases, so that in the field of politics there was little to distinguish the France of the 1950s from the Third Republic of pre-war days.

A French economic recovery had, however, already begun. A sweeping, but final, programme of nationalisation removed that divisive topic from the political arena once and for all; a practical five-year plan was launched, and economic planning, regarded with so much suspicion north of the Channel, was generally accepted; the celebrated 'Grandes Ecoles' provided men of quality and the highest professional training for industry, science and administration; and waiting patiently at Colombey-les-Deux-Eglises for a call to save his country and revive its glory was the one Frenchman whose war record made him internationally famous, General Charles de Gaulle. He was passing the time by writing his memoirs in the purest of literary styles, so that even those who disputed the contents could not fail to be dazzled by his use of the language.

Recuperation was thus making good progress and there were already the first signs of a European urge to associate, exemplified by the creation of a Council of Europe, with a parliamentary Assembly at Strasbourg, of the Organisation of European Economic Co-operation and, within a few months of the Queen's accession, of the European Coal and Steel Community. Even in the United Kingdom, the European Movement, publicised by clarion calls from Churchill in London, Strasbourg and Zurich while he was still in Opposition, had established its right to be heard and to be taken seriously.

The North Atlantic Treaty Organisation, founded in 1949 because of Russia's evident antagonism and the realisation that she had no intention of releasing her grip on the occupied territories of Eastern Europe, was of more immediate practical value. It was NATO which provided the framework for the continuing presence of America's influence and armed forces in Europe, a presence without which the political stability and economic recovery of France, Germany, Italy and indeed Spain would have been impossible. It was based on realism rather than idealism, and the British, having decided to embrace the internationalism which membership of NATO implied in the matter of European defence, accepted the situation, not merely with resignation but with enthusiasm.

Nevertheless the recovery of Europe and the Far East had far to go in 1952. The Big Three, the United States, the Soviet Union and Britain, were still considered arbiters of the world's destiny, although certainly the Americans and probably the Russians thought that the British, exhausted and impoverished by six years of war (against four for each of them) were not quite in their own top league. With Churchill at 10 Downing Street they would not have dared say so; and the three were, after all, the sole members of that most exclusive of all clubs, The Nuclear, to which the Soviet Union was a recent and by no means welcome addition. The defection of a number of British and American scientists and administrators had provided Stalin with the keys to the club. It was more than eight years before France, the next candidate for election, exploded her first atomic device and it was not until 1964 that China followed suit.

For a further three and a half years Britain's status as one of the Big Three was virtually unchallenged and unchanged. Churchill had regular meetings with the President of the United States. He was far from pleased when, in December, 1954, Eisenhower insisted that the French also be invited to a conference at Bermuda, because francophile though he was at heart, he believed the inclusion of France in discussions which had hitherto been bilateral would detract from their uninhibited intimacy and thus alter their character. The Americans, for their part, said with entire frankness that they acknowledged and valued a special relationship with the United Kingdom, but they would be embarrassed to make such an admission publicly. The French must come, if only for the sake of appearances.

When in April, 1955, the mantle of Churchill fell upon Sir Anthony Eden, a new and, in the event, momentous change occurred. This was not because Eden's views on broad matters of policy differed profoundly from Churchill's; but they had been in serious disagreement on two matters. The first was a new relationship with Russia. Churchill, who had failed to rouse the world against Bolshevism after the Russian Revolution, but nearly thirty years later had succeeded in so doing by his Iron Curtain speech at Fulton, proceeded to devote his last two years as Prime Minister to an unsuccessful effort to bring an end to the Cold War. On succeeding Churchill, Eden, though warier than his predecessor of the demoralising effect which appeasement of the Russians might have on Western European defence efforts, himself decided that an attempt to improve relations with the Soviet Union was desirable. He invited Bulganin and Khrushchev to London. A few years later, Mr Harold Macmillan also made an exploratory expedition to

Moscow; but neither of these initiatives was any more successful than that on which Churchill had placed so much store. Mr Harold Wilson's endeavours in the 1960s were equally barren. The bear, as Churchill would have put it, was occasionally prepared to dance, but was consistently reluctant to be tamed.

It was the second disagreement between Churchill and Eden which had eventual consequences of a lasting nature. Churchill had obstinately resisted Eden's proposal, supported by most of the Cabinet, to withdraw all British troops from the Suez Zone in Egypt and to replace their expensive watch on the Canal by a treaty with the Egyptian Government which, under the revolutionary leadership of General Neguib, had recently deposed the pleasure-loving King Farouk. It would be carrying the imagery too far to declare that there was war in heaven, but there was certainly discord in the Cabinet. Churchill gave way in 1954 because the Americans exploded a hydrogen bomb, which he thought was further removed from the atomic bomb in the sheer size of its destructive power than high explosive shells, or even the atomic bomb itself, had been from the bow and arrow. The whole concept of world strategy seemed to require revision because of this single event, and Churchill saw no further advantage in retaining a garrison at Suez. So Eden had his way and a solemn treaty of friendship was signed with Neguib's successor, Colonel Nasser, whereby civil contractors replaced British troops in the Canal Zone. It was understood that the Anglo-French Suez Canal Company would retain responsibility for the Canal itself and for the provision of pilots.

In July, 1956, the impetuous Colonel Nasser nationalised the Canal without warning or consultation. The British and French were justly incensed. Anthony Eden in particular, having argued with Churchill in favour of trusting the Egyptians, felt personally aggrieved. Matters were not improved by the shameful tergiversation of the American Secretary of State, Mr John Foster Dulles. Having advocated the refusal of American aid for the Egyptian project of a giant dam at Aswan, he began by encouraging the British and French Governments to display firmness in the Suez Canal dispute, not excluding the use of force. Then at the critical moment he withdrew his moral support and demanded appeasement. The

23

Israelis, in direct contact with the French and also, though less openly, with the British, attacked Egypt on a convenient date and there followed a landing by British and French forces in the Canal area with the purely nominal object of putting a stop to the Israeli-Egyptian war. These landings and the operations which immediately followed were a carefully planned and successful military achievement. They were to be consummated by a triumphal march southwards to Suez and it was hoped that the Egyptians would then see the error of their ways and remove the objectionable Nasser, while an international body assumed responsibility for ensuring the maintenance and free navigation of the Canal.

This was the last serious attempt at gun-boat diplomacy and it was a dismal failure. The United Nations condemned the Anglo-French initiative as aggression. The Americans, especially angry because the landings took place on the day of their Presidential Election, threatened to impose oil sanctions on Britain and France, both of which were deprived of their normal Middle Eastern supplies by the very nature of the war. The Commonwealth was deeply divided, though the Australian Prime Minister, Menzies, loyally supported Eden. The British at first reacted in favour of the adventure. Indeed, Mr Hugh Gaitskell, Attlee's successor as Leader of the Opposition, was heard to complain that his natural supporters in the country were all behind Eden, whereas most of the intelligent Tories that he knew supported him in condemning the Government's action. The Liberals at first voted with Eden and then, two days later, against him.

Nothing fails like failure. Once the British and French troops had bowed to American pressure and withdrawn without even reaching Suez, the people divided their displeasure between their own Government and the Americans, particularly when it became necessary to reintroduce petrol rationing. From the Russian point of view the Suez affair could not have been more timely and convenient, for it deflected world censure from their own contemporary measures to stifle, without scruple or restraint, a liberal insurrection in Hungary. It was also a useful opportunity for them to proclaim a newly-discovered friendship for the Arab world which, they could now insist, far exceeded that of the British or the French. A year later the Americans, oblivious of their moral objections to the Suez venture, themselves took unilateral action by landing armed forces in the Lebanon; but when in May, 1958, the Arab apple-cart was again upset, by the assassination of the young Hashemite King of Iraq, and of Britain's stalwart friend, Nuri Pasha, not a shot was fired nor a paratroop dropped to prevent a clique of russophile revolutionaries seizing power in Baghdad. A combination of British and French impetuosity with American indecision delivered to the Russians latch-keys for several Middle Eastern doors.

There were to be, in the years ahead, a few small gun-boat initiatives aimed, for the most part successfully, at averting injustice by showing strength. Anthony Eden, as Foreign Secretary, had already used the threat of British arms to dissuade Saudi Arabia from seizing Abu Dhabi's oasis at Buraimi; in 1961, the British military presence in the Persian Gulf was sufficient to deter Iraq from occupying Kuwait and thus quadrupling its own oil wealth; later still, in 1969, Mr Harold Wilson sent a frigate to the West Indies to restore peace between St Kitts and the island of Anguilla; and in the 1970s a late-flowering species of gun-boat diplomacy emerged when Britain waged a confused, long-drawn-out and, in the end, ineffective Cod War with the Icelanders, who sought to exclude British trawlers from waters within two hundred miles of their shores. Ships were rammed, trawls were cut, tempers were frayed, but the Navy fired no shots and, having been permitted to achieve nothing at all, the gun-boats were finally withdrawn. At the end of 1976, the British, with their traditional disdain for logic, supported and acclaimed the decision of the European Economic Community to impose a two hundred-mile fishing limit in European waters.

It was clear by 1957, when Mr Harold Macmillan became Prime Minister, that the days of unilateral action were over for Britain. Short, sharp military excursions were left to the Israelis, who in July, 1976, showed greater aptitude than the British or Americans had ever displayed for such exercises by sending an aerial commando force to Entebbe to rescue a hundred hostages held by terrorists and General Amin. In future Britain's foreign, defence and indeed economic policies must be concerned and concerted with groups rather than with individual States. The United Nations, hamstrung first by the constant use of the Soviet veto in the Security Council, and then by the manipulation of the Assembly in the interest of groups of small countries with vested interests, lost whatever hold it may originally have had on the faith of the British people. In Parliament lip service was paid to its authority. Indeed, it became standard practice for the Opposition to suggest, whenever an intractable problem in foreign affairs presented itself, that before any action was taken the matter should be referred to the United Nations, even though it was well understood that this would be a futile procedure. If the United States required chrome from Rhodesia she would acquire it whether or not the United Nations had imposed sanctions. If Britain chose to stay in Gibraltar, she would do so, however many resolutions to the contrary were passed in New York. But positive action on any but the smallest scale must henceforward be taken by the joint endeavour of groups of countries with common aims.

The London Conference of 1954, dominated by Anthony Eden, had strengthened the position of European security, principally represented by the forces of NATO. Thus, even before the Suez episode, the advantages of grouped defence resources were acknowledged. All the same it was the continuing presence of American soldiers in Europe, and the warm feeling of reassurance they provided, which was felt to be the strongest shield for the British Isles against Eastern military designs; and when, in 1953 and 1954, the creation of a European Defence Community was under discussion, it was regarded in London solely as a method of uniting the French and the Germans in a common cause. Nobody in the Government seriously suggested the British should join what Winston Churchill described as a 'sludgy amalgam': Britain's 'manifest destiny', in defence as in many other things, was identified with that of the United States and it so remained in the eyes of Her Majesty's Government until at least 1960.

Meanwhile the more powerful countries of Western Europe were actively engaged in planning an ambitious European experiment, convinced that although they had all been dependent on American assistance, and were still relying on the ultimate safeguard of American nuclear power, their united strength could provide the proud independence to which they aspired. There were some in

Britain who shared these hopes, but few who believed that the ancient nations of Europe, divided by language, tradition and historic divergencies could, for many years to come, form a United States of Europe in any way comparable with the United States of America. A free trade area certainly; but a Federated Europe seemed to most people, and certainly to the British Government, the insubstantial mirage of a far, far distant Utopia.

In 1955 the incorrigible Europeans nevertheless held a conference at Messina (to which the British declined an invitation) and in March, 1957, went on to sign the Treaty of Rome in the face of strong British and Scandinavian arguments in favour of an alternative Industrial Free Trade Area. British collaboration would, it was thought, alienate the members of the Commonwealth (who had long counted on the preferential tariff treatment they received from Britain), subject British industry to dangerous European competition, raise food prices and discriminate in favour of European farmers against their British counterparts who were more efficient, more productive and more highly mechanised. Parliament, in this instance accurately reflecting the undoubted prejudices of the people, would not have been willing to contemplate accession to the new Common Market, and as there was to be a General Election in 1959, a policy of adherence to Europe, involving immediate hardship to the consumer whatever the ultimate benefits, would have led to a catastrophe at the polls for whichever party sponsored the idea.

An era of mystifying initials began. There was EEC and OEEC; there was CAP and the CET; all in addition to the existing UNO, NATO and SEATO. Now the Scandinavians, with strong British approval, invented EFTA, which came into being in 1959 as an answer to the Common Market. It was a free trade association of seven European countries, of which Britain was far the biggest, with no common external tariff and thus nothing to antagonise the members of the Commonwealth; nor was there much danger of British farmers, who were handsomely subsidised themselves, having to give anything away to foreign competitors or of British housewives having to pay more for their food.

Mr Harold Macmillan had become Prime Minister in 1957, following Sir Anthony Eden's illness and subsequent resignation. He had been an early supporter of a United Europe, when Churchill was beating the drum at Zurich and Strasbourg in the late 1940s. The ardour both of Churchill and Macmillan had been stoked by the keenest and most deeply convinced of all the believers in European unity, Churchill's son-in-law, Duncan Sandys. The two main obstacles, the Commonwealth, with its fervent addiction to Imperial Preference, and the peculiar problems of British agriculture, might be insuperable objections to Britain signing the Treaty of Rome, and membership of EFTA was now an additional complication; but Macmillan was not wholly convinced. In 1960, with electoral considerations in abeyance after a triumph at the polls in the previous autumn, he instructed the Secretary to the Cabinet, Sir Norman Brook, to examine the obstacles. The result was not encouraging, but nor were the alternatives. British trade was declining, EFTA was too small a unit to stimulate a renewed commercial expansion, and the solution of reversing the decision of 1776 and seeking a close, formal association with the United States was unlikely to appeal to Congress, to the American business community or to the majority at home. Britain had indeed reaped some of the harvest of the affluent society which had developed throughout the Western world in the wake of the Korean war, and of the rise in production the war had stimulated; but the underlying prospects for the future were less alluring. When Macmillan spoke of the Wind of Change, he was referring to the British Empire: what he had failed to say was that a Wind of Change must blow in Britain itself. He now saw that the time had come to fan such a breeze.

In the summer of 1960 Macmillan appointed three dedicated Europeans to high office in his Administration. Duncan Sandys became Secretary of State for Commonwealth Relations, for Macmillan required a resolute advocate of European unity to face the opposition which he expected from the Commonwealth countries and which he indeed received in full measure. Edward Heath was appointed Lord Privy Seal and Foreign Office spokesman in the House of Commons; and another of Churchill's sons-in-law, Christopher Soames, was moved from the War Office to the Ministry of Agriculture. Soames went to 10 Downing Street in December to insist that, whether or not the goal of entry into Europe was achieved, there must in any event be drastic changes in the form of support given to British farmers. The Prime Minister summoned his wise and experienced Conservative colleague, Mr R. A. Butler, to listen to the Soames arguments. Butler agreed with them and as Macmillan himself was convinced that a European solution must be sought, he submitted the proposal to the Cabinet. They declared themselves in favour of applying for membership of the European Community.

Throughout 1962 Heath, supported by Duncan Sandys and, on the agricultural front, by Soames, toiled at the negotiating table in Brussels. With one exception all the members of the Community welcomed the prospect of British membership. The exception was France, of which General de Gaulle had become President and Chief Executive in 1958, sweeping into oblivion the graceless relics of the Fourth Republic. De Gaulle suspected the British of preferring, and being entirely unwilling to discard, their special relationship with the United States; and he had never forgiven the Americans for their hostility towards him during the war. He therefore sent to Brussels two dedicated hatchet men, Monsieur Wormser and Monsieur Couve de Murville to repel the British boarders. De Gaulle did not himself believe in a Federated Europe. He shared none of the idealism of Monnet, Schumann or Spaak; but he did accept the idea of *L'Europe des Patries*, an association of sovereign states offering each other trading advantages. Its main difference from EFTA, in De Gaulle's calculation, was that France would be its undisputed leader; and the inclusion of the British might be damaging to that important prospect.

De Gaulle's spoiling tactics were assisted by two events. At a meeting of Commonwealth Prime Ministers in the autumn of 1962 several of the participants, and notably the Canadian, Mr Diefenbaker, were outspoken in their opposition to Britain joining the Common Market. Secondly, when the British bought from America *Polaris* missiles for their nuclear submarines, de Gaulle asserted that this was proof of British half-heartedness towards Europe and that Britain was determined to be the lap dog of the United States. Thus, early in 1963, the effort to join the Common Market was thwarted by the obstinate and obstructive behaviour of Charles de Gaulle, whose ingratitude was notable since, had the British not championed him twenty years before, it was by no means certain that anybody would have heard of him.

Angry and frustrated, the British negotiators left Brussels for a full ten years. Where was Britain now to go? Her share of world trade was falling year by year; Germany and Japan were beginning to dominate markets which had long been British preserves; Peugeots and Volkswagen replaced the products of Coventry, Dagenham and Luton in the parking places of Lusaka, Lagos and Singapore, and were increasingly noticeable on the roads of the British Isles. The shaft had gone home when a year or two previously Dean Acheson, former American Secretary of State and an undoubted anglophile, said: 'Britain has lost an Empire and failed to find a role.'

The ensuing years were consumed by internal problems, by Mr Harold Macmillan's illness and by two General Elections; but in 1967 the Labour Government, with Mr Harold Wilson as Prime Minister and Mr George Brown as Foreign Secretary, reached the same conclusion as Macmillan: Britain must join Europe or decline. Unfortunately a serious balance of payments crisis in 1967 led to the devaluation of the pound, so that the intransigent de Gaulle was able to declare that Britain's economy was too unstable for her candidature to be seriously considered. The advance was therefore rebuffed once again, but the suitor remained ardent and in 1968 Wilson took the unusual step of inviting a leading member of the Opposition, Christopher Soames, to go to Paris as British Ambassador and persuade the General to be more amenable. To what extent he might have become so remains an open question, for in April, 1969 he fell from power and was succeeded by the equally nationalistic, though less intransigent and less despotic Monsieur Pompidou.

A year later, Harold Wilson made an electoral miscalculation. The Opinion Polls were markedly favourable to the Labour Government and to Wilson personally. In June, 1970 he advised the Queen to dissolve Parliament, and informed the sceptical electorate that the Opinion Polls had not influenced his decision at all: it had been based on plans he had made as long ago as 1964. There was a General Election as the result of which the Opinion Polls were shown to have been misleading and Mr Edward Heath became Prime Minister. He at once devoted himself heart and soul to his cherished ambition of entry into Europe and, backed by the negotiating skill of Mr Geoffrey Rippon, he was successful. He was supported in his task by the genuine enthusiasm of Germany, Italy, Holland, Belgium and Luxemburg. The French without the General were temporarily like bees who have lost their queen. They buzzed but they did not sting.

At home, the Labour Shadow Cabinet was torn by internecine strife. The pro-Europeans, led by Mr Roy Jenkins, were opposed by equally dedicated anti-Europeans. Mr Harold Wilson, as Leader of the Opposition, found himself athwart a spiky, uncomfortable fence. He was therefore obliged to compromise by proclaiming that the terms of entry Heath would negotiate were sure to be unacceptable and that when the Labour Party returned to office they would at once renegotiate them or else leave the European Community. It was difficult for the Labour leaders to convince all their supporters that the terms Heath did succeed in negotiating were in fact unacceptable and more than sixty Labour Members of Parliament, led by Roy Jenkins, were too honest to pretend that they had been so convinced. Thus the proposal to join the Common Market was approved by a large majority in the House of Commons, and in 1972 Britain signed the Treaty of Rome. Denmark and Ireland did so too, and the Six Common Market countries became the Nine.

However, there was still sufficient insular sentiment in the Labour Party, among a few Conservatives and in the Trade Unions, for Harold Wilson to feel obliged to insist, when he returned to power in 1974, that the whole matter must be reviewed, that Heath's deplorable terms of entry must be revised and that (contrary to the traditions both of representative government and of adherence to signed international treaties) the question whether to stay in Europe or to denounce the Treaty should be decided by a referendum. Everybody knew that Wilson himself was dedicated to staying in; but though an undoubted patriot he had seldom found it expedient to subordinate the internal stresses and strains of his Party too straightforwardly to the national interest, and his tactics on this occasion, while responsible for the raising of countless eyebrows at home and abroad, at least left the vociferous anti-Common Market minority with no immediate riposte. In June, 1975, after the other Common Market countries had good-naturedly agreed to a few unimportant amendments enabling Wilson to claim that the terms of entry had been renegotiated, a nationwide referendum was held for the first time in English history and a huge majority voted to stay in Europe. Insularity did not die, but it suffered a severe heart attack.

One of the few parts of the world in which the British, even in the days of dominion over palm and pine, had neither interest nor influence was Vietnam, the former French Colony of Indo-China. When the Communists, controlling the northern half of the country, took steps to implement by force the policy of reunification with the non-Communist southern half which they had been advocating for several years, a civil war broke out. It seemed as if it might be another Korean War, for the circumstances were not dissimilar. But in the Korean dispute the United Nations, taking advantage of the temporary withdrawal of the Russians, had authorised military action against the northern aggressors and after a bloody conflict, in which the principal contestants were not the Koreans themselves but the Chinese and the Americans, the *status quo* was restored. In the early 1960s, when hostilities threatened in Vietnam, the United Nations were incapable of taking action, but the Americans, under three successive Presidents, J. F. Kennedy, Lyndon Johnson and Richard Nixon, rushed into the fray on behalf of South Vietnam.

In Britain the intervention of the Americans was resented by the left-wing of the Labour Party, and by their supporters among students and intellectuals, with almost the same emotional intensity that had characterised the attitude of a previous left-wing generation to the civil war in Spain, another country in which Britain had had little interest and no influence. During the war in Vietnam, the Labour Government was by no means anti-American, but internal pressures were such that Mr Harold Wilson and Mr George Brown thought it expedient to try their hand as honest brokers. They even contemplated flying to Saigon to inaugurate discussions between the opposing forces. Their worthy intentions were rebuffed and Britain's interference in disputes with which she had no connection, past or present, was seen to be of no avail. If the days of gun-boat diplomacy had passed, so had those of grandiose diplomatic initiatives at the conference table in the style of Disraeli.

This had an unfortunate side-effect, for while Mr Wilson and Mr Brown were concentrating their thoughts on how to solve the dispute in Vietnam, civil war broke out in Nigeria. This vast country,

containing nearly half the population of black Africa, and a quarter
of that of the entire continent, had become independent from
Britain in 1960 and had been endowed with the usual legacy of two
Houses of Parliament, complete with a mace and a bewigged
Speaker, a Judiciary steeped in British legal tradition and a well-led
Civil Service. Unfortunately, tribal antagonisms were strong and
in 1967 armed hostilities began. Unlike Vietnam, Nigeria was a
country where British influence was still strong. An immediate
initiative in support of the Federal Government might have stifled
the flames before they caught hold; but when the British High
Commission in Lagos asked urgently for instructions, they found
that the Prime Minister and the Foreign Secretary were too im-
mersed in their plans to resolve the Vietnamese problem to pay
attention to the fire in their Nigerian back garden.

To the surprise of most people Wilson resigned in March, 1976,
became a Knight of the Garter and retired to the back benches of the
House of Commons. Although it was clear to all that Mr James
Callaghan would succeed him, there was a delay of three weeks
while the Parliamentary Labour Party, by the slow process of elimin-
ating rival claimants in successive ballots, formally established their
preference for Callaghan. The inheritance was an uneasy one, for
the pound sterling plumbed depths never reached before, the
Government majority in the House of Commons was uncertain,
Parliament was log-jammed by scores of incomplete and highly
controversial bills (for which there was no obvious support among
the Electorate), Northern Ireland was in a bloodier ferment than
ever, the Scottish and Welsh Nationalists were in a position to exact
heavy pounds of flesh for the support which alone could sustain the
Government, and although the Trade Union leaders were willing
to support the Labour Party in fighting inflation, there was fierce
opposition by the left-wing to the cuts in public expenditure which
Callaghan knew to be essential.

Britain's economic decline, by comparison with her European
neighbours and Japan, is the subject of another chapter in this book.
Her gross national product, her share of world trade, the international standing of her currency, the productivity of her labour
force, and the growth of her industrial production: all these have been
overtaken and surpassed by countries such as France, Germany and

Japan which lagged far behind her in 1952.

Thus in 1977 Britain's standing in the world is in economic respects far lower than in 1952, though a chronic imbalance of trade and payments was even then apparent and the once unshakeable pound had already been devalued in terms of the dollar. Had it not been for the establishment of English as the most important of the world's languages, her new and potentially exciting opportunities as a member of the European Economic Community and a handful of inherited treasures, Britain would by 1977 have been relegated in the eyes of foreign countries to a status lower than that of a second-class power. But she does possess some treasures denied to others and they include a number of sparkling jewels which, despite the fecklessness of some of her citizens, she has adamantly refused to take to the pawn shop.

One is the Commonwealth. It is not indeed Britain's, as the Empire once was; but whatever the occasional aberrations of some of its members, it has inherited the British traditions of justice, equality before the law and respect for the sensitivities of others. It is often incoherent, individual members may suspend the law of *habeas corpus*, there may have been friction, as between Kenya and Uganda, or even active hostilities, as between India and Pakistan; but the broad panorama of understanding and shared ideals is one which because the Commonwealth is in its essence of British origin has redounded to the continuing credit of its founder.

Secondly, Britain shares with her own, long-emancipated child, the United States of America, the reputation of upholding the liberty of the individual. It should not escape notice that even those whom the British have imprisoned in time of stress, Gandhi and Nehru, Kenyatta, Makarios, Nkrumah, Hastings Banda and even the Palestinian terrorist, Miss Leila Khaled, have seldom, if ever, borne a grudge against the gaoler; nor have those who were most outspoken in their attacks on Imperial rule failed to seek sanctuary in London when they themselves were rejected. The safe harbour used by Kossuth, Karl Marx, Lenin and Napoleon III, by White Russians, German Jews and Italian anti-fascists, among many thousands of other 19th and 20th century refugees, was also available to President Azikwe of Nigeria, to Ayub Khan of Pakistan, to Asians expelled from Kenya and Uganda, and to many who have fled from oppressive régimes in South Africa, Chile and Greece. It is not just that asylum has traditionally been available to all who do not seek to disrupt the United Kingdom itself; but in Britain the degree of liberty and right of unbridled criticism of the Government is equalled in few lands and surpassed in none. There have indeed been attempts, especially in the 1970s, to restrict freedom by law, and some of them have been successful; but the very imposers of these restrictions are for the most part men and women who genuinely believe in freedom of speech and freedom from arbitrary arrest. In so far as they have restricted liberty, they have done so in the sacred, if sometimes incompatible, interest of equality. Even the diminishing number who live under democratically elected governments in Europe, Asia, Africa and South America, do not fail to recognise the special qualities of Anglo-Saxon liberty and to give due credit to the Barons at Runnymede, to the village Hampdens and to the great liberal reformers, from whichever political party they came, of the 19th and 20th centuries.

Freedom for others is, however, something which Great Britain no longer has the strength to champion. Nor, indeed, has Western Europe. The days when British influence was exercised on behalf of oppressed Poles, down-trodden Balkan peasants, Armenians threatened by massacre and Garibaldi's Red Shirts, are long past; nor could the ambitions of a latter day Hitler be challenged by Britain alone. The terrible wrongs and atrocities inflicted by the Khmer Rouge in Cambodia, the Chinese in Tibet and the rulers of Ruanda Urundi, Uganda and Equatorial Africa are left to the ineffective, easily thwarted censure of the United Nations Organisation which, by a tacitly accepted conspiracy of silence, seldom debates the denial of human rights east of the Berlin Wall. Britain, once proud to be the world's policeman, can only enforce the law and an element of civilised behaviour within her own frontiers.

A third jewel, and a pearl of great price, is stability. When Irish bombs exploded in Belfast, and even in Birmingham, Glasgow and London, the shock was temporarily profound; and the violent crimes in the streets of the great cities which were already disturbing in the 1960s have become doubly so in the 1970s. Demonstrations against the American war in Vietnam, the rule of the Colonels in Greece, the Junta in Chile, apartheid in South Africa and other foreign affairs for which the British Government had no responsibility, and about which they could do nothing but make deprecating noises, became occasions for the display of noisy hooliganism; but a nation of animal lovers was outraged when, to the indignation of millions of television watchers, the hooligans went so far as to let off fireworks under the hoofs of police horses. There was violence, organised by a few extremists, during the picketing of mines, factories and power stations in a series of strikes in 1972 and 1973. There were race riots at Notting Hill in 1958 and again, at the end of a sweltering August, in 1976. All these disturbances were, however, recognised as unpleasant gusts of wind in a world which was subject to storms of far more lethal strength beyond the coasts of the British Isles.

The country's reputation for social and political stability is little damaged, and the mere fact that the people have faced unpleasant events, to which they have gradually become accustomed, with the imperturbability expected of them, and without a trace of panic, has strengthened their reputation. There are few countries in Europe and fewer still anywhere else, which entered the last quarter of the 20th century with as great a faith in internal security or are acknowledged by the rest of the world to have such an inbuilt institutional and emotional stability.

Before the unsavoury Poulson episode in the 1970s, which revealed a disturbing measure of corruption in local government in the north of England, incriminated one high Civil Servant and was even alleged to have infected Parliament, it would have been tempting to include incorruptibility among the virtues still distinguishing Britain from other Western countries. It is not easy to chart the ill-defined strip of territory dividing corruption from the provision of legitimate incentive, and none but the ingenuous believes that business executives, politicians and local government officials do not sometimes stumble over the border. However, in years when bribery was rife in the United States, widely practised in many European business communities and apparently endemic in the newly independent countries of Asia and Africa, the British record was at least clean by comparison. The Central Government has been above suspicion and so have the higher ranks of the Civil Service. The City of London has had its annual scandal or two, but can legitimately boast that its leading institutions are unspotted; and if exporters have found that in certain markets the provision of inducements is essential to the winning of a contract, they have been more selective in their largesse than many of their foreign competitors. When, in 1976, the Lockheed Aircraft bribery scandal rocked the Governments of Japan, Italy and the Netherlands and caused tremors in Germany, Britain, which had close connections with Lockheed in producing engines for its Tristar aeroplanes, was one of the few countries where there were no slanderous whispers to which even the most credulous could attach importance.

The fourth, and one of the most precious of Britain's surviving treasures, is the Crown itself. As the political power of the Monarchy declined, or at least lay dormant, its influence on the country's standing overseas increased and it became an asset of diplomatic strength. Pomp and circumstance alone, greatly as they are admired in a world of tarnished and tawdry official procedure, would not have sufficed. It would have been easy for the British Monarchy to degenerate into a meaningless pantomime, in which the magnificent scenery was no more than an alternative to a night at the opera or a Hollywood extravaganza. It has not done so. The Queen's tireless visits abroad have done more to remind people that Britain still exists, to build goodwill in foreign and Commonwealth countries alike and to stimulate British exports, than any number of ministerial conferences and diplomatic protocols, and than all the garish posters, sponsored tours by municipal dignitaries and libraries staffed by the British Council, useful and beneficial though these most certainly are. To almost the entire world the image of Britain is linked with one of the Queen.

There were, in 1976, two royal occasions of particular significance. The first was the visit to London, in the blazing June sunshine, of the President of the French Republic. A good understanding between the British and the French is vital to the European experiment, but it has long been thwarted by a present clash of interests and a past sense of grievance. The French remember Fashoda, when as long ago as 1898 the British drove away a French expedition in order to seize the Sudan for themselves. They remember, too, the sinking of the French fleet at Oran in July, 1940, as untoward an event as when the British and French jointly sank the entire Turkish fleet at Navarino in 1827, but justified in the eyes of the British (and originally of General de Gaulle too) by the necessity of preventing the French ships falling into German hands. The British for their part remembered the mutinies in the French Army in the summer of 1917, which obliged Lord Haig to stage a diversion that bears the accursed name of Passchendaele, and the French surrender of 1940 which left Britain alone to face the German onslaught. These distant memories were revived by the refusal of de Gaulle to allow Britain into the Common Market and by the French conviction that Britain would continue to look westwards to America rather than southwards to Europe. By the mid-1970s the British and the French had reached one common conclusion: they each preferred the Germans.

Monsieur Valérie Giscard d'Estaing's State Visit to London was an outstanding event. The only overt result was a decision that the French President and the British Prime Minister should henceforth meet every year; but the change in attitude, at the Quai d'Orsay and the Elysée no less than in the Foreign Office and 10 Downing Street, was of importance for the future of Europe. It did not come about at the expense of Germany or of any other Power. It was, according both to the President's entourage and to British officials, largely due to the Queen in person and to the unaffected simplicity with which, amidst all the magnificence of a State Occasion, she received and entertained the French President. The Entente Cordiale established by King Edward VII had long receded into history; there had been a time in the 1960s when, as Mr Julian Amery put it, nothing remained but an Entente Concordiale based on the one remaining joint enterprise, the building of a supersonic air liner. Now, at last, there was hope of genuine co-operation for the future.

In July, 1976, the Queen and Prince Philip, aboard the royal yacht *Britannia*, sailed into Philadelphia, where the Declaration of Independence had been signed two hundred years before. The Americans had by no means written the United Kingdom off the map, but being a hard-headed people, only moved by sentiment when they are outside their Government Departments, their factories and their counting-houses, and then very emotionally indeed, they had ceased to regard Britain as much more than a formerly stable ally, whose people were more comprehensible, on linguistic grounds, than other foreigners, but who had lost their initiative, run down their defences, abandoned competitive habits, forgotten both how to manage and how to work and were not far from the precipice of bankruptcy.

By her first words when she landed in Philadelphia, the Queen disarmed the Americans, who are generous-minded even when the sacred cows of their history are under discussion. 'I speak to you,' she said, 'as the direct descendant of King George III.' George III and the Red Coats were thenceforward tacitly removed from the Agenda for the remainder of the visit. She went on to admit that the Founding Fathers of the United States had taught Britain an invaluable lesson: 'To know the right time and the manner of yielding what it is impossible to keep.' Without that lesson, she said, the British could never have transformed an Empire into a Commonwealth.

The visit to the United States had no immediate political objective. It touched deeper chords. It was an emphatic and successful demonstration that after two hundred years of political separation Britain and the United States are still closely linked by history, sentiment and moral purpose. The Queen did not neglect more mundane commercial considerations. She lent *Britannia* for a meeting between fifty American and fifty British businessmen, thus repeating a successful experiment she had made on earlier visits to Brazil and Mexico and incidentally demonstrating that the royal yacht is not just the luxurious appendage of the Crown which some members of the House of Commons believe it to be. Nor was it a useless extravagance to entertain the President of the United States to dinner on board, for there could have been no more impressive way of returning Presidential hospitality; and over five hundred boats put to sea to escort *Britannia* as she sailed from Newhaven to Newport. Arrival by air could never have produced a comparable effect.

The Queen's gift for combining informality in conversation with dignity of bearing won respect in Washington. Her readiness to mix with the crowds thronging Wall Street appealed to the gregarious New Yorkers. In Boston, scene of that Tea Party in 1774 which was the immediate cause of all the trouble, the crowds roared their welcome to George III's successor, and whenever an Irish American voice was raised in formal protest it was silenced by a thousand cheers. It is no exaggeration to claim that Queen Elizabeth II was greeted with an American warmth that no other visiting Head of State has ever known; and they said, in their enthusiasm, that 'it made us all feel better'.

From the United States the Queen and Prince Philip went to Montreal to open the Olympic Games and to see their daughter compete for Britain in the equestrian events. There had been forebodings of a hostile reception by republican groups, and even of danger. In the event the French Canadians showed no such animosity. No doubt many stayed at home, but those who went out to welcome the Queen of Canada smiled and approved as she drove through the streets in an open car, a gesture last made by General de Gaulle when he was seeking to establish France's ancient claim to the loyalty of French Canadians.

It was thus that in 1976 North America was forcefully reminded of Britain's continuing significance, as the Germans had been by a royal visit in 1965, the Japanese in 1975, and the French both in 1957 and 1972. No Prime Minister or Foreign Secretary could have attracted such attention and aroused such enthusiasm. It is not the Queen alone who keeps Britain 'on the map'; but perhaps she makes the largest single contribution.

The very institution of the Monarchy, and its now traditional disengagement from party politics, can claim much credit for calming the waters at home and ruffling them with an exhilarating breeze abroad. So can the fact that the King or Queen of Great Britain, unlike the transitory head of a republican state, acquires knowledge of people and experience of events over many years. But the primary reason for the contribution the Crown has made to the maintenance of Britain's position in the world lies in the personality of the Queen herself.

It must be a record unique in the annals of a thousand years that a British Sovereign has reigned for twenty five years without once putting a foot wrong, though it may be argued that Queen Elizabeth I, who both ruled and reigned, reached her Silver Jubilee without making obvious errors of judgement. The Queen owes much to her upbringing: a father who was by no means clever, but had an unflagging sense of duty and developed great shrewdness; and a mother who supplied warmth, affection, a capacity to laugh at misfortune and irresistible charm. She owes much, also, to a husband with the ability, in any other circumstances, to be chairman of a great industrial enterprise; and to an unbroken family life which arouses admiration even among those who fail to emulate it. She has at least four qualities of her own without which all the gifts of the good fairies would have been of little avail. Those gifts are energy, patience, honesty and wisdom.

To travel as the Queen travels, with seldom a day of rest between official functions and tiring visits, and at the same time to read the Cabinet Papers, the Foreign Office telegrams and the countless documents requiring approval and signature by the Head of the State: this, interspersed with frequent audiences, investitures and dutiful entertaining at home and abroad, demands a vitality, combined with an unwavering attention to duty, such as few human beings could maintain over twenty five years, however pleasant it may be to be relieved of the fatiguing necessity of buying the food, paying the household bills and travelling by public transport. To perform these royal duties gracefully, and even to enjoy them, is more difficult still.

Patience is not a virtue for which those in positions of authority are usually noted. To listen for hours to speeches of welcome; to be studiously polite to people who may not naturally be bores but are overcome by shyness and by uncertainty how to behave; to watch school-children performing gymnastics in Australia which are little different from those performed in Canada, Fiji or Brazil; constantly to attend and usually to preside at long-drawn-out official functions; to think of things to say to total strangers with undisclosed personal interests; never to be able to fidget because every eye is on you; and always to be expected to smile: these and many other professional requirements call for a patience beyond what may reasonably be demanded of human beings. They are, in addition, combined with the serious political and economic worries of which the Head of State cannot be oblivious and with the diplomatic functions which the Queen, as Britain's leading representative, must always be ready to perform. By sheer strength of will-power the Queen controls the impatience she must often feel, and never fails to look imperturbable. Nothing is better calculated to win the esteem of her subjects, whether resident in the United Kingdom or beyond its shores.

Honesty in its true sense means a refusal to act a part in which you disbelieve, determination to live in accordance with the principles you accept, and an unwillingness to compromise on what you think morally wrong, however much you may be ready, for the sake of peace and understanding, to compromise on what you desire. It is not among the commonest of good qualities; but it is certainly among the most golden, and the British have been singularly fortunate to discover it in their Queen.

In June, 1953, when the Queen was anointed – 'as Solomon was annointed by Zadok the priest and Nathan the prophet' – the Archbishop prayed that she might receive 'the spirit of wisdom and government, the spirit of counsel and ghostly strength, the spirit of knowledge and true godliness'. Wisdom is denied to many brilliant men and women. It is a gift as easy to recognise as it is difficult to define, and it is as precious as it is rare. The Queen has had seven Prime Ministers in the United Kingdom alone, and although we be denied, perhaps for many decades, the knowledge of the extent to which they have been guided by her occasional advice – for it must be doubted if she makes a habit of offering it except when her experience or feminine intuition imperatively prompt her to do so – it is still more doubtful whether any of the seven would deny that she is wise. Impetuous words, let alone impetuous deeds, are dangerous to all connected with affairs of State, and to none more so than Constitutional Monarchs. The Queen has never once been heard to say anything that could give political offence. It need not be assumed that in the privacy of an Audience she has refrained from saying much that was of political, social and administrative advantage.

CHAPTER 2

Empire into Commonwealth

The transformation of the British Empire, the largest and most beneficent the world has known, into a free Commonwealth of Nations had begun a few years before the Queen came to the throne. The Indian sub-continent split into two antagonistic states and while one of them, Pakistan, was temporarily content to retain the British Crown as the symbol of its new sovereignty, the other, India, was determined to become a Republic. It had long been accepted that while the numerous British Colonies were directly subject to policies approved in Whitehall, the self-governing Dominions were independent countries whose only link with Britain was common allegiance to the throne. Now India, on receiving the freedom of Dominion status, was unwilling to recognise the King of England either as Emperor or King of India.

There were many, in the other Dominions as well as in Britain, who held that in such circumstances India must sever her relationship with the Commonwealth and Empire. Jan Smuts of South Africa and Robert Menzies of Australia were of this persuasion and so, in his heart of hearts, was Winston Churchill. However, the Prime Minister, Clement Attlee, was determined that if India would not stay within what was called 'the magic circle of the Crown', she should at least be offered every inducement to keep her connection with the Commonwealth. In this laudable objective he was ardently supported by the last Viceroy of India, Lord Mountbatten of Burma, whose close friendship with the Indian leader, Jawaharlal Nehru, turned the scales. The King, with sorrow but realistic good sense, renounced the proud title, Emperor of India, which his great grandmother had assumed seventy years before, and signed himself 'George RI' for the last time on 1st January, 1948. India, under the influence of Nehru, became and remained an active member of the Commonwealth.

In February, 1952, a substantial area of the map was still coloured in the red of the British Empire. In addition to the United Kingdom and the four old-established White Dominions, there were now three self-governing nations in Asia; for in February, 1948, Ceylon had followed India and Pakistan into independence and only Burma had chosen the road to separation. The rest of the Empire was intact. Measures were, however, already in hand to widen the participation of African leaders in the administration of their own countries and to lay the foundations, legislative as well as executive, for self-government. Such faint whispers of discontent as were audible at all came from a few black intellectuals whose views, formed by the London School of Economics or by American anti-colonialist influences, were held to be unrepresentative.

The Coronation, in June, 1953, was an occasion of loyal Imperial solidarity unmarred by any sign or sound of dissent. In her solemn Oath, the Queen swore to govern the peoples of her numerous 'Possessions, and the other territories to any of them belonging or pertaining, according to their respective laws and customs'. She promised that she would 'cause Law and Justice, in Mercy, to be executed' in all her judgements and in all her dominions. At that time, not only did quiet reign in the Colonies, but Ireland, north and south, was free of all but fringe agitation. The dismal Irish troubles were a fading memory and if partition was still proclaimed as an issue between Ulster and the Republic, it seemed likely to remain peacefully dormant, or at any rate a matter of words rather than of action. De Valera, like so many revolutionary tigers, had been tamed by age and responsibility.

Consolidation rather than immediate independence was thought to be the prime Imperial duty. Mr Attlee's Labour Government originated the idea of federating the self-governing Colony of Southern Rhodesia with the two strictly Colonial territories of Northern Rhodesia and Nyasaland. Their Conservative successors adopted the proposal with an enthusiasm which was guarded, at least as far as some members of the Cabinet were concerned, but in 1953 the Federation was established on a trial basis for seven years. A Governor General, in the person of Lord Llewellyn, and later of Lord Dalhousie, represented the Queen, and it was intended that if the experiment proved a success the Federation should in due course become, like Canada or Australia, a self-governing Dominion.

The idea had much to recommend it. There would be notable economic advantages in the close association of the three Colonies, a dam could be constructed at Kariba to produce power for the benefit of both Rhodesias, and it was hoped that a genuine multi-racial community would emerge in contrast to the ruthlessly white-dominated Union of South Africa on the Federation's southern border. It was not to be; for the nationalist leaders of the two black Colonies suspected it was a trap to subjugate them to the white rulers in Salisbury; and the latter feared it would delay the full Dominion status for which they had waited so long. In 1960 Mr Harold Macmillan appointed the Monckton Commission to examine the situation, hoping that after they had listened impartially to all the evidence they might be able to make recommendations which would enable the Federation to survive and to prosper; but the suspicions of Northern Rhodesia and Nyasaland were irremovable. The experiment, made with high hopes and noble intentions, foundered in mistrust and, as some maintained, in bad faith. Before the Queen's Silver Jubilee could be celebrated there was to be a long, unhappy period of ill-will and uncertainty which caused deep distress in Britain as well as in the whole continent of Africa.

The other attempt to establish a Colonial Federation also failed, though neither the attempt nor the aftermath left any legacy of ill-will. This was the Federation of the West Indies established in January, 1958, with Lord Hailes, the former Conservative Chief Whip, as Governor General. The distances between the islands were too great, their disparities of government and temperament too profound. In 1962 Jamaica and Trinidad each declared their wish to become independent Monarchies within the Commonwealth and gradually, as the other larger islands followed suit, this short-lived Federation was in its turn dissolved.

In October, 1952, came the first stirring of dissension in Africa. The Mau-Mau organisation in Kenya, a blend of nationalist fervour and primitive witchcraft, began its campaign of terrorism. The leader was a fanatic called Kimathi who used hypnotic despotism to dominate a group of Kikuyu tribesmen in the Aberdare forests and mountains. The Colonial Office pinned the blame for the insurrection on Jomo Kenyatta. He was indeed the leader of nationalist political agitation, but not the organiser of terrorist atrocity. He was interned and then, after the final destruction of Kimathi's gang in 1956, the Kikuyu became disenchanted with Mau-Mau, and in the best tradition of British political prisoners, Kenyatta emerged to lead his people to independence, to membership of the Commonwealth and to friendly co-operation with those who had fought and derided him.

The flames of sedition had scarcely been extinguished in Kenya when the Gold Coast seemed on the verge of catching alight, although nothing comparable to Mau-Mau was threatened. The leader was an attractive and vigorous nationalist, Kwame Nkrumah, who was ill-content with the slow, evolutionary process towards internal autonomy favoured by the Colonial Office. He was not spiritually, or even intellectually, uplifted by the prospect of parliamentary democracy on the Westminster model, at which the gift of a Speaker's Chair to the embryonic Gold Coast House of Commons seemed to hint. There were riots and there was civil disobedience, and the British Government, bowing with a good grace to evident impatience with a period of apprenticeship longer than Nkrumah and his supporters were prepared to accept, recognised the independence of the Gold Coast in March, 1957. A former Labour Minister, Lord Listowel, was appointed Governor General to represent the Queen, the name of the country was changed to Ghana (in deference to ancestral memories of an ancient African Empire lost in the mists of time) and the pattern was set for a succession of many Independence Ceremonies. The Queen sent Princess Marina, Duchess of Kent, as her representative, the Union Jack was lowered and the new flag raised with becoming decorum, and in an atmosphere of general good-will the Duchess of Kent opened the State Ball at Christianborg Castle by dancing with Nkrumah. The United States were represented by the Vice President, Richard Nixon. It was said that he noticed a pensive African leaning against a pillar in the ball-room. Seeking to be friendly, he asked: 'Well, my friend, how does it feel to be free?'

'I wouldn't know,' was the reply. 'I come from Alabama.'

After three years of independence, Ghana became a Republic and Nkrumah established himself as dictator, imprisoning the Opposition leaders and reducing the Parliament to an organ of one-party government. He declared his country's non-alignment with East or West in the world struggle for influence, and he paid visits to Moscow and other Communist capitals in order to cultivate the friendship of the 'Soviet bloc'. To this there was added galloping megalomania and unbridled corruption, but neither his flirtation with the Soviet Union nor his self-appointment as the Osageyfo (or Messiah) deterred him from remaining a warm supporter of the Commonwealth. His attendance at the meetings of Commonwealth Prime Ministers was constant and his interventions were, for the most part, constructive. In November, 1961, in spite of the security risk involved – for there had been bomb explosions in Accra, an attempt on Nkrumah's life and a further contraction of internal freedom – the Queen insisted on paying a ceremonial visit to Ghana. Grave doubts had been expressed in Britain, where it was feared that the Queen's life was being needlessly risked, but her courageous determination to go was acknowledged by the Cabinet, and amply rewarded by the fervid warmth of her reception and the consolidation of Ghana's loyalty to the Commonwealth connexion, a loyalty which survived the fall of Nkrumah and many subsequent changes of régime.

The independence of Ghana was followed, a few months later, by that of Malaya, recently saved from terrorist domination by the brilliant waging of jungle warfare under the leadership of Field Marshal Sir Gerald Templer. Then it was the turn of Cyprus, where, after a bloody insurrection aimed at uniting the island to Greece, Greeks and Turks were temporarily reconciled under a tri-partite guarantee given by Britain, Greece and Turkey, and the Cypriots became content to accept membership of the Commonwealth. They declared the island a Republic.

In 1960 the Federation of Nigeria, rich in oil prospects and containing so vast a proportion of the of the whole African population, obtained its independence. The country was united under the leadership of a great, humble and incorruptible Moslem, Sir Abubakar Balewa, who began his administration with faith in parliamentary government and with almost universal good-will. Three years later, Sir Abubakar, who had been instrumental in erecting a statue of the Queen by a skilful Nigerian sculptor in front of the Lagos Parliament building, explained that it was difficult for Nigerians to accept a European lady as their Queen, much as they respected her as Head of the Commonwealth; and so the Governor General, Dr Azikwe, became President of the Republic. The Nigerian experiment had a tragic set-back when in 1966 Sir Abubakar, the Golden Voice of Africa, was murdered in a *coup d'état* staged by Ibo officers. A year later the northern Moslems sought revenge by murdering thousands of Ibos. There followed three years of civil war in which the Ibos fought the rest of Nigeria, and although the number of casualties was wildly exaggerated by unscrupulous propagandists, the country suffered misery and dejection. In Britain there was vocal sympathy for the Ibo resistance, but the Labour Government gave firm support to the Federal cause, and to the astonishment of many the victorious Federalists showed a truly Christian clemency which was mainly inspired by their leader, General Gowon. Unfortunately he proved less adept at governing the country than at winning the war and sparing the vanquished. In spite of its tribulations, Nigeria remained united and became rich as the oil began to flow.

What Mr Harold Macmillan had described as the Wind of Change grew into a gale. Colony after Colony claimed and received its freedom, almost invariably taking its seat at the council table of a rapidly expanding Commonwealth. There was, however, one large and significant casualty. In 1960 the Union of South Africa, to which Britain had restored independent government after the Boer War with a magnanimity only equalled by that of the victorious Federal Government in Nigeria sixty years later, held a referendum on the question of Monarchy or Republic. The nationalist government of Dr Verwoerd wanted a Republic, to which all the British inhabitants of South Africa and many of the Dutch were opposed. The Republicans won by the narrow majority of 52% of the votes cast. It had by now been well established, with the agreement of the Queen, that a Republican constitution was no bar to membership of the Commonwealth of which all the members, Monarchies and Republics alike, recognised her as Head. The change of status did, however, require the formal approval of the other Commonwealth countries, and in the case of South Africa this was no mere formality.

In keeping with so much British practice and tradition, the rule that members of the Commonwealth should refrain from interference in each other's internal affairs is accepted but unwritten.

48

Nevertheless, a community of nations which is multi-racial could not, however deeply ingrained its belief in tolerating diversities, accept that the political and social segregation of whole sectors of a nation is solely a matter of domestic significance. The hearts of the South African nationalist government had hardened towards their black and coloured fellow-citizens as their parliamentary power increased, so that by comparison with their Afrikaaner predecessors, Smuts and Botha, they seemed to echo the biblical words of King Reroboam: 'My father chastised you with whips; I will chastise you with scorpions.' Feelings had been exacerbated by the brutality of the South African police in massacring over sixty African demonstrators at Sharpeville in March, 1960, a tragedy which was re-enacted with still higher casualties in Soweto and Cape Town in 1976.

The ideal of racial equality was, of course, new. The Government of George III had not included among its reasons for challenging the rebellious colonists of 1776 the fear that the Red Indians would be maltreated; nor had the British Liberal Government of 1906 had any qualms about returning to the defeated Boers freedom to rule South African natives by the use of the sjambok or whatever other instruments they might choose. Now a far more tender social conscience had developed in Britain itself; and with Nigeria and Ghana, as well as India, Pakistan, Ceylon and Malaya, having equal voices at the Conference of Commonwealth Prime Ministers which assembled in London in March, 1961, it became clear that if South Africa remained, more than half the others would go. Nor would any newly-enfranchised Colonies have joined. The British Commonwealth and Empire would have degenerated into a small white society whose membership became decreasingly coherent as new generations of Canadians, Australians and New Zealanders forgot or disregarded the ties with which kinship and a shared ordeal in two world wars had bound them to the mother country. In the face of the hostility shown by almost all the Commonwealth Prime Ministers, South Africa withdrew her application to remain in the Commonwealth on changing to a republican constitution.

Thus one of the richest and most enterprising of the former British Dominions entered an isolation ward, which became more restrictive as the 1960s gave way to the 70s, as the members of the

United Nations expressed their growing disfavour and as events in Rhodesia and the former Portuguese Colonies cast a menacing shadow southwards. Only five years before she came to the throne, the Queen had accompanied her father and mother on a triumphal tour of South Africa and had broadcast to the Empire from Cape Town on her 21st birthday. Now the accession to power of a group of honest but benighted disciples of the Old Testament who ignored the lessons of the New, and who were supported by a bare half of the white population and by none of the black majority, threw South Africa into an isolation which was far from splendid. A poll of all the inhabitants of the country would undoubtedly have produced a happier and healthier result.

The Commonwealth survived several other skirmishes with but light casualties. In Canada the perennial antagonism of British and French Canadians was accentuated in the 1960s as nationalist and separatist movements, albeit representing a minority of the French-speaking people, raised a loud clamour in Quebec. In 1964 the Queen and Prince Philip, despite grim warnings of a hostile reception, visited the town. Their courage in so doing – and indeed physical courage was required – was rewarded by an unexpectedly calm reception and an acknowledgement throughout Canada of the pacifying influence they had exerted. The situation was not improved by the tactlessness of General de Gaulle. He visited the Province in 1967 and, with a loud disregard of international good manners, reminiscent of Kaiser Wilhelm II before the First World War, shouted: '*Vive le Québec libre.*'

In 1967 the British left Aden, a Colony of a hundred and thirty year's standing which had once been a vital coaling station on the shipping route to India, and no less important as a base for the Royal Navy in its control of the Indian Ocean, the Persian Gulf and the Red Sea. Its Imperial value fell with the advent of air transport, the evacuation of the British military bases in Egypt and, for nearly twenty years after the Suez episode of 1956, the closure of the Suez Canal. After a painful confrontation with nationalist guerillas, aided by Colonel Nasser and the Soviet Union, the British Government abandoned Aden, which changed its name to the People's Democratic Republic of Yemen and did not seek inclusion in the Commonwealth. An earlier casualty, of even less importance, was the arid territory of British

Somaliland. On receiving independence in 1960 it joined its neighbour, the former Italian Somaliland, to form a new Republic of Somalia and quaintly chose the anniversary of the Battle of Trafalgar as its national day.

A greater loss to the Commonwealth, at least on sentimental grounds, was Pakistan. The antagonism between India and Pakistan was, for totally distinct reasons, matched by that between the western part of Pakistan, known as the Punjab in British Imperial days, and the former province of East Bengal. In 1971 a separatist movement in the east, led by Sheikh Mujibur Rahman, won an election and during an ensuing confrontation between the Sheikh's supporters and the Pakistan army India declared war on Pakistan in support of Sheikh Rahman. The Indians won a short campaign and the eastern part of Pakistan seceded to form the new State of Bangladesh which was admitted to the Commonwealth, with strong Indian support, in April, 1972. The aftermath was a sad one. Pakistan, defeated and disillusioned, withdrew from membership of the Commonwealth, and Bangladesh, ravaged by famine, floods and disease, renounced its initial democratic aspirations and was converted into a one-party state. In 1975 Sheikh Rahman, the country's founder, was overthrown and assassinated.

The gnawing and, as it seemed, incurable pain of Rhodesia was the most distressing problem in Commonwealth relations as the Queen's Silver Jubilee approached. It stemmed from the disintegration of the Rhodesian Federation; for when in 1964 Northern Rhodesia, renamed Zambia, and Nyasaland, renamed Malawi, broke away to become independent Republics within the Commonwealth, Southern Rhodesia remained as it had been before Federation, a Colony which was internally self-governing but still short of that independence, including defence and foreign affairs, which other less advanced communities had attained. The old, moderate leaders of the white community were replaced by obstinate men demanding immediate equality with the other self-governing states, but still professing fervent loyalty to the Queen and to Britain.

The British Government made strenuous efforts to dissuade the Southern Rhodesians, under the leadership of a gallant former RAF fighter pilot, Mr Ian Smith, from impetuous decisions which must eventually lead the country to disaster. They failed in their endeavours and, with singular ineptitude in the choice of date, the Southern Rhodesians made a Unilateral Declaration of Independence on Remembrance Day, 1965. Throughout 1966 the British Prime Minister, Mr Harold Wilson, was indefatigable in trying to negotiate a settlement that would satisfy the wishes of moderate African leaders for eventual majority rule, and yet allow time for education and experience to qualify the Rhodesian Africans, many of whom were still in a primitive stage of development, for the responsibilities which would one day be theirs. The precedent of Kenya, which had become independent in 1964 and in which the white minority, though not, alas, the Asian, were considerately treated by the new African rulers, seemed to offer hope of a comparable Rhodesian settlement in the years ahead; but the Rhodesian white settlers numbered some 250,000, in contrast to the 40,000 in Kenya, and it was their industrious enthusiasm and managerial skill which in less than one man's life-time had created out of scrub and bush a thriving modern community, with prosperous farms, fine cities, successful mining operations and the basis of an industry.

In spite of this Harold Wilson did succeed in persuading Ian Smith to accept a solution that would have given the European population twenty years in which to create a sound multi-racial society before they were numerically outvoted by the Africans. This had required courage as well as skill on Wilson's part, for the settlement would have been contested by the left-wing members of his own Labour Party who, from their distant ivory towers, advocated the totally unrealistic solution of immediate majority rule on the basis of one man – one vote. They failed to notice that this formula, bequeathed by the British, had already been discarded by the new, indigenous rulers of almost every African state. Wilson was saved from party embarrassment by the action of Ian Smith's colleagues in declining to endorse the settlement on which he and Wilson had agreed.

The Unilateral Declaration of Independence was an act of treason, but although some African members of the Commonwealth murmured briefly about Britain's duty to intervene with armed force, it was clear to most men that the British could not mount a military expedition in sufficient strength at short notice. Nor would it have been reasonable to require British troops to fight and kill their own kith and kin, many of whom, like Mr Smith himself, had fought for King and Country in the war. At Britain's request, sanctions were imposed on the rebellious Rhodesians by the United Nations, but many countries lacked diligence in enforcing the punitive measures, and as Rhodesia's traditional supplier, Britain, closed her trading doors, the Portuguese, Swiss and South Africans cheerfully entered the market place. French and German firms were not slow to seize their opportunities, and even the United States found Rhodesian chrome irresistible.

Retribution was at hand. The Portuguese Colonies of Mozambique and Angola fell into left-wing nationalist hands; the attempts made by Kaunda of Zambia and Nyerere of Tanzania to induce caution and achieve compromise foundered against the stony obstinacy of the Smith Government; and in 1976, as trained guerillas assembled on her frontiers, Rhodesia drew daily closer to a state of siege. In the autumn of 1976 hopes rose again when the Rhodesian Government accepted proposals made by the American Secretary of State, Henry Kissinger, for a transfer of power to a black majority in two years. In November a conference took place in Geneva, at which the Rhodesian nationalists and Mr Smith were present; but it was evident that a wide gap divided them. Rhodesian courage is to be admired as much as her folly is to be deplored. The episode has created strains within the Commonwealth, laid the foundation of potential disaster for South Africa and brought to an end, at least for the time being, the high hope of creating a multi-racial society in which Africans and Europeans could live side by side in good-will and learn to share the responsibility of government. The fulfilment of that hope might have pointed a moral of rare value not only to Africa, but to Great Britain, with its own racial tensions, to the United States, where the problem is still deeper-rooted, and to the entire world.

The British Empire was built over a span of two hundred years. It was dismantled and transformed in less than thirty. None but the ideologically blind and those nurtured on propaganda in place of history will dispute the benefits which it bestowed on its subjects; nor should either the fashionable predilection for self-abasement when referring to Britain's Imperial past, or the entirely different purpose and ideals of the modern Commonwealth, be allowed to distort history and diminish the achievements of Colonial administrators in the 19th and early 20th centuries. Not only were swamps drained, modern technologies introduced, roads and railways built and education provided, but the inestimable boons of peace, sound administration and impartial justice were offered to a third of the world's surface and a quarter of its population. The burning of widows on funeral pyres, the infanticide of twins and capital punishment at the whim of a ruler were firmly suppressed. The missionaries, often abused for their pains, were zealous guardians of their flocks against the petty tyranny of Colonial rulers and native chiefs alike.

The Empire brought wealth to Britain by providing raw materials for her industry, and in the process it enriched the economies of many subject peoples, not as fully as might have been desired, but to a degree far higher than the subsistence levels of pre-Imperial times. Peace, in some parts of the Empire, departed with the British troops, just as Britain herself succumbed to tribal feud and foreign invasion when the Roman Legions left her shores. The legacy of sound administration, of which the Indian Civil Service was the most renowned exponent, but for which the Sudan and Nigerian Civil Services and the unself-seeking members of the Colonial Service also deserve to be long remembered, was not universally rejected when the white officials went home. In almost all the lands trial by jury and the rule of law were, at least in theory, embodied in the new constitutions. The older generation in Britain look back nostalgically to an Empire in which they felt undiluted pride. For them, and indeed for many of their children, the heterogeneous Commonwealth which has succeeded it arouses no comparable surge of emotion. In 1977 they should nevertheless pause to consider what a remarkable achievement the Commonwealth in fact is and the extent to which both its survival and its utility are due to the personal inspiration, ceaseless travels and unwavering faith of the Head of the Commonwealth herself and of her husband, Prince Philip.

The Commonwealth in 1977 is an organisation united not, like NATO or the European Community, by treaty but by association. That association is in origin historical; and the link between its members is their common acceptance of the Queen as their Head.

There are thirty six self-governing members, of which twelve accept Queen Elizabeth as their Sovereign, nineteen are Republics and the remainder have their own hereditary or elective rulers. They have no common foreign policy, they are not averse to quarrelling with each other, they only share defence arrangements if they chance to belong to NATO or SEATO or some other mutual defence organisation. Nevertheless, in a divided world, where the United Nations Organisation has forfeited the faith of millions, and proved largely incapable of enforcing its resolutions, the Commonwealth is a multi-racial entity unique in its ability to discuss without prejudice, above the clash of races and colours, matters of interest to all its members. If thirty six Finance Ministers, or thirty six Ministers of Education, can meet to describe their problems and to hear the experience of others, the contribution to world sanity is greater than that made by any other international body. When the Heads of State and the Prime Ministers meet, as they have regularly met since the Commonwealth began, there is an opportunity for the Prime Minister of Canada to talk to the Prime Minister of Guyana, and for Zambia to meet New Zealand or Fiji, in the conditions of comfortable relaxation which are at their most congenial in a private club. To describe the Commonwealth as a club has become a cliché already long in the tooth (if indeed clichés have teeth, which is all too seldom the case). The analogy is none the less apt, for in a club members can say things which they would hesitate to mention outside, and the mere fact of common membership induces a probability of good-will and a strong possibility of companionship.

If this were all, the regular association of so many disparate nations would still be worth preserving, though there be no longer a formal political link between the members and they cannot be counted on to co-operate on issues of major international policy or even of defence. They do, however, share traditions of law, language and recent history, as well as an important range of common services. In broad terms, they accept the same standards of good international behaviour. Moreover, there have been, from the Colombo Plan onwards, joint endeavours to ensure social and financial collaboration. These have included the provision of large sums of capital by the developed countries of the Commonwealth for the benefit of their less prosperous fellow-members. Until the mid-1970s the currencies of all the members except Canada were tied to sterling, and the links between the City of London and the main Commonwealth financial centres have survived the weakness of the pound.

The great British trading companies are widely represented in Asia, Africa and North America: and the Commonwealth Development Corporation, the Commonwealth Development Finance Corporation, the London Merchant Banks, the Commodity Markets and the Insurance Companies all make a substantial contribution to capital investment and to the marketing of exports. They have helped to finance projects of industrial and agricultural importance, to build hydro-electric stations and other public utilities, and to expand those already in existence. Technical aid has been sent from the public and private sectors and not only from those of Britain, Canada and Australia; for India and Ceylon have been providers as well as recipients. Inspired by Voluntary Service Overseas, which started in Britain in the 1950s, the young people of all Commonwealth countries have been mobilised for service beyond their own frontiers and for youth exchanges between the members.

Personal and professional ties are stronger still. Englishmen do not need to regard themselves as foreigners in a Commonwealth country, in spite of new migration formalities necessitated by the violence of the modern world; nor are visiting Commonwealth citizens expected to feel they are abroad when they tread the streets of London, Edinburgh or Liverpool. Appeals to the Privy Council are now rare events, but British lawyers are in constant demand and doctors still more so. There is scarcely a capital without a high quota of resident and visiting businessmen, doctors, teachers and technical experts from other Commonwealth countries; and parliamentary delegates are seldom absent from the scene for long. An amiable relationship has been established in press, radio and television circles. There has long been an intimacy of association in the world of sport, exemplified by the Commonwealth Games and by the interchange of visits between cricketers, footballers, athletes and hockey players. This was regrettably marred, at least temporarily, by a dispute between New Zealand and the African countries which, heated by outside intervention, erupted at the Olympic

Games in July, 1976 and created the unfortunate precedent of confusing sport with racial politics.

In the academic field, the universities of all the Commonwealth countries have formed an Association. Its members hold regular meetings and congresses. Help is constantly given to students seeking places in the universities and technical colleges of other Commonwealth countries. A scholarship scheme, approved and subsidised by the Governments, went into successful operation a few years after the reign began, providing opportunities for students from all Commonwealth countries to study in each other's higher educational establishments. Many go to British universities, but British students for their part have accepted places in those of India, Ghana and Malaysia; nor have Canada, Australia and New Zealand been anything but generous in opening their academic doors.

In London a Commonwealth Institute, with a Board including all the High Commissioners, provides displays and exhibitions as well as devoting itself assiduously to educational and cultural activities. The Commonwealth Foundation fosters interchanges between a wide variety of professional bodies, and the Commonwealth Parliamentary Association maintains a full hundred branches. Lawyers, doctors, journalists, broadcasters, architects: these are but a few of the long list of professional men who have established associations to maintain institutional links between all the countries of the Commonwealth.

The emphasis in recent years has thus been on social, professional and financial links rather than on political co-operation. Nevertheless, in 1965 the Commonwealth Governments unanimously agreed to establish a Secretariat in London, not only to act as a clearing centre for communication between them, but also to resolve problems and promote understanding in all the spheres, including the political, where their interests either coincide or may be liable to collide. The first Secretary General, Mr Donald Smith, was a Canadian, and his successor, Mr S. Ramphal, is from Guyana. Without claiming a status of personal authority comparable to the Secretary General of the United Nations, he acts as the communicating link between all the member countries and fulfils many of the roles once assumed by the Dominions Office or its successor, the Commonwealth Relations Office; and the Commonwealth Secretariat has played an invaluable part in arranging technical assistance programmes and development projects, in the activities of youth organisations and in educational exchanges. The Queen gave Marlborough House, long the palatial residence of Queen Mothers and Princes of Wales, to be its headquarters and she follows its activities with close attention.

The Empire is no more; the Colonies are a mere handful, their status retained solely for peculiar reasons of local importance; but just as Imperial Rome left a legacy of law, language and literature which has lasted two thousand years, so Imperial Britain has left a still richer legacy which is capable of immediate enjoyment by her heirs and successors.

Since the Queen came to the throne, she and Prince Philip, jointly or severally, have paid no less than 167 visits to Commonwealth countries and the Queen herself has spent over 570 days in her Commonwealth travels. Some of these journeys, such as that to India in 1961, were of historic significance, for it had been fifty years since a British Sovereign set foot on Indian soil and in the interval the ruling Congress Party, which greeted the Queen with affection and acclaim, had struggled against all that the British Monarchy seemed to represent. Many of the other visits were long tours, lasting for weeks and penetrating into remote areas far from the capital cities. On formal occasions such, for instance, as the reception of the diplomatic corps by the Queen of Australia in Canberra, or the Queen of Canada in Ottawa, the Commonwealth High Commissioners are the first to be received and are then invited to stand behind the Queen with her personal Household while the representatives of foreign powers are presented.

On all matters relating to the Commonwealth, successive Prime Ministers of the United Kingdom have been as punctilious in consulting the Queen as ever Disraeli or Gladstone were in referring questions of foreign policy to Queen Victoria. Thus, Mr Macmillan kept the Queen informed and sought her views at every stage of the vexed affair of South Africa's expulsion from the Commonwealth and of the fruitless endeavours to save the Rhodesian Federation from dissolution; nor were Sir Alec Douglas Home, Mr Wilson, Mr Heath or Mr Callaghan any less exact in submitting for royal approval the proposals, in principle and in detail, for the long series of

Colonial Independence negotiations which stretched from Ghana in 1957 to the Seychelles in 1976.

Obviously the Queen, in spite of her frequent visits to many of the leading Commonwealth countries, neither can nor would wish to follow the internal affairs of nations which have their own Governors General or Heads of State with the same close attention as is her constitutional function in the United Kingdom itself. But when an initiative by one member of the Commonwealth has a bearing on the development or activities of the whole, it is the Queen's right and duty to be informed and, if she so wishes, to express her views and give her advice. Ministers of Commonwealth Governments on their way through London, are frequently received in Audience and, if opportunity allows, the Queen also receives Ambassadors accredited to a foreign country by a member of the Commonwealth.

Occasions of particular importance are the regular meetings of Commonwealth Heads of State and Prime Ministers. They are normally held in alternate years and there have been fifteen since the reign began. The early gatherings invariably took place in London, but as *the British Commonwealth* gradually, and without any formal decision, came to be regarded as *the Commonwealth*, it was appropriate that other capitals should also receive the Prime Ministers.

In 1971 they met in Singapore. This was the only Conference which the Queen did not attend, and while the Prime Ministers were engaged in their deliberations one of their number, Mr Obote, was forcibly ejected from his leadership of Uganda by a *coup d'état* in Kampala organised by Idi Amin, whose subsequent aberrations were responsible, first, for an undeclared war between Tanzania and Uganda, and then for a grave dispute with Kenya. Amin, who created himself both a Field Marshal and a Doctor, and then awarded himself the Victoria Cross, might have been regarded as a mere joke in bad taste, but the atrocities committed under his orders, and his overt support of the terrorists who hijacked an Air France plane in June, 1976, brought him into disrepute throughout the civilised world, effectively destroyed the East African economic community, and were a sore embarrassment to Uganda's fellow-members of the Commonwealth. At the end of July, 1976, Britain withdrew the entire High Commission Staff from Kampala. This was the first time diplomatic relations with a Commonwealth country had been severed; but it was equally the first time that a rogue elephant had been at large in the community, alarming his neighbours, terrorising his subjects and causing acute embarrassment to his fellow-members of the Organisation for African Unity.

In 1975 the Queen of Jamaica travelled to Kingston to receive the Prime Ministers and to be present in the city in which they were conferring. For 1977, on account of the Silver Jubilee, London has been selected as the meeting place. In large measure the Commonwealth owes its survival as an effective and, by its example, an influential body in the world of 1977, to the tireless enthusiasm of the Queen and Prince Philip and to their refusal to be discouraged by the set-backs, disappointments and occasional crises (of which disagreement over Suez was the most severe) that have been met sometimes as small pebbles and sometimes as menacing boulders along the way.

In spite of the Commonwealth's high traditions and distinguished origins, it might well have been found that it was built on sand so that, as time passed and old-established ties were loosened, it crumbled into a meaningless, ceremonial ruin as remote from modern reality as the Holy Roman Empire in its declining years. That it has not done so, and has retained its hold on the imagination and loyalty of Asians and Africans, West Indians and Malaysians, on the Old Commonwealth and the New, to an even greater extent than on the British themselves, is in large part due to Royal encouragement and enthusiasm. In a paradoxical society, where the assertion that all men are equal has been matched by the growth of racial tension throughout the world, the Queen and Prince Philip have never shown the slightest inclination to abandon their conviction that neither race nor religion nor colour should be taken into consideration in the judgement of men or of nations.

Papua New Guinea is not among the largest or best known of Commonwealth countries; but there is significance in the fact that in 1975 the inhabitants of those distant islands in Oceania, after a visit by the Queen during the previous year, tore up their draft republican constitution and invited Her Majesty to become Queen of Papua New Guinea as soon as they attained their independence from Australia. Those who, unlike the people of Papua New Guinea, prefer an indigenous Head of State, are none the less welcoming in the reception they give to the Head of the Commonwealth when she alights on their territory; but had Queen Elizabeth II and her husband been less assiduous in their attentions, less energetic in their travels and less genuinely devoted to a task which they alone can fulfil over so long a period, it is at least possible that during the last twenty five years the once proud Empire would have left no worthwhile succession to its finer traditions. Instead it has been transformed into a free association of Sovereign States. Few of them readily admit, at any rate openly, to pleasure or even profit from their Imperial past, but none resent the looser bonds which now unite an adult family.

CHAPTER 3

Defence of the Realm

By the end of the war it was clear that although the junior of the three Services, the Royal Air Force, might continue to march on last at ceremonial parades, it must be given priority in the defence of the realm. Nevertheless, in 1952, Britain still possessed an immense battle fleet with capital ships, aircraft carriers and a long retinue of cruisers and destroyers; while the army, supplied with a constant intake of National Service recruits at home, was using regular troops to fight in Korea, was occupying North Germany and was supplying garrisons for Singapore, Hong Kong, Cyprus, the Canal Zone and many other outposts of the Empire. But it was also clear to the Labour Government that the United Kingdom itself could only be defended by means of an Alliance of which the United States provided the backbone of men and material. To this end the North Atlantic Treaty Organisation (NATO) had been created, and nuclear-armed American aircraft were in operation from bases in Britain. It was a far cry indeed from the spring days of 1918 when all the heavy equipment of the American Expeditionary Force to Europe had been supplied by the British and the French.

With the threat of Russian aggression, recently exemplified by the blocking of overland routes to Berlin, the demands of active service in Korea and the necessity of policing half the world, as well as supplying a strong contingent to NATO, additional defence expenditure rather than retrenchment seemed to many responsible men an urgent necessity. Mr Attlee's Government had reached this conclusion. The resignations of Mr Aneurin Bevan and Mr Harold Wilson had been due less to the Cabinet's refusal to sanction the supply of free spectacles and false teeth than to their objection to spending more on defence. It was ironical that when a Conservative Government was returned to office, financial stringencies prevented them from including in the 1952 Estimates their Labour predecessors' proposals to raise the military budget.

Defence of the Realm

The RAF, vital though its role was admitted to be, was equipped
with aircraft which would soon be out of date. It had squadrons of
Meteor jet-fighters, and three months after the Queen's accession a
Canberra jet-bomber broke a record by flying to Australia in just
under twenty four hours; but in the nuclear age even these spec-
tacular machines were of limited value. The sole effective defence
against an enemy's atomic bombs was seen to be the ability to
retaliate. In spite of NATO and the presence in the United Kingdom
of American bombers, a British nuclear deterrent became the
principal preoccupation. Britain was already manufacturing her own
nuclear weapons, a fact which led to frantic demonstrations by the
supporters of the Campaign for Nuclear Disarmament, some of
whom were inspired by noble pacifist ideals and others by Communist ambitions to weaken the Western powers.

The first British atom bomb exploded in the Monte Bello
islands in October, 1952. Could Britain also produce the means to
deliver one? As one balance of payments crisis succeeded another
the answer became steadily more negative, but a determined effort
was made to dispute this unpalatable fact. A series of V-Bombers,
first the *Valiant* and then the *Vulcan* and the *Victor*, were designed
with the ability to carry an atom bomb and drop it directly over the
target. One such type of bomber would have sufficed, but national
pride, which some described as *folie de grandeur*, decreed that there
should be three. They were duly built, and were still in service in
the mid-seventies, but it was apparent that their chance of reaching
a strategic target against defence by radar-controlled guided missiles
would become slighter year by year.

The politically disastrous, though militarily successful, Suez
operation of November, 1956, was a watershed for strategic
planners. Till then the old, deep-rooted convictions of the imperial
past were predominant. The sea-lanes to India and the Antipodes
must be kept open; garrisons and bases all over the world must be
defended; Britain's mission to police her Empire and the seas must
be sustained. After Suez, the waters flowed down the other side
of the mountain and fully three years were devoted to discussing the
country's future role in a nuclear world, in which the British Isles
were neither geographically defensible nor materially powerful
enough to stand alone, with or without the support of the British

Commonwealth and Empire. The first British thermo-nuclear device, or hydrogen bomb, was exploded in 1957, but whatever the dreams of an independent nuclear deterrent, Splendid Isolation was a dream of the past. Partnership with the United States and active co-operation with NATO were now dominant themes accepted by all political parties.

It was already clear by 1957 that the value of the V-Bombers, with 'falling' bombs but no guided missiles, would be short-lived for any but tactical purposes. So, at great expense, a guided missile called *Blue Steel* was designed. It could be released from an aircraft at a range of little more than a hundred miles from the target. Unfortunately, there was every prospect that some equally well-guided rocket would soon be able to destroy the bomber before *Blue Steel* was close enough to be released. So the experts became interested in a ballistic missile called *Blue Streak*, which was a copy of the American *Atlas*. This would travel thousands of miles with commendable accuracy and could be launched from concrete pits in East Anglia, or wherever else was considered suitable by the authorities (though not, of course, by the local inhabitants, who were sure to become a primary target for nuclear attack by the enemy, especially as the liquid oxygen fuel would have to be stored in visible, and therefore vulnerable, surface installations). Luckily for the peace of mind of the East Anglians, the experts decided that the provision of atom-proof sites for *Blue Streak* would be expensive and many of them believed that it was, in any case, the wrong kind of weapon for British defence purposes. So, after spending a large sum of money on the preparatory manoeuvres, Her Majesty's Government decided to proceed no further.

In 1960 the undaunted planners became obsessed by another ballistic missile called *Skybolt* which would be fired not from vulnerable ground sites but from aircraft. The Americans, who had invented it and spent many millions of dollars on its design and development, themselves held divided views on its merits. The Defence Secretary, Mr Robert McNamara, thought it an extravagant project: the US Army Air Force wished to develop it further. In offering it to the British instead of to his own Air Force, Mr McNamara said that he would make no charge at all for the expensive development costs to date. Still more generously his

Department privately informed the British scientists why they themselves thought it unworthy of further expenditure. In spite of this, the Royal Air Force, by now desperate in their search for a modern weapon, wished to develop a *Skybolt* missile in conjunction with the French, and they tried to persuade the Government to approve the heavy cost of final development. Mr Harold Macmillan was wise enough to refuse. Instead, he went to Nassau in 1962 and made an agreement with the Americans to buy *Polaris* missiles. British-made thermo-nuclear warheads were affixed to them, thus providing the armament for the latest submarines. Everybody was content except the Royal Air Force, who saw the Navy taking over their deterrent role, and General de Gaulle, who pretended that the Nassau agreement was proof of that Anglo-Saxon solidarity which he deemed an incontrovertible reason for denying Britain entry into the Common Market.

In 1964 the Conservative Party took the curious decision to fight a General Election with the inclusion of 'Independent Nuclear Power' in their manifesto. As they lost the election it will never be known how they would have implemented this prohibitively expensive promise; but the victorious Labour Party were at once faced with difficult decisions on defence. They were sufficiently realistic to see that Britain's military role in the world of the 1960s, while it should match her responsibilities to NATO, must also match her resources. The temptation was to carry the economies too far, for the Labour leaders were enthusiastically wedded to spending more than the country could in any case afford on increasing social security, improving the Welfare State and authorising expenditure on every kind of public service, building and commitment for the future.

The Minister of Defence, Mr Denis Healey, was assaulted on one side by his own service advisers, demanding bigger and better weapons, and on the other by his parliamentary colleagues pleading that the claims of milk for school-children, new schools, more hospitals and higher old age pensions were superior to those of aeroplanes, submarines, tanks and missiles. The Cabinet ordered a huge decrease in the Defence Estimates. In obedience to his colleagues' decision, Healey cut several Gordian Knots. He cancelled the TSR 2 fighter aircraft, a British-designed model with fixed wings which contained every known electronic device and cost a fortune. Instead he sought to buy the American F111. It was scarcely less expensive but, because it was a swing-winged model, it was adjudged more up-to-date. There were, however, doubts whether it could fly, whereas the TSR 2 prototype had already proved its ability to do so.

The F111, too, fell by the wayside in the drastic cuts in expenditure which the Government were forced to make after the devaluation of the pound in 1967; and because the French were also chilled by a cold economic wind in that year, an Anglo-French project for a 'variable geometry' fighter was cancelled. The only British aircraft which the RAF were allowed to commission was the Hawker-Siddeley Vertical Take-Off *Harrier*, an invention of revolutionary ingenuity which contributed much to Britain's reputation in the field of aircraft design once it had survived a temporary cancellation of development expenditure, caused by the RAF's wish to substitute a supersonic version of the same aircraft called the P1154. This was technologically more advanced than any design that had been conceived on an American or European drawing-board.

There was thus, between 1956 and 1970, much wavering and indecision about aerial defence and nuclear deterrents. The judgement of Governments and experts was an expensive failure precisely in the years when financial stringency limited the choice which was available and required that firm orders be placed. Many millions of pounds were wasted because wrong decisions were taken, and in the event Britain's defences and striking power are no less dependent on the ultimate strength of the United States in 1977 than they were in 1952. In fact they are more so.

In the cuts imposed on the Defence Forces during the middle and late 1960s, and again in 1976, the deprivations of the Army were different from those of the other two Services. It was ordained that all three should reduce expenditure, but the principal savings naturally came from the cancellation of ship construction and aircraft development. The Army equips men whereas the Navy and the Royal Air Force man equipment. Thus the Army's contribution to economy was made by decrease of manpower. All establishments were reduced. Some regiments were disbanded. Others were amalgamated, and local loyalties were gravely disturbed. The Argyll and Sutherland Highlanders, in particular, fought their sentence of death with an offensive spirit worthy of their record in action; and they were reprieved after the Conservative electoral victory in 1970.

Meanwhile drastic changes had been made in the organisation of the Defence Staffs and Departments. In 1952 there were still the three separate departments of the Admiralty, the War Office and the Air Ministry. The Chiefs of Staff were almost exactly as they had been before the war. The Ministry of Defence was a small co-ordinating department, little different in size or scope from the war-time Office of the Minister of Defence which Churchill had set up under General Ismay in 1940. The first change was made in 1956 when Marshal of the Royal Air Force Sir William Dickson was pro-moted to be Chairman of the Chiefs of Staff Committee, presiding over the three Chiefs of Staff with a wider responsibility than he had had as Chief of the Air Staff; and in 1959 this new post increased in importance, largely because of the driving personality of its new incumbent, when Lord Mountbatten succeeded Dickson and was appointed Chief of the United Kingdom Defence Staff.

Mr Harold Macmillan reached the conclusion that in the world of the 1960s three distinct Service Ministries were no longer efficient instruments for the control of national defence. On his inspiration plans for rationalising the system were set in train. Thus, in 1964, while Sir Alec Douglas Home was Prime Minister, the long-estab-lished Service Departments lost their identity and were merged in one monolithic Ministry of Defence under Mr Peter Thorneycroft. The flag of the Lord Commissioners of the Admiralty was hauled down in the presence of the last First Lord, Lord Jellicoe, whose father had commanded the Grand Fleet at the Battle of Jutland and who had himself been First Sea Lord. The Queen assumed the ancient title of Lord High Admiral, which has been in commission for over two hundred and fifty years. The offices of Secretary of State for War and for Air vanished for ever. In keeping with modern requirements, the high policy of all the defence forces was concentrated in the hands of one Secretary of State and the detailed affairs of the three services were relegated to subordinate Ministers, whose rank Mr Harold Wilson subsequently reduced to Parliamentary Under Secretary. They were housed with most of the civil and military staffs of the three Departments in one large and architecturally repellant office-block on the Victoria Embankment.

The Royal Navy was deprived of its battleships shortly after the beginning of the reign. One nuclear shell or bomb would have meant their immediate destruction and it was too expensive to retain even the latest of them, *HMS Vanguard*, for prestige or ceremonial purposes. One by one these magnificent emblems of maritime supremacy were towed away to be broken up. The cruisers went too, the last, *HMS Belfast*, being preserved near Tower Bridge as a monument for the rising generation to visit and admire. By 1960 there were already more Admirals on the Active List than Ships in Commission. The aircraft-carriers fought sturdily for survival and there was, until 1965, a project to build a new carrier of great size and still greater modern gadgetry. The Royal Air Force which, even before the war, regarded the Navy with a hostility otherwise reserved for the Axis Powers, maintained their vendetta by arguing that the F111 fighters which they were then expecting to acquire would be adequate to cover troop landings a thousand miles away. They declared that both aircraft-carriers and the Fleet Air Arm were unnecessary luxuries and Mr Healey, searching earnestly for something expensive to scrap in the interest of further expenditure on the Welfare State, greeted their arguments with joyful relief. In February, 1966, the Parliamentary Under Secretary for the Navy, Mr Christopher Mayhew, who believed Mr Healey to be wrong, said so publicly and resigned. So did the First Sea Lord, Sir David Luce.

It was not only the ships that were scrapped, but the bases too. Malta became independent and its famous harbour, placed in charge of civilian contractors, could thenceforward be regarded more as a port of call than a permanent base; Aden fell into hostile hands; Singapore was held to be too expensive and, with memories of 1942 still fresh, untenable in war; Simonstown in South Africa was discarded because the Labour Government thought it wicked to rub shoulders with the Afrikaaner supporters of apartheid and chose to turn a blind eye to the growth of Soviet naval power in the Indian Ocean; and in 1968 the decision was taken to withdraw the Royal Navy from the Persian Gulf in three years' time, despite the practical value of its presence to the small oil-soaked Arab Sheikdoms when they were threatened by their larger neighbours. Although temporarily halted by the return of the Conservatives to power in 1970, the withdrawal from the Gulf finally took place in 1975. Cyprus remained, its utility decreased by the division of the island between Greeks and Turks; and Gibraltar was kept less because of its value as a base than because the inhabitants, many of whom have the political advantage of belonging to the Transport and General Workers Union, were steadfastly opposed to incorporation in Spain.

Britain still has a small, well-equipped modern navy, which is perennially short of the money needed to build new ships and convert old ones, but which is capable of playing its part in meeting the country's obligations to NATO and might, from time to time, quell a dissident movement on a Caribbean islet; but the Royal Navy of 1977, although maintaining its inherited quality and traditions of service, stands in much the same relationship to the navy of 1952 as a well-groomed mouse to a mammoth. Mammoths are too expensive to feed nowadays.

The *Polaris* submarines do, of course, dispose of a destructive power many times greater than all the battleships which ever sailed the seas. But this is the ultimate power and if it were ever used it would be at a time when the world was being depopulated in a final, gigantic holocaust. In the more probable event of limited hostilities, while the nations were reeling unsteadily back from the precipice of mass suicide, the nuclear submarines would lie motionless at their allotted stations. Thus the Royal Navy of 1977 cannot aspire to be more than one highly professional unit in an allied contingent, itself outmatched in size, though not necessarily in efficiency, by the widely-deployed naval forces of the Soviet Union.

It is no longer sufficient for Naval Officers and Ratings to be men of good character, well-trained seamen and, in the case of Officers, specialists in gunnery, signals or engineering. They must be qualified to handle complex equipment and to master the skills of an entirely new kind. If the order to 'make and mend' ever be given in a nuclear submarine, it is to be hoped that it retains its traditional meaning of permission to relax; any attempt to interpret the order literally would give justifiable grounds for alarm; but it is a fact of modern naval life that a submarine sailor, at sea for weeks or months at a time without ever seeing salt water or breathing fresh air, must be an expert and a professional in matters which bear little relationship to the element in which he serves.

This is not true to the same extent of the other services, but both the Army and the Royal Air Force use equipment which, as the years go by, becomes scarcely less complicated than that supplied to the Navy. Until manned aircraft become obsolete the RAF will undoubtedly retain the dash and the proficiency by which their fame was created and their place in the history books assured. The Army, for its part, has had the experience of using its equipment in action, first in Korea, with as yet little advance on the methods and armaments of the Second World War, and later in Aden, Cyprus, Oman and Northern Ireland. In the early 1960s thirty thousand British troops were operating in Malaysia on account of the so-called 'Confrontation' between that Commonwealth country and President Sukarno's Indonesia about the possession of North Borneo. It was a long assignment, no less demanding in patience and the skills of jungle warfare than the earlier struggle against the Communist guerillas who terrorised the Malayan rubber plantations in the 1950s. The military problems were handled with indisputable efficiency and the operations, which ended in 1966, were successful. In spite of this, and the number of troops involved, the 'Confrontation' was largely ignored by Parliament, the Press and Television so that the Public were scarcely aware of the campaign.

In Cyprus during the late fifties and in Northern Ireland during the seventies, the Army faced with disciplined courage the horrors of civil insurrection, the stabbing and shooting in the back, the ambushes and the land mines. The last National Servicemen returned to civilian life in 1964, and Britain's only peace-time experiment in conscription came to an end. An entirely professional army required and obtained conditions and rates of pay which would have astonished the soldiers of a previous generation, and this was achieved with an increase of efficiency and no decline in discipline.

The Army has, in essence, been mechanised. Royal Marine Commandos fight under its command on land and it has been trained to co-operate with the other services and with allied forces, realising that an important part of its duties will henceforth be to fight if not in, at least from, the air. The amateur soldier has vanished.

In his place there are highly qualified professionals and particular emphasis has been laid on training NCOs in leadership. The dull routine of the barracks square has been diversified by adventurous exercises, with stress on the part to be played by the individual soldier and the imagination he is expected to use. The iron rigidity of military life and the chasm which separated Officers and Other Ranks have been replaced by a relaxed, but none the less efficient and generally accepted, discipline depending on the mutual respect of the leaders and the led. In 1977 the British Army compares well in morale and experience with any in the Western world, nor is it short of voluntary recruits.

The old Territorial Army which provided such a vital backing for the Regulars in two world wars was abolished in 1967, but the Government's endeavour to make a small retrenchment by this un-imaginative step met with such resolute opposition that a new Territorial and Army Volunteer Reserve was created to provide a supporting body of trained officers and men who can be used as re-inforcements. It is much smaller than the former Territorial Army, but unlike its predecessor it is equipped with modern weapons, is well integrated with the Regular Army and includes specialists in the various military trades. It is too small to be an effective reserve of trained manpower in a serious emergency, but it would be capable of reinforcing certain vital elements of the British Army of the Rhine where, in 1977, the main strength of the nation's land forces is deployed on their important but unspectacular duties in support of NATO.

The royal family extended their traditionally close association with the armed forces. The Queen, Colonel of the Grenadiers before she came to the Throne, and as much concerned with regimental affairs as a woman could be, married a serving officer of the Royal Navy who had been mentioned in despatches for his part in the Battle of Matapan. Their eldest son was not content with the honorific colonelcies and commands which would, in any event, be conferred on the Prince of Wales. After his studies at two universities, Cambridge and Aberystwyth, he went to Cranwell, obtained his Wings as a pilot in the Royal Air Force and was appointed a Flight Lieutenant. Then, in 1971, he joined the Royal Navy in which he served actively for five years, until the time of his mother's Silver Jubilee, rising to the command of *HMS Bronington* entirely on his own merits.

The Defence of the Realm in 1977 conjures up a picture totally different from that in days gone by. It is no longer a matter of repelling foreign invaders or fighting for civilisation in the trenches of Flanders and the sand-dunes of North Africa. The Verse of the National Anthem which called on God to 'scatter her enemies and make them fall', to confound their politics and frustrate their knavish tricks, has fallen into disuse. This is regrettable, for there are still enemies who are much disposed to the employment of knavish tricks. Whatever the danger of Russian aggression, neither the Soviet land forces, armed with nuclear weapons, nor those of any other power, are comparable to the French under Napoleon or the Germans under William II and Adolf Hitler; for to-day a full-scale military attack would almost assuredly be the signal for a world holocaust, consuming civilisation long before the armies could be deployed. Therefore, the duties of the soldiers, sailors and airmen of the Queen bear little resemblance to those familiar to their fathers and grandfathers.

Except in Ulster, it is sixty years since troops were used to give active support to the civil power. In a national emergency, the Army may still be required to unload ships or guard public utilities against organised disturbers of the peace, but police duties are a function which no government willingly orders soldiers to assume. There have been occasions in the present reign, and there may be others, when British troops were sent to restore order in foreign lands, such as Cyprus, Oman or Malaysia, because it was a British responsibility to quell disorder, or because the local authorities appealed for help. To-day, however, the primary role of all three services is to form part of an international Defence Force dedicated, by its armaments and its efficiency, to deter aggression. Only if, by some unlikely chance, a war were to be waged with conventional weapons, would the armed forces of the Crown be called upon to fight and die for the survival of principles which the peoples of the Western world, whatever their internal political squabbles, hold sacred.

Part II

THE GOVERNMENT
OF BRITAIN

CHAPTER 4

The Three Estates

The fact that the Royal House descends in direct line from King Alfred was considered important in the genealogically conscious 19th century, although even then a Poet Laureate could write:

> 'The gardener Adam and his wife
> Smile at the claims of long descent.'

The present generation is, in the main, indifferent to such considerations; but the great majority are none the less well content with the institution of a hereditary Monarchy, perhaps more so than they have been for a hundred years. There can be few who would willingly exchange the Queen for a drab superannuated politician as President of the British Republic. Some, disenchanted by the Houses of Parliament and by the present system of Cabinet Government, might conceivably be tempted to welcome an experiment in Presidential Government, on the American or French pattern; but there can be no doubt at all that most of Her Majesty's subjects would, if consulted, express a strong desire to retain their present status and are in favour of distinguishing the Head of the State from the Head of the Government. As Winston Churchill used to proclaim: 'A battle is won, crowds cheer the King: a battle is lost, the Government falls.' The British have no objection at all to symbolising their patriotism in the person of their Sovereign.

This preference is based to some extent on sentiment, to some on a natural inclination to accept what has always been, and by no means least on personal affection for the Queen and her family. It is, nevertheless, expedient to examine the institution of the Monarchy itself, the changes that have taken place in its power and influence, and the relevance of a hereditary system in the last half of the 20th century.

Some similes, however hackneyed, are indispensable. They include the likening of ancient institutions to a river. In the case of the

British Monarchy the comparison is entirely apt, for rivers run fast near their source, flow through steep gorges, become torrents difficult to navigate, are joined by tributaries, fall over dangerous rapids and sometimes sweep ruthlessly away everything that blocks their passage. As they near the sea, they broaden into a quieter, even-flowing stream, irrigating the countryside through which they pass and attracting the people not only to construct their houses, their factories and their great cities on the banks, but also to dam the flow of the waters, to build bridges and to take measures to prevent the river overflowing its natural course. Such has been the story of the Monarchy from the Plantagenets to the House of Windsor.

Queen Elizabeth II inherited a Crown shining brightly because of the example which her father and her grandfather had set, and the love they had inspired. In 1952 it was, however, already a different Britain, for the two greatest wars in history had shaken the foundations of society. The map of the world and the outlook of the human race were much changed since the day in 1911 when her grandfather was crowned. Moreover, she was a woman and she was only twenty five years old. The Prerogatives of the Sovereign were, in theory, intact; but many of those on which Queen Victoria and Edward VII had always insisted, such as the right to be consulted personally in all affairs relating to foreign policy, had lapsed when the dynasties ruling other European countries vanished from the political scene. The undoubted influence of the Sovereign on the choice of Ambassadors, Bishops and even Cabinet Ministers had also waned. Queen Victoria constantly intervened in affairs of state and as late as 1892 personally chose Rosebery as Prime Minister in preference to Harcourt; Edward VII kept a stern eye on the activities of his Ministers; George V played a principal part in the formation of the 1931 National Government; George VI never hesitated to argue with Winston Churchill about appointments, and in 1945 was responsible for persuading Clement Attlee to reverse his original intention of appointing Ernest Bevin Chancellor of the Exchequer and Hugh Dalton Foreign Secretary.

The new Queen had in Winston Churchill a Prime Minister who paid deference to the rights of the Sovereign, but he had no ambition to play the part of Lord Melbourne nor, since the Queen was married to a man of high intelligence and dynamic personality, was there the slightest need for that avuncular training which Queen Victoria had gratefully accepted from King Leopold of the Belgians, as well as from Melbourne. Labour Members of Parliament had adopted the principle of electing their leader, a process which some people still thought unconstitutional, since it effectively obliged the Sovereign to send for the Member thus elected when Labour won a General Election. Yet it would have been difficult to dispute that it was the Queen's essential right and duty to select her Prime Minister and to exercise her own judgement if the issue was in doubt. When Churchill resigned in April, 1955, the matter of his successor was not mentioned in his final Audience. Before he finally left Downing Street he caused this to be recorded together with the opinion, expressed as one who had had a longer practical experience of the workings of the Constitution than anybody else, that no outgoing Prime Minister had the right to volunteer a suggestion about his successor unless the Sovereign specifically asked for advice.

The point was not immediately relevant, for there was no doubt, in the Conservative Party or elsewhere that the bespoken successor to Churchill was Sir Anthony Eden. It was, however, a relevant point in January, 1957, when Eden resigned, for a choice had to be made between Mr R. A. Butler and Mr Harold Macmillan; and in 1963, when Macmillan was taken ill, there were a number of contestants for the Prime Ministership. The Queen had to decide, though not without securing the best advice available to her. In 1957 the Lord Chancellor and Lord Salisbury took a poll of the Cabinet and reported the result to Buckingham Palace, while the Queen sought the views of Sir Winston Churchill, Lord Chandos and Lord Waverley. The Cabinet poll and the views of the elder statesmen left her in no doubt that she should send for Mr Macmillan. In 1963 the Conservative Party was divided in its preference: some were for Mr Butler, others for Lord Hailsham. The Queen, who had not consulted her outgoing Prime Minister in 1955 or in 1957, decided to do so in 1963; and in consequence she sent neither for Butler, nor for Hailsham, but for Lord Home.

Home generously resigned the leadership of the Conservative Party some months after his narrow defeat in the 1964 election. The Conservatives then decided to follow the practice of their opponents and to invite the Members of their Party in the House of Commons to elect a new leader. There was a contest between Mr Edward Heath and Mr Reginald Maudling, which Mr Heath won. Meanwhile, on the death of Mr Hugh Gaitskell, the Labour Members of Parliament had held a contest between Mr Harold Wilson and Mr George Brown, which Mr Wilson won. Thenceforward the hands of the Sovereign were in all normal circumstances tied, for whichever Party won an Election, she would in practice be bound to send for the man or woman chosen by the Members of that Party in the Commons. A further precedent was established in 1976. Mr Harold Wilson publicly announced his intention of resigning as soon as the Labour Members of Parliament chose his successor. He postponed doing so for three weeks until the Labour Members, in their third ballot, selected Mr Callaghan, whom the Queen then invited to form a Government. It was the first time there had been a change of Prime Minister while Labour was in Office.

Thus a political function of the Sovereign, which is of great practical importance, but which might in certain circumstances bring the Monarchy into the political arena, was reduced almost to vanishing point in the 1960s. But it was not abolished and it is always possible that circumstances may arise in which any Head of a parliamentary state, whether Royal or Presidential, is obliged to make a personal decision who shall be Prime Minister, so that the government of the country may continue without serious interruption.

The other Royal Prerogatives are unlikely to be used again unless Parliamentary Government, democracy and internal stability are in danger of crumbling into ruins. Queen Anne vetoed a bill; but no Monarch has done so since the beginning of the 18th century and the only, scarcely conceivable, situation in which the royal veto could be used would be to thwart a decision by an irresponsible majority in the House of Commons to prolong the life of Parliament in order to establish single-party rule, or to change the system of government without first holding an Election so as to discover the will of the people.

William IV was the last King to dissolve Parliament without the advice of the Prime Minister, and it is hard to imagine conditions which could lead to the repetition of such a royal initiative. Refusal of a request for a Dissolution is improbable but conceivable; for it is the Queen's duty to ensure that the Country is governed in accordance with the will of Parliament, and if a Prime Minister sought a Dissolution without the full support of his colleagues, or when another Party or combination of Parties seemed likely to command a majority in the House of Commons, it might be the Queen's uncomfortable duty to refuse a Dissolution until she had satisfied herself that no alternative Government could be found. With approximate equality between the two major parties in the Commons, and a number of small groups offering a variety of governing combinations, such an eventuality cannot be entirely excluded.

Whatever the hypotheses about the future, the Queen has, in practice, lost one potentially embarrassing political power which she possessed in 1952: that of choosing whom to invite to form a Government when there is no single incontrovertible candidate. Her other royal Prerogatives are dormant, as they had been for many years before she came to the throne. Most of them could only be revived in the case of an unprecedented national emergency, and it must therefore be the fervent hope of the Queen and her subjects that they will always remain as they are to-day, a historic survival of royal powers inappropriate to the well-ordered functioning of a Constitutional Monarchy. Hurricanes do, nevertheless, occasionally blow at unexpected times and from unexpected quarters. Therefore, given the immense safeguards of precedent and, in normal circumstances, of ministerial advice, it would be an imprudent nation which demanded the formal revocation of the latent powers of the Crown.

It is in her capacity as Head and chief representative of her peoples, rather than as constitutional Head of State, that the Queen's position is different from that of her forebears. She has not, like previous Monarchs, been the symbol of loyalty and patriotism in war, for there has been no nationwide appeal to fight 'For Queen and Country'. On the other hand she has had, and used, opportunities to be seen and to be known which her predecessors never had. George V made a royal progress to Delhi to be crowned Emperor of India; George VI, whose reign was largely consumed by war and its aftermath, went to the United States and Canada in 1939, and made a lengthy tour of South Africa and Rhodesia in 1947; Elizabeth II, Head of a huge Commonwealth in the Jet Age, is a constantly travelling Monarch and when she is not opening Parliament in a distant realm, or paying an official visit to some foreign land, there is no shortage of towns, schools, regiments, ships, factories, hospitals and benevolent institutions anxious to welcome her in the United Kingdom.

Thus, the first Estate of the Realm, with its active political powers reduced by precedent to the right to be informed, to encourage and to warn, also fulfils a function which no other Estate, ancient or modern, can usurp. It is clear that in one important, and indeed crucial, aspect, the institution of the Monarchy has radically altered. Its influence, and perhaps its very existence, depends on the personality of the Sovereign. As recently as 1936, when Edward VIII abdicated, the institution was seen to be of greater strength and significance than the King himself. In 1977 Elizabeth II keeps her hold on the loyalty and affection of her subjects still more as an individual than as Queen. 'Receive,' the Archbishop said, 'these bracelets of sincerity and wisdom . . . for symbols and pledges of that bond which unites you with your Peoples.' Perhaps none of the symbols of the Coronation was more appropriate to their recipient. There have been some among her Ministers who regarded the Monarchy as an outdated and expensive relic, which served no practical purpose but, on the contrary, perpetuated both class distinction and the pernicious doctrines of inherited advantage. It may be doubted whether Mr Richard Crossman was alone in changing his mind when, as Lord President of the Council, he found himself frequently in the presence of the Queen; and those who have discovered that State Visits to Britain do more than dislocate the London traffic admit the notable diplomatic value of a Sovereign whose long experience of public affairs enables her to offer visiting Kings, Presidents, and the important political and official entourage which accompanies them, a great deal more than splendid pageantry; although that is in itself an invaluable contribution to success in impressing foreign dignitaries. It remains none the less true that at the end of the 20th century, the British Monarchy would be unlikely long to survive an unwise, self-centred, headstrong, corrupt or even a self-indulgent Monarch.

*

In 1952 the second Estate of the Realm, the House of Lords, was much the same in composition, though not in power or influence, as it had been a century earlier. There were many more peers, because 20th century Prime Ministers were lavish with their recommendations, and therefore a high proportion of those with seats in the Lords were of the first or second generation; but, except for the Bishops and the Law Lords, all held their seats on a hereditary basis. It was an exclusively masculine gathering, for peeresses in their own right were excluded. There were 860 members who included the two Archbishops, 24 Bishops, 16 representatives for Scotland, elected by their fellow Scottish noblemen at the beginning of each new Parliament, and five surviving Irish representative peers who under the system existing until 1922 had been elected for life.

The right of the Lords to reject legislation had in practice been reduced to a delaying power by the Parliament Act of 1911, and even this was denied to them if the Speaker of the House of Commons certified that a bill sent from the Commons was a 'money bill'. In 1949 Mr Attlee's Government curtailed this power still further, so that the period of delay might only extend to one year from the date of the Second Reading of a bill in the House of Commons. The practical function of the House of Lords became one of examining legislation passed, often in a hurry, by the Commons, spotting imperfections and proposing amendments which were then sent back to the Commons for approval or rejection. It also happened from time to time that because business in the Lower House was congested, Government bills, or Private bills on matters of specialised rather than general concern, were initiated in the Lords where they received their first scrutiny.

Twenty five years later, the powers of the House of Lords are unaltered, although the method of exercising them has evolved; but the constitution of the Chamber is radically different. There are 1,117 members including the Bishops and the 16 Law Lords. Many hereditary peers have, for the duration of a Parliament, renounced their right to be summoned. Women are admitted, whether because they are hereditary peeresses in their own right or because they have been created Baronesses for life; all the Scots, but none of the Irish (unless they happen also to be peers of the United Kingdom) have the right to take their seats; and the total includes 282 Life

Peers. There are still a few survivals of the past: for instance the age of Commoners entitled to vote in Parliamentary and local elections has been reduced to 18, but peers are not eligible to sit in the Lords until they are 21; and although the offspring of what Sir William Gilbert called 'that annual blister, Marriage with Deceased Wife's Sister', have ceased to be bastards, it is considered that the ancient prejudice would still apply in the case of succession to a peerage. All who do legitimately succeed have the right to renounce their title and their seat in the Lords; but as a counter-attraction peers are now paid a daily tax-free allowance when they choose to attend.

One important change came about as a result of the 1963 Peerages Act, which was based on the recommendations of a Committee established in the late fifties under the chairmanship of Lord Swinton. Its provisions included the voluntary renunciation of a peerage for the life of the new holder. He or she would be obliged to make the decision within one month, if already a Member of Parliament, and within twelve months if not. Some eldest sons of peers elected to the House of Commons had a strong, but long-frustrated, desire not to be translated to the Upper House when their fathers died and thus be forced to abandon certain political ambitions. Among those ambitions was the prospect of being either Prime Minister or Chancellor of the Exchequer. No heir to a peerage had ever felt keener to avoid an obligatory coronet than the Hon. Anthony Wedgwood Benn, MP, who became annually more distressed by the prospect of becoming the 2nd Viscount Stansgate. On the other side of the House of Commons there sat until 1950 the Hon. Quintin Hogg, who had then succeeded his distinguished father as the 2nd Viscount Hailsham. They each had political ambitions and natural abilities. Mr Wedgwood Benn's earnest arguments on this matter wrung many political hearts, but the gracious decision of Mr Macmillan's Conservative Government to heed his prayers had results that were not foreseen. Under the 1963 Act all existing peers, other than those of the first creation, were given an initial period of six months in which to decide whether to renounce for life. The 2nd Viscount Hailsham, a much favoured candidate for the succession to Mr Macmillan, did so. His example was followed by the Foreign Secretary, whose claims to be Prime

Minister had not until then been widely canvassed, the 14th Earl of Home.

In no country but Britain would a hereditary Second Chamber have been considered anything but fantasy in the 20th century. There were, by the law of averages, sure to be some brilliant men among eight or nine hundred peers. Such were, for instance, the 3rd Earl Russell, more generally known as Bertrand Russell and the Earl of Halifax, a Fellow of All Souls. There were men of distinction in all walks of life on whom peerages had been conferred in recognition of their services. There were also bound to be dunces, dunderheads and the occasional lunatic. A system which might be thought defensible when both power and responsibility were represented by land, and most of the great landowners sat in the House of Lords, was impossible to justify in the 1950s on any grounds but tradition, sentiment or a decreasingly held belief in hereditary excellence.

There have been many endeavours to reform the House of Lords and to introduce the principle of life peerages. They failed because the House of Commons was jealous. A more logically selected Second Chamber could scarcely be denied additional powers to amend or reject bills passed by the Commons. As long ago as 1855 it had been decided to make an eminent Judge, Sir James Parke, a Life Peer. There were angry debates; the Committee of Privileges protested; and in the end the problem was resolved by converting Sir James's incipient life peerage into a hereditary one with the title of Lord Wensleydale. Future controversies of the same kind were averted by the decision, in 1876, to create Law Lords, who took their seats in the House on a non-hereditary basis; but it was not until the middle of the 20th century that Lord Simon, who had been Lord Chancellor in Churchill's war-time coalition, proposed that a dozen non-legal life peerages be created. This sensible suggestion was opposed by Lord Salisbury and others on the grounds that a breach of the hereditary principle in the House of Lords would be damaging to the conception of a hereditary Monarchy. The fact that the stability of the three Scandinavian Monarchies and those of Holland and Belgium had never been disturbed by the absence of a hereditary Second Chamber was, for the purpose of the argument, disregarded.

By 1958 these objections were overcome and a Life Peerages Act

was passed, applicable to women as well as to men. This innovation
was seen to have the dual advantage of removing what was undoubtedly an anomaly (though the creation of hereditary peerages
was not debarred), and of introducing into the Lords people of experience who would swell the number of daily attendances and add
strength to the debates. The intention and expectation was that this
transitory nobility would make a notable contribution to the
business of the House. In fact both Mr Harold Wilson and Mr
Edward Heath created many life peerages for honorific purposes, or
in order to offer a graceful retreat to those whose services they no
longer required. Much adverse comment was caused when, in 1974,
Mr Wilson made his secretary, Mrs Marcia Williams, a peeress. Fuel
was added to the flames both because Mrs Williams, who assumed
the resounding title of Falkender, took no part in the affairs of the
House of Lords and because Mr Wilson's resignation Honours List
in 1976 included a number of peerages bestowed on men who seemed
unlikely to make a contribution to the business of the House. It was
soon clear that the innovation of life peerages had made no difference
to the standing of the House of Lords, for in 20th century Britain a
non-elected Second Chamber, however its members were chosen,
could be entrusted with no effective or permanent checks on the
decisions of the Commons. More peers did indeed attend debates:
the daily average rose from 50 to 250; but this was understood to be
due to the tax-free allowance rather than to the enthusiasm of the
newly-selected legislators.

The admission of women in 1958 was achieved without serious
obstruction, though an elderly Scottish nobleman, Lord Glasgow,
did oppose it, on the grounds that insufficient sanitary facilities were
available for ladies in their Lordships' House. In spite of this shortage
of conveniences, hereditary peeresses in their own right were also
allowed to take their seats in 1963. However, the one serious endeavour to reform the powers of the Lords, proposed in 1967 by an
all-party Committee under the Chairmanship of the Lord Chancellor, Lord Gardiner, was rebuffed by the House of Commons where
two such determined adversaries as Mr Enoch Powell and Mr
Michael Foot joined forces to mount a successful assault on a scheme
which was seen to endanger the Commons' legislative monopoly.

Easy though it is to discount the importance of the House of

Lords, and dangerous as the situation may well be when an all-powerful House of Commons, obedient to the fiat of the Executive but perhaps far from reflecting the true opinion of the country, can impose its will on the other two Estates of the Realm, it is wrong to suppose that the House of Lords has no power and serves no useful purpose at all. Now, as before, many of the members who do attend have specialised knowledge and long experience in wide fields. The amendments it makes to bills are, as often as not, accepted by the Commons, which may have had insufficient time to consider the implications of a clause or a schedule in detail. On controversial issues, too, when the Lords are satisfied that it is in the national interest for a decision not to be hurried, and for public opinion to have a chance to crystallise, amendments by the Upper House may provide a salutary opportunity for further deliberation. Provided the Speaker of the House of Commons is satisfied that there are reasonable arguments in favour of the amendment, and that the House of Lords is not merely shuffling clauses of a bill backwards and forwards, enjoying a game of parliamentary ping-pong and scheming to delay legislation unpalatable to its Conservative majority, the House of Commons may be impelled to give second thoughts to measures which it had originally approved with care-free abandon. In the last analysis, however, it is still true in 1977, as it has been for more than two generations, that in a dispute between the two Houses the will of the elected Commons must prevail.

*

In essence, the third of these traditional Estates, the House of Commons, changed even less than the other two. There was much rowdiness, which the country as a whole found juvenile and distasteful, but this was certainly no more pronounced than it had been in the late forties or indeed in Queen Victoria's reign. There has been some redrawing of constituency boundaries, but insufficient to provide a due balance between the numbers of voters registered in each. Thus, in 1977 Meriden had nearly 100,000 voters and Newcastle Central only 25,000. There is talk of electoral reform so that the Liberals, who polled over six million votes in 1974 but won only 14 seats, might be more fairly represented; but there are no serious signs of progress in this direction. Committees have been established in both the Lords and the Commons to recommend changes in procedure without the smallest expectation of such changes being either proposed or approved for several years: and the rules set out in the compendious work of Erskine May have been, throughout the period, the Bible of the House of Commons.

What has changed is the quality and the quantity of the fare served up in the House of Commons and the method of digesting it. The first two or three Administrations during the reign did not over-burden the House with legislation. Under Sir Winston Churchill much parliamentary time was devoted to denationalising Steel, which the Labour Party renationalised twelve years later, and Road Transport, which it did not. By and large, however, the Churchill and Macmillan Governments paid more attention to governing the country as they thought the situation demanded than to initiating legislation. It was not till the sixties and seventies that Governments took leave of their senses.

In the short Labour Government of 1964–65, which had a majority of four and no clear mandate, 65 Government bills were placed on the Statute Book. After the 1966 General Election Parliament was swamped by indigestible and often scarcely comprehensible material. Less and less time was available to debate great issues; and Members of Parliament were submitted to detailed legislative pressure which many, on both sides of the House, found well-nigh insupportable. Yet in his book of memoirs, Mr Harold Wilson boasts of 'the highest legislative productivity in our history'. Apart from agriculture, it was the only sector of British life for which such a boast of high productivity could be made.

The consequence of this frenetic desire to legislate, on matters great and small, was that not only were the ablest members obliged to restrict their energies and attention to subjects in which they specialised, and thus hardly able to contemplate the wider issues before Parliament and the Country, but the machinery and time-tables of both Houses suffered from jams and bottle-necks by com-parison with which the roads leading out of the great cities on a Friday evening might be considered easily negotiable. Governments resorted to delegated legislation: laws which were placed on the Statute Book by means of some wide Enabling Act, being scarcely considered and never debated at all. By the end of 1976 it was calculated that for every thousand pages of Statutes there were three thousand pages of delegated legislation of which Parliament had but indirect cognisance.

This was not the only way in which the Executive imposed its will on Parliament, with but little evidence of ordinary Members having the courage or the means to rebel. There was a second, and superficially democratic, development: the irruption of Manifesto Government. The practice of issuing Election Manifestos goes back well into the 18th century, and it may be that in the days of Gladstone and Disraeli, or even of Salisbury and Campbell Bannerman, when men read their newspapers with care, at least the politically conscious members of society took note of Party Manifestos. It was, however, understood that a Manifesto represented the optimum a Government might hope to achieve if time stood still, no military or economic interruptions occurred and peace reigned at home. By the 1960s and 70s it may be doubted whether anything approaching 5% of those who voted at General Elections read the Manifestos of the Party they decided to support, and it was precisely in these circumstances that both the major Parties fell victims to an epidemic of Manifestitis.

After the 1950 General Election, Mr Attlee, with a majority of only six, said that his Government had no mandate to introduce drastic new measures. Sir Winston Churchill thought it the duty of his Administration to govern, to build houses and to abolish rationing rather than to legislate. Sir Anthony Eden held similar views, but was much affected by the single issue of Suez. Mr Harold Macmillan faced matters of grave importance to the country as a whole, such as the Wind of Change in Colonial affairs, the withdrawal of South Africa from the Commonwealth, the reorganisation of Defence and the first attempt to join the Common Market. Sir Alec Douglas Home had but a year in which to restore unity in his own Party and prepare for an election. Manifesto Government began in 1964 but was hampered by sharp industrial and economic tremors; Mr Heath persisted with it in 1970; and Mr Wilson, the Labour Party and the Trade Unions pronounced it to be Holy Writ after 1974.

Even in 1966, despite a handsome parliamentary majority of 99, the Labour Government received less popular votes than the

Conservatives and Liberals combined. In 1970 the Conservatives polled less than Labour and the Liberals. In the first 1974 Labour Government, Mr Wilson scored, in all, 230,000 votes less than Mr Heath, and the Liberals had more than half as many votes as either of the two major Parties; and in the second Labour Government of 1974, only 28% of the total Electorate voted Socialist. Yet with this lack of support from the General Public, and at one stage no parliamentary majority at all, the Government had, before the end of 1976, forced through Parliament 140 bills, many of them controversial, few representing the ascertainable will of the people, and the majority passed thanks to the complaisance of a handful of Scots, Welsh and Northern Irish nationalists who had only the slightest interest in anything but their own sectional aspirations.

It was not surprising that as the Silver Jubilee approached and the Government, striving to master the intractable problems of a floundering economy, was seen to be at odds with its own more vociferous supporters, the House of Commons was increasingly discredited and there was a mounting demand both for electoral reform and for an immutable Bill of Rights. The day when Mr Attlee had considered that his small majority gave him no mandate other than to govern to the best of his ability was distant indeed. Yet the fault did not lie with the House of Commons itself. It lay with an Executive that had usurped, year by year, more of the authority of the Legislature, had contrived the means of imposing its will on those who should have been its masters, and was obsessed by the malign conviction that virtue lay in heaping statutory Pelion on legislative Ossa.

CHAPTER 5

Three More Estates

Three entities which had existed for many generations, and which had always influenced the policy of the Government and the lives of the people, attained so much more power in the first twenty five years of the reign that they may now themselves be considered Estates of the Realm. They are the Executive branch of government, the organs for disseminating news and views (commonly called the Media) and, by no means least, the Trade Unions.

The fact that in Britain there has never been a separation of powers between the Legislature and the Executive, such as is written into the American Constitution, has for centuries been taken to mean that the members of the Government, and of the Civil Service which supports and advises them, are, though servants of the Crown, also the servants of Parliament and the people. The House of Commons was long jealous of its power to censure Ministers who acted without its authority, or at least approval, and since Ministers used for the most part to spend many years on the back benches of the House before they were given office, their instinct was to follow this tradition without demur. The Queen's first Prime Minister, Sir Winston Churchill, paid much more than lip service to Parliament. He said that he was the servant of the House of Commons, and he meant it with all sincerity.

His last term of office was, at any rate in his own eyes, the continuation of his war-time Administration. There had, however, been an interval of six years during which changes of far-reaching importance had taken place. Vital sectors of industry had been nationalised; universal social security, proposed by Beveridge and others in the plans they prepared for the War Coalition, had been provided by Acts of Parliament during Mr Attlee's Labour Government; and Sir Stafford Cripps had initiated the novel process of Economic Planning. It was the policy of both the big political parties to ensure full employment and this meant more continuous intervention in the management of the nation's economy than would have been considered tolerable before the war. It was clear that the Executive, and in particular the Civil Service, would be required to assume new powers and acquire new skills.

The Queen's First Government cared little for these things. After denationalising Steel and Road Transport, they concentrated on removing the relics of war-time austerity and on governing the country with as little new legislation as possible. Mr Eden's Cabinet followed the same principles, until his Government collapsed in the bitter aftermath of Suez. Meanwhile, the surviving nationalised industries, Coal, Electricity, Gas and the Railways, were accepted by the Conservatives as necessary evils and were given active help from Whitehall in the planning and reorganisation which was urgently required.

The standard of unquestioned integrity and political impartiality, which has always been the pride and hallmark of senior Civil Servants in Britain, was well illustrated at the beginning of this period by such men as Sir Edward Bridges, Secretary of the Treasury, and Sir Norman Brook, Secretary of the Cabinet. They, and their colleagues at the head of the great Departments of State, were men with intellect, experience and capacities which in those days would have earned them salaries four or five times higher than they received from the Crown, had they chosen to leave Whitehall for the City, commerce or industry. The burdens they carried were more onerous than those born by the chairman of a great bank or a leading industrial company, and they received no public recognition of their achievements except, from time to time, in the Honours List. In days when the Government made less direct intervention than now in the affairs of commerce and industry, they were seldom required to involve themselves in business decisions or even to understand such matters in any but the broadest outline. They were dedicated servants of the State who remained discreetly in the background, accepting the decisions of Ministers but never fearing to argue with them; and they rated the fulfilment of duty higher than pecuniary reward.

Those who followed them were also men of worth and calibre. It would be invidious to list them, but special mention may be made of Sir Norman Brook's successors as Secretary to the Cabinet, Sir

Burke Trend and Sir John Hunt; nor should the distinguished services of men like Sir Douglas Allen and Sir William Armstrong at the Treasury, or Sir Richard Powell, successively Permanent Under Secretary at the Ministry of Defence and the Board of Trade, or Dame Evelyn Sharp, the first woman ever to be a Permanent Under Secretary, be lightly forgotten. These, the so-called Mandarins of the Civil Service, were the trusted advisers of Conservative and Labour Governments alike, entirely unaffected by their own political predilections; and none of the changes which have taken place in the skills required in Whitehall has made their replacement by men and women of wisdom and broad experience any the less necessary to the government of the Kingdom. The increasing disappearance of their anonymity is to be deplored, if for no other reason than their inability to reply to personal criticism and attack.

During the 1950s, recruitment into the Civil Service fell below the level of ability desired, precisely at a time when expansion and more diverse training was becoming important. Industry, recovering from the direction of its activities necessitated by war, and stimulated by the opportunities which the boom after the Korean War was providing, recruited able young men and offered higher rates of pay and better conditions of employment than the State. The universities and the schools tended to abandon the long-established habit of recommending the Civil Service as a career to their brightest pupils.

When Mr Harold Macmillan became Prime Minister in 1957, he realised that a degree of planning was necessary and although he was, like Churchill, a dedicated House of Commons man, he was convinced that the Government must look beyond the confines of the Departments of State to the wider world of industry. The Chancellor of the Exchequer, Mr Selwyn Lloyd (whom Mr Macmillan shortly afterwards dismissed to the surprise and dismay of many of his followers) established a National Economic Development Council, commonly known as NEDDY, with a staff chosen largely from outside the ranks of the Civil Service. The Chancellor was Chairman and the members were drawn from the Cabinet, from the leaders of the private and nationalised industries and from the Trade Unions. It was destined to play a major part in decisions of economic policy and it was only indirectly, through its ministerial members, accountable to Parliament; but it did establish a soundly-based, impartial meeting ground for the two sides of industry, and it was intended to be instrumental in providing a solution to the 'stop-go' problems which had so bedevilled the economy since the end of the war that every time industry was buoyant, and full employment apparently assured, a serious balance of payments crisis necessitated turning the traffic lights abruptly to red.

Meanwhile the Civil Service painstakingly adjusted itself to changing circumstances. Recruitment, and the quality of the recruits, improved as the financial inducements were raised. Less emphasis was placed on the performance of examinees and more on the proficiency of their work during their first few years in the service. It was made possible for Civil Servants to retire (or be encouraged to retire if they were found unsuitable) with a pension proportionate to their length of service. As time passed, the Fulton Report advocated changes in organisation, modern training methods and better conditions of employment. Seeds were planted which would germinate and bear good fruit in distant years ahead.

When a Labour Government took office in the autumn of 1964, one of the first most enterprising, and, in the event, most disappointing, measures was the production of a National Plan. The preparation and supervision of this plan was deemed to require not only a new Department of Economic Affairs, but the temporary secondment of highly-skilled businessmen from the City and Industry. Its activities were in theory subject to Parliament, but it was a novel form of governmental activity, with functions difficult to define, so that despite Mr George Brown's frequent endeavours to explain the objects of his Department, Members of Parliament found themselves entering unexplored territories for which no easily intelligible maps were available. Although the work on the plan achieved little, it did underline the need for Civil Servants of a kind different from those traditionally established in Whitehall.

Apart from the Department of Economic Affairs, the other institutions which had expanded in scope and activity, such as the Health Service, the Customs, the Post Office, the Inland Revenue and the Ministry of Aviation, now had to be staffed by men with the knowledge and practical experience to control organisations which employed large numbers and were usually both technical and decentralised. The old-fashioned Civil Servant who advised his Minister on policy was still required, but beneath and alongside him there must be men and women with qualifications hitherto regarded as irrelevant to Government Departments. The basis of training had to be reviewed and revised, for the additions to the Whitehall establishment were management enterprises, akin to great industries, and Civil Servants were to be put in charge of them without being subjected to the commercial discipline of profit and loss accounts and with no accepted yardstick for measuring their capacity to conduct business affairs.

The lack, at least temporarily, of Civil Servants to fill the highest appointments in the Nationalised Industries, and in other green, or supposedly green, pastures of Government patronage, has meant that search must be made elsewhere. Ministers holding, or at least professing, socialist sentiments of varying hues from pale pink to deep carmine have been obliged to send urgent invitations, and even plead for help, in areas of undiluted capitalist blue. The Treasury and the Cabinet Office keep a list of bankers and industrialists whom they call 'The Good and the Great', from which they submit to Ministers men they think best qualified for the job. Many of the Great and quite a lot of the Good decline these invitations, preferring their established activities to cruising in uncharted waters where the pleasures are limited and the chances of drowning particularly grave; for, by the very nature of a nationalised enterprise, the freedom of manoeuvre allowed to the head of it is sure to be unpalatably circumscribed. Sometimes three or four candidates have refused before a man of the requisite courage and self-sacrificial character could be corralled. Nor have the rewards been commensurate with the risks, and parliamentary wrath has frequently been roused by the embarrassed announcement of a large gross salary which, after tax, is almost always far less than the obliging chairman earned in his former commercial or industrial activities. There has been a marked reluctance to consider the claims of men who, though unquestionably able, are still comparatively young and might therefore be readier to accept the challenge. A nation which once accepted and applauded a Prime Minister twenty four years old, now recoils with horror from the idea of a man under fifty in a top position of authority. Perhaps it is unjust to say that the nation recoils; but the Treasury certainly does.

It became necessary for successive Governments, Labour and Conservative, to rationalise the structure of the Whitehall Departments. Defence and Foreign Affairs, which had formerly been held to warrant eight Cabinet Ministers, were now restricted to two. Giant Departments were created: the Department of the Environment took possession of a concrete palace in Great Smith Street. It swallowed and digested the Ministries of Housing and Local Government, Transport and Works. The Department of Trade and Industry, housed behind glass and concrete in Victoria Street, devoured the Board of Trade and the Ministries of Supply, Power and Aviation, becoming the arbiter of trade, industry and energy. Lest any should be so rash as to believe himself up-to-date with the machinery of Government, the Department was subsequently divided yet again into separate Ministries of Trade, Energy and Industry. The Department of Health and Social Security assumed responsibility for all the citizens, whether they liked it or not, from the cradle to the grave. The Ministry of Labour changed its name, for the sake of appearance, to the Department of Employment, because the old theory that there was dignity in labour was felt to be outmoded. The stolid, unshakeable Home Office kept its name, surrendered its Children's Department to Health and Social Security, but otherwise retained its functions, its 19th century office and its 19th century procedures.

The purchase of Government supplies was reorganised in the hope of saving money. This was just as well, because by 1975 there were twice as many Civil Servants as there had been when war broke out in 1939, and every time a call for reduction in man- and woman-power became irresistible, some new Act of Parliament was sure to entail the opening of an additional Government Office. Thus in 1976, the Sex Discrimination Act, greeted with mirth by the majority of the population, both male and female, as soon as they heard about it, none the less necessitated the opening of a brand new Government Office. However, economies were made in one of the most costly regions of Government expenditure by the creation in 1971 of a Defence Procurement Executive, which thenceforward bought all the requirements of the armed forces and was the biggest supply organisation in the land. This was followed by a Property

Services Agency which became responsible for the management of the Government's buildings and property.

However well the necessity of retraining, and of recruiting men and women with new aptitudes, was recognised, successive parliamentary measures, increasing as much in complexity as in number, obliged Civil Servants to shoulder obligations which neither their background nor even the new methods of training equipped them to bear. They were expected to supervise activities in private commerce and industry of which their knowledge was necessarily limited. Had the object been solely to lessen the chance of fraud and exploitation, it would have been a laudable one, but in the seventies there has been a noticeable tendency for the Departments of State to interfere in the smooth running of well-organised industries, imposing conditions for which they had no difficulty in obtaining parliamentary authority, however little the implications were understood by those who gave legal validity to statutory instruments that had never been debated in Parliament.

The insurance industry provides one example. It had always enjoyed freedom from Government control, and this, together with a world reputation for integrity, enabled it to develop a flexibility in its conduct of business that established Britain's profitable role as an international market for insurance. In the late sixties there were one or two failures by recently established companies whose policy holders were rescued by judicious intervention. Thereupon, a huge structure of State supervision was erected, almost entirely duplicating the work of existing auditors and actuaries. Detailed and intricate returns were required by the Department of Trade so that the position of each insurer might be meticulously and superfluously analysed. Further legislation called for the disclosure of even the most tenuous, indirect connections between agents and insurers, and produced rules of sufficiently laborious complexity to ensure that time which might otherwise have been fruitfully spent in helping to increase the country's invisible exports was devoted to the unproductive task of completing mountains of forms. The insurance industry was not the only victim of this manic burgeoning of bureaucratic intervention, for by 1976 one in ten of the working population was a Civil Servant and the Country was weighed down by the burden of over-administration.

The introduction of special advisers from outside the Civil Service was not new, but those whom Ministers imported into their departments had normally been experts without any strong political affiliation. Thus Churchill had imported Professor Lindemann from Oxford, promoting him in due course to ministerial rank with a seat in the House of Lords, and Macmillan followed suit with Sir Percy Mills. When Harold Wilson became Prime Minister in 1964, he inserted two men in the highest echelons of Whitehall, Professor Thomas Balogh and Dr Nicholas Kaldor, both of whom had strong Labour party affiliations but were, at the same time, well-known as economists in the academic world. They, like Lindemann and Mills, in due course wended their way to the House of Lords, becoming Parliamentarians and, in the case of Balogh, a Minister of the Crown. In 1970 Edward Heath followed the same pattern. With the willing connivance of Marks and Spencer he temporarily deprived that company of the services of Mr Derek Rayner, who had special qualifications to advise on the organisation of the new Defence Procurement Executive and in due course took charge of it. Shell were equally co-operative in lending Mr Richard Meyjes to be head of a Business Team which Heath created as an adjunct to his Administration.

Heath established in the Cabinet Office an organisation called the Central Policy Review Staff, which because of its unwieldy designation and also because it was to devote itself to the consideration, in detail as well as in principle, of matters requiring specialist knowledge and planning experience, was immediately called the Think Tank. Its duties are to study and make recommendations on subjects about which the Cabinet requires advice, to address itself to issues affecting two or more Government Departments, to provide Ministers with competent briefs on matters falling outside their own departmental knowledge and to review the strategy of the Government. Heath chose as its head a distinguished scientist, Lord Rothschild, who had been a Fellow of Trinity College, Cambridge, and subsequently Research Director of the Royal Dutch-Shell Group. In the interval Rothschild had won the George Medal and had become a leading member of the Central Advisory Council for Science and Technology. Neither Mr Rayner nor Mr Meyjes had any party affiliations, nor were they translated to the House of Lords; and in so far as

Lord Rothschild had ever expressed political opinions, they were not Heath's; for he had sat on the Labour benches in the Upper House.

The Think Tank was an earnest and unusual attempt by a British Government to lay plans for the future of the economy, and to do so not only for the duration of its own likely tenure of office, nor with an eye to the immediate political programme and an election Manifesto, but on the basis of a rational analysis of probabilities made with the best professional advice that was available. It may be that scientific planning is a Utopian dream in a parliamentary democracy, for sectional interests, the imperative demand for full employment and the ever-present, overhanging consciousness of a forthcoming General Election are tank traps, especially Think Tank traps, of formidable efficiency. Governments woo the Electorate by declarations of policy, usually expressed in turgid prose and embodied in a Manifesto. Manifestos neither convince nor convert any but an already chosen few; but professional politicians believe that they do. In consequence, much attention is paid to the tactics of gaining immediate electoral favour and little to the strategy of a campaign for future prosperity. As Lord Rothschild had said, with a cynicism which may be forgiven: 'A policy, in my experience, usually consists of what is left, if anything is left, of a plan after the politicians have worked it over.'

If the alternative to planning is to drift from one hastily contrived life-saving operation to another, until finally there are no life-boats within hailing distance, then Mr Heath's foundation of the Think Tank, which his successors, Mr Wilson and Mr Callaghan, did nothing to discourage, may prove to be an innovation of far-reaching importance. The freedom of Civil Servants to give advice has always been unlimited, but in practice they can seldom make proposals to Ministers, with any chance of success, unless those proposals are politically acceptable. The planner, on the other hand, conceives it to be his duty to be objective: to study the facts, to deduce the probabilities and to draw attention, without political fear or Ministerial favour, to the course of action most likely to provide the ultimate benefits required. Unlike the Minister and the Civil Servant, the professional planner is unable to compromise. I quote Lord Rothschild again: 'You cannot have half a Channel Tunnel. Perhaps we shall find out to our cost in the next five years that you cannot even half devolve.' What, however, the Think Tank, of which Sir Kenneth Berrill is now in charge, can and does do is to consider such vital matters as what the country's energy requirements will be by the end of the century, whence they will most profitably be drawn, how North Sea Oil may contribute, and at what level of miners' pay the nation's vast coal reserves can be economically extracted. There is not, in 1977, likely to be a shortage of matters on which the Cabinet demands immediate recommendations nor of long-term problems to which the Think Tank, without relying on a crystal ball or diverging from a rational analysis of known facts, can be invited to devote its skill. In 1952 the Government had at its disposal nothing but a central statistical office, Lord Cherwell, and an unlimited supply of crystal balls.

One of the functions of the Think Tank, namely the provision of briefs for Ministers on matters before the Cabinet which have little or no connection with their departmental responsibilities, illustrates a change in Cabinet practice and procedures over twenty five years. Before he became Prime Minister, Churchill had always been conspicuous for declining to restrict the expression of his views, within and without the Cabinet, to matters relating to his own Department. As First Lord of the Admiralty he constantly intervened in the affairs of the War Office and the Foreign Office; as Colonial Secretary he followed with interest the policies of the Ministry of Agriculture and the Home Office; as Chancellor of the Exchequer he excluded no Department from his animadversions. When he was Prime Minister he discouraged his colleagues from trespassing to quite the same uninhibited extent; but he did consider it the function of all Cabinet Ministers to be prepared to discuss in a generally well-informed manner any topic of national importance. The fewer papers they had before them and the less their remarks were recorded the better. Cabinet Minutes should, he believed, contain nothing but an account of the conclusions reached. As affairs of State grew more complex, the weight of ill-digested paper that Ministers were required to read grew heavier. The entire conduct of Governmental business became more specialised. The Cabinet was less and less a group of wise men and women with time to reflect even on their own narrow field of policy, let alone on that of the nation as a whole.

The existing machinery of government is inadequate to provide a remedy. Ministers arrive at meetings of the Cabinet or of Cabinet Committees having hurriedly glanced at their papers in the car. Sometimes the brief from a Permanent Secretary may even be that a particular item on the agenda is of no interest to the Minister. Collective responsibility survives in theory, but in practice questions of importance may be decided with scarcely any consideration at all by those whose duty it is to ponder on their wisdom and effectiveness. The briefs provided by the Think Tank are an attempt to remedy this ill; but the ill itself demonstrates the extent to which, in recent years, matters of significance to the nation have been decided without full consideration by the Members of the Administration entrusted with the Government of the country, let alone by the elected representatives of the people in Parliament.

The return of the Labour Party to office in March, 1974, was the signal for developing on a large scale a habit which had hitherto been followed only rarely and with caution. It is a practice of dubious merit. Almost every Minister brought into his office one or more outside advisers. Few of them had any claim to expert knowledge of the affairs with which the Department was concerned, but they all had strong political ties. Some were believed to have equally strong political ambitions. The intention was, no doubt, to establish a nursery for future Labour Ministers; but in so far as this thundering herd of juvenile politicians had access to official information, it was feared there might be a risk of breaches of security. The irritation of the professional Civil Servants, though well disguised by their habitual urbanity, was the more understandable because the new outside advisers, apart from their academic qualifications and their keenness to advance their Party's cause, appeared to have little to offer that was not readily available to the Civil Service.

All these developments, some of them fruitful and only a few positively harmful, contributed to the growth of a *de facto* separation of powers. The Executive was decreasingly subject to parliamentary control, however much the external forms continued to be respected. This was due partly to the complexity of modern administration and to the speed with which decisions had to be taken, with or without subsequent ratification by the Legislature. It was due still more to the impatience Ministers felt with the slow, cumbrous procedures of the House of Commons and their technocratic determination to reach their goals by the quickest means available. It was due to the independence from direct parliamentary control of the many Boards, Executives and Committees which, though responsible to the Government, were not within the administrative ambit of a single Minister. It was due, above all, to the lack of vigilance shown by Parliament itself and the willingness of Members ultimately to accept, however much they might immediately complain, the fiat of the Cabinet.

The device of subordinate legislation, whereby powers of grave significance were granted underneath the cover of a wide Enabling bill, was a convenience to the Executive, for it provided the Government with the legal right to act on many matters to which Parliament had never given consideration. It was also a potential danger to the liberty of the individual. In earlier days it had frequently been the duty of Civil Servants to explain to their political masters that one decision or another could not be taken because there were no statutory powers to enforce it. In the sixties and seventies it became the practice for Ministers to meet such an obstruction by replying that they would make a statement of their intentions in Parliament, and if no serious objection was raised they would proceed, whether or not the specific powers existed.

Worse still was to follow. Ministers concluded that if an awkward situation arose and they were prevented from giving immediate effect to the remedy they thought appropriate, they might nevertheless act as if they already had the requisite authority and inform the House of Commons that retro-active legislation would be introduced in order to set the record straight. An early example of this dangerous practice was the action of Mr Charles Pannell, Minister of Public Buildings and Works, who informed the House in 1965 that Industrial Development Certificates would thenceforward be required for all business premises with an area greater than 10,000 square feet. This was doubtless a wise provision at a time when too much of the national wealth was being squandered on speculative office buildings; but Mr Pannell had no power at all to make such an order. Retro-active legislation would, he said, be laid before the House in due course. Before there was time for the necessary bill to be presented, there was a General Election. Had the Government lost that election, there was no guarantee that the bill would ever have been introduced, so that without one iota of legal authority property developers would have been restrained from activities which, however economically undesirable, were nevertheless allowed by law.

Thus, the House of Commons, over-burdened by legislation, exhausted by long sessions and all-night sittings, and so obedient to the Party Whips that on any matter but one of deep principle the Cabinet is sure to get its way, has surrendered every year to the Executive more and more of the power which it is its duty to exercise. The doctrine of 'Open Government' has been loudly preached. Information, in the form of indigestible White Papers, Green Papers and Consultative Documents, has been made available both to Parliament and the general public on a scale far more lavish than ever before; but the House of Commons is ill-equipped to challenge the Executive on the complex and detailed issues which are laid before it, and which are frequently incomprehensible to any but the expert. Modern Parliamentarians, though denied the staff support and technical assistance which a Member of the American Congress takes for granted, are certainly more assiduous in their attention to the business of the House, and in their efforts to scrutinise the legislation laid before them, than were their predecessors. They have in effect become professional politicians with neither the facilities nor the remuneration that such a status should confer. They have not, however conscientious their habits, the means or the time to explore in depth the intricate proposals with which they are presented, at too fast a rate and in too great a bulk, in every succeeding session. The Executive, whether King, Cabinet or Cabal, was always powerful: in the reign of Queen Elizabeth II it has become close to being omnipotent.

Of course, in the British system of Parliamentary Government, which has slowly evolved from the Glorious Revolution of 1688, supreme power nominally resides in the Queen in Parliament. For all the reasons given in this chapter, real power is exercised by the Cabinet alone, wielding authority with or without the connivance of the Civil Service, using the instrument of an obedient, bewildered and harshly Whipped House of Commons, and contemptuously disregarding bursts of spirit from an emasculated House of Lords. It can be exposed by the Media or even by diarists within, such as Mr Richard Crossman; it must bow to the Trade Unions; but one stalwart defender of society against arbitrary action is the Judiciary, until such time as its intervention can be overriden by a new Act of Parliament.

When the Archbishop of Canterbury invested the Queen with the spurs and the sword at her Coronation, he said:

'With this sword do justice, stop the growth of iniquity, protect the Holy Church of God, help and defend widows and orphans, restore the things that are gone to decay, maintain the things that are restored, punish and reform what is amiss, and confirm what is in good order.'

These are among the functions of the Queen's Justices, who have been as punctilious in performing them as the noblest traditions of the legal profession demand. They have shown no fear in interpreting decisions against the wishes of the Government if they judged them to be in contravention of the law. Their most distinguished representatives, men such as Donovan, Devlin, Kilbrandon and Wilberforce, have presided over Commissions set up to examine matters of disquiet to the general public. The ancient framework of Justice has been amended. Assizes, over which itinerant Judges presided with the pomp and ceremony of the medieval Justiciars, were abolished after consideration of a report on the judicial system by Lord Beeching, and in their place Crown Courts were established. The Magistrates, still in great part Justices of the Peace who give their services to the community on a voluntary, unpaid basis, have less authority to settle disputes or impose penalties by summary decision; and many cases that would, in the 1950s have been handled expeditiously by a bench of Magistrates, are now submitted to a Crown Court with consequent delays in the administration of justice. Nevertheless, although the Judiciary, endeavouring on the Queen's behalf to fulfil the duties laid on her at the Coronation, have been signally unsuccessful in their efforts to 'stop the growth of iniquity', their help and defence of widows, orphans and others of Her Majesty's subjects have been a comfort and relief to those threatened by the spreading tentacles of executive and bureaucratic power.

There are, moreover, two other alert watchdogs. One, the Media, is prohibited from biting, lest an Editor be committed to the Clock Tower of the Houses of Parliament, but however much Ministers may resent the fact, nothing can stop the barking. The other, the Trade Unions, can and does bite. It is convenient to consider first the changes in the form and impact of the barker.

*

At the Queen's accession a total monopoly of broadcasting, whether by television or wireless (as it was then generally called), was held by the British Broadcasting Corporation, established by Royal Charter in 1926 with a Chairman and Governors all appointed by the Crown. In 1952 the Prime Minister, Winston Churchill, submitted to the Queen the name of Sir Alexander Cadogan as Chairman. He had been Permanent Under Secretary at the Foreign Office during the war and was subsequently British representative at the United Nations. Another of Churchill's ablest and most trusted wartime assistants, Lt General Sir Ian Jacob, was appointed Director General in the same year. The BBC was in safe and competent hands.

Although television was, in the main, a British invention and the BBC had been offering limited programmes since the early 1930s, the main concern of the Corporation was still with sound broadcasting. There were fewer than 1.5 million television licences in issue. Twenty five years later there are approximately 18 million. Thus an influence scarcely conceivable in 1952 developed between the Accession and the Silver Jubilee and now penetrates the living room of almost every home in Britain. The French and German standards of living quickly caught up with the British, long though Britain's lead had been in 1952; but either because the British are less frugal, or more probably because they have a better developed hire purchase system, they have always owned more television sets than the citizens of any other European country.

The televising of the Coronation inside Westminster Abbey was the signal for rapid advance. The Coronation Executive Committee opposed the suggestion. So did the Archbishop of Canterbury and the Dean of Westminster; so did the Prime Minister; and so did the

Cabinet. They all thought the glare and heat of the lighting would put an unbearable strain on the Queen in a supremely moving, but long, solemn and exhausting ordeal, during which her every movement would be watched by millions of eyes. The Queen overruled them all. It was her Coronation; she took her dedication to serve the country seriously; and she determined that all her people, not just the few thousands in Westminster Abbey, should see her anointed and crowned. The televising was achieved with near perfection, and though in 1953 transmission could only be in black and white, two colour films, one using technicolour and the other the new Eastman Kodak process, were taken inside the Abbey and shown in cinemas throughout the Kingdom. But it was at the live television broadcast, watched in public houses, clubs and shops by those who had no sets of their own, that the people marvelled.

In the following year, a group of Conservative back bench Members of Parliament formed themselves into a pressure group to promote the idea of a second television organisation, in competition with the BBC. It would be financed by the sale of advertising. The Labour Party were horrified at the suggestion that the State broadcasting monopoly should be broken in favour of private enterprise. They were not alone. Churchill and Eden were repelled by the suggestion, as were the entire Cabinet with the exception of the Home Secretary, Sir David Maxwell-Fyfe. The Postmaster General, Lord De La Warr, whose task it would be to supervise the passage of a bill through Parliament, was no less opposed than Churchill and Eden to such a vulgar innovation.

However, in those days the Executive, as represented by the Cabinet, was less omnipotent than it subsequently became. The back benchers won. The Cabinet reluctantly bowed beneath the weight of opinion and Lord De La Warr, to his credit, sponsored the measure with skill and determination once the decision had been taken. In July, 1954, an Independent Television Authority was created. It was authorised by Parliament to interview and select programme companies. It did so with speed under the chairmanship of Sir Kenneth Clark, encouraged by the driving force of Mr Norman Collins, formerly an outstanding figure at the BBC where he had, however, found insufficient scope for his ideas and energies. They chose as Director General another dynamic entrepreneur, Sir

Robert Fraser, who had until then been head of a governmental body, the Central Office of Information. He remained at his new post for sixteen eventful years.

While the BBC was anchored in London, Fraser, with the advantage of franchises to offer to separate and competing programme companies, advanced to other regions as well. The first ITV transmission was made in London in September, 1955. Only five months later, two selected groups began to broadcast television programmes from Birmingham and there were soon further companies at work in the north of England. Scotland followed, and then Southern Television with its tentacles on the south and south east of England. At the time of the Silver Jubilee there are fifteen independent programme companies in operation. The early years were hard, anxious times for the ITV companies, partly because many of the sets in existence could only receive BBC transmissions; but before the 1950s were over, so successful were the advertisements with which the companies interspersed their programmes, that the big advertisers began to direct their national sales policies in relation to the territories covered by the various television programmes. The boundaries originally established by Fraser for the first five licences are still today much the same as those used by the leading firms for the division of their marketing activities.

As the independent companies grew in number, they had an important advantage over the BBC. For every one expert or department in the BBC dealing with a particular subject such, for instance, as current affairs, the ITV companies could field at least five. However, the BBC fought hard for the national audience. Sir Hugh Carlton Greene, appointed Director General in 1960, saw his opportunity in the new fashion for satirical and irreverent revue which had been popularised by such productions in London as 'Beyond the Fringe' and was supported by increasingly uninhibited tendencies in the newspapers. He captured a huge audience with a programme entitled 'That Was the Week that Was' introduced by David Frost who, moving with the informality of the times, started calling everybody, including Cabinet Ministers, by their Christian names. Impertinence came to be considered an asset, if not actually a virtue. From 1957 to 1962 Carlton Greene employed John Freeman, formerly of the *New Statesman* and subsequently British Ambassador in Washington, to interview famous men and ask them searching questions. On one occasion he reduced his victim to tears. The BBC held its audience.

ITV struck back. As early as 1955 and 1956 Mr Aidan Crawley, first editor of Independent Television News, recruited Robin Day and Christopher Chataway. Ludovic Kennedy was soon added to this talented group. Later, when the Chairman of ITA, Dr Charles Hill, ordered two of the leading companies, ABC and Rediffusion, to merge under the direction of Howard Thomas with the name Thames Television, a long series of brilliant documentaries, such as 'The World at War', began to attract away from the BBC some of its most dedicated viewers. It was perhaps to be expected that ITV would surpass the BBC in the quality of its light entertainment. It is questionable whether it has done so, but it has surprisingly outstripped its rival by far in the presentation of news. At least, it is apparent from the polls regularly taken that the viewers think so. Competition is intense, research and production are every year more professional, and when in 1963 the BBC started its new channel, BBC2, audiences were given a choice of three programmes to watch. They did so more and more, and in consequence television has become a major social and political power in the land.

Its impact, and its capacity to entertain, was increased still further by the arrival of colour television in 1970. There was no British colour system, which many thought a regrettable backsliding by the heirs of John Logie Baird's original invention; and so the choice lay between the American colour system, generally agreed to be unsatisfactory, or one of two European systems. While General de Gaulle was busy trying to sell the French SECAM to the Russians, the British, who at that time had good reason to be displeased with the General, declared their preference for the German system, PAL. They undoubtedly made the right choice and the colour on British television is as good as any in the world. By the end of 1976 almost half the licences issued were for colour sets.

The industry is one in which youth has its chance. Thames Television, for instance, has seven programme departments, all with Controllers in their late thirties or early forties and two of them women. The Directors of Programmes of all the five major ITV Companies are in their forties and the BBC has a comparable record.

A new type of journalist is being bred, for one third of the programme on each channel, and in the case of BBC2 two thirds, is information as opposed to entertainment. Thus television recruits journalists as well as trained researchers and a staff to cater for the tastes of the public and to diagnose their reactions. There are challenging opportunities, too, for dramatists and musicians; and almost all new films are directed by men trained in television.

A heavy responsibility lies with the Programme Directors, who now occupy positions as powerful and important as the editors of newspapers. Judgement and sensitivity are vital because although the BBC must, by the terms of its Charter, be impartial, and Parliament has insisted the ITV be equally so, there is danger in the inevitable cutting of words in the mouths of those interviewed and in the speeches of politicians. The complaints so often directed at newspapers that phrases are printed out of context can be still more sharply directed at the abbreviation of interviews recorded on television; and such complaints must needs be more satisfactorily answered than by the newspapers, for the impartiality binding on television has never been required or expected of the Press.

The political leaders of the 1960s and 70s soon realised that television was indispensable to their influence. In the early years of the reign, Churchill, who disliked bright lights, would never face a television camera if he could avoid it, though he would in all probability have been an exceptionally gifted TV performer. Neither Sir Anthony Eden nor Mr Harold Macmillan, used as they were to different kinds of hustings, originally seemed at ease on television, although they both, and Mr Macmillan in particular, proved themselves brilliant impresarios in retirement. Sir Alec Douglas Home was equally ill-at-ease with the new phenomenon. It was, however, inescapable for Wilson and Heath, and the cruel facts of biochemistry became apparent, for Wilson swam on the TV screens like a duck enjoying itself on the lake in St James's Park, and Heath, for all his undoubted integrity and the quality of his speeches, was unable to win the confidence of television audiences.

It may be that those in authority have taken criticism by the media too seriously. Cabinet Ministers have nearly always been sensitive to Press criticism, often unduly so. They have had too high an expectation of the treatment they should receive, and with the advent of television this is on the verge of becoming an obsession. Perhaps they have a false idea of what the media can achieve for them. A politician's main audience should be in Parliament, but it is significant of the power which this new Estate of the Realm exerts that modern Ministers and Members of Parliament seem more conscious of the effect they make by transitory, quickly forgotten appearances on the television screen than by their speeches and conduct in the House of Commons. No doubt the broadcasting, and eventually the televising, of parliamentary debates will prove a wholesome corrective, for it is a fact of modern life that unless something scandalous or at least salacious occurs in the Houses of Parliament, few people bother to read the debates and even the serious newpapers print but short extracts.

Important though television has become, radio, which was so much more widely received than television in 1952, is still the morning fare of most households. The wide distribution of the portable transistor set in the late fifties and sixties was instrumental in holding the attention of housewives who would otherwise have been working beyond the range of their fixed, plugged-in apparatus. Imports of radio sets, mainly transistors, rose from a mere 85,000 in 1960 to 1,620,000 in 1963, and to over six million in 1973. Car radios too, though less frequently installed in British cars than in the United States or in the affluent parts of Europe, none the less provide many thousands of listeners throughout the day.

In 1967 the BBC divided its broadcasts between four channels so that its listeners could be offered an extensive choice of programme. The more staid opted for Radio 4, the more serious could turn to Radio 3 and the majority divided their favours between the advanced and popular musical talents of Radios 1 and 2. In the same year the BBC opened a local station at Leicester and began cautiously to extend its interest further into the provinces.

In 1970 the Conservatives returned to office and proceeded to introduce a bill for the establishment of local radio stations, financed by advertising, on a basis comparable to the independent television companies. The issue was no longer one of political principle, for Labour politicians had found the independent sector as useful as had their opponents. Lord Aylestone, who as Herbert Bowden had been

Labour Chief Whip, was Chairman of the ITA, to which he was appointed in 1967 when Mr Wilson submitted the name of his predecessor at the ITA, Lord Hill of Luton, to be Chairman of the BBC. As Lord Hill, better known as the Radio Doctor, had been a Conservative Minister for eleven years and Lord Aylestone was presiding over a citadel of at least tolerably free enterprise, the separation of broadcasting politics from party politics was seen to have arrived. This disengagement was consecrated by Mr Heath's appointment of the principal of Edinburgh University, Sir Michael Swann, as Chairman of the BBC in 1973 and Mr Wilson's choice of Lady Plowden, highly distinguished in the field of education and public service, but totally unconnected with politics, to succeed Lord Aylestone in 1975.

The Conservative bill was accepted with little demur in 1973. The Independent Television Authority changed its name to Independent Broadcasting Authority, not with the usual objective of confusing the public for the fun of it, but because radio as well as television was now within the demesne. It was resolved that up to sixty local radio stations should be established under the auspices of the IBA which was to be responsible for choosing the programme contractors and would make provision for transmitting the programmes to the selected areas.

Nineteen local stations were selected for the first phase. They had all been financed and equipped, and had started to broadcast, before midsummer 1976. They provided, as was required of them, local news and national news; they played the kind of music they thought their listeners would find agreeable; they canvassed local opinion on every subject they thought suitable for discussion; they supplied helpful information to bewildered old-age pensioners and broadcast, with equal facility, birthday greetings or emergency messages; they organised ingenious competitions; they treated politics with the fine balance required of them; they exuded late 20th century respectability; and in a remarkably short space of time they captured the local audiences and captivated the advertisers. By the end of 1976 the nineteen stations, mostly small in staff and economic in overhead costs, were earning a combined revenue of some £12 million; and many of them had the allegiance of more than half the listeners in the area reached by their broadcasts.

Just as local newspapers have a natural appeal to town and country dwellers outside the great metropolitan districts, so local radio, from the very start of its transmissions, was set to engage the loyalty of men and women more interested in local events than in distant earthquakes and civil disturbances, and to be regarded as no less a local possession than the Town Hall or the football ground. The attitude of the local newspapers varied. In some places, believing that local radio would increase the total amount of advertising and thus directly benefit them, they co-operated willingly. In others, making a virtue of necessity, they acknowledged an unavoidable state of affairs. Yet in others, they adopted the old nursery tactic of shutting their eyes and pretending the radio station wasn't there.

There is, no doubt, a difference between the impression made on the eye by television and that made on the ear by radio; but it is unlikely that either is as lasting in its effect on the thought and memory as the written word. Thus the newspapers, however little news they can aspire to offer in competition with television and radio, are still the most important suppliers of comment and opinion to the reasonably well-informed public. The less reasonably well-informed who, being true hedonists, prefer to remain in that state, demand neither comment nor opinion but take pleasure in the new tabloids with their ample supply of sport and nudes. Perhaps it is as well, for as world communications improve there is too much news, and inflation of news is like every other kind of inflation: the more that is produced, and the faster it circulates, the higher the price to be paid in misunderstanding, hasty judgement and impetuous deduction.

Nevertheless, even if the great majority care little about the more important national and international news, not registering it in their minds and still less attempting to remember it, the minority who govern, direct and manage are affected by the presentation of opinion. They no longer feel an obligation to read the Parliamentary Debates, unless they happen to be Members of one House or the other, but they do read the thoughtful articles in the thoughtful papers. Thus, what has befallen the Press in this period is of real significance.

In 1952 newsprint, rationed in the war because of enemy submarines, was still rationed because of financial stringency. By the time of de-rationing in 1957, the cost of newsprint had soared and all the newspapers saw their expenses rise to a scarcely supportable extent. The days of the Press Lords, who made fortunes from their large circulation papers, seemed to be over. Advertising revenues have fluctuated, being alarmingly reduced at times of financial crisis (of which there were a great many during the period); and circulation, if not actually lowered by television and radio competition, has in many cases been restrained from further growth. To add to the troubles of Fleet Street and the provincial newspapers, a series of disunited Trade Unions, the leaders of which, though not perhaps the largely inattentive members, have tended to be aggressive in their militancy, have continually held the proprietors, the management and the public to ransom.

In 1952 there were nine national daily newspapers published in London and three evening papers. Some of the better known provincial papers, such as the *Manchester Guardian, Yorkshire Post, Scotsman, Glasgow Herald* and *Birmingham Post* had circulations of varying size outside their own local areas. With the rise in costs and fall, or at best maintenance, of circulation, closures and mergers took place. In 1960 two well-known papers, originally owning allegiance to the Liberal Party, the *News Chronicle* and the *Star*, ceased publication. Already in 1959 a large, beneficent but late-flowering specimen of the dying breed of Press Lord, Lord Thomson of Fleet, who like Lord Beaverbrook was a Canadian, and who had already bought the *Scotsman* acquired the *Sunday Times* and its myriad of magazines and provincial papers from Lord Kemsley. Then in 1961 the *Daily Mirror* bought Odhams Press, owning even more magazines than Lord Kemsley, and controlling the *Daily Herald* which, because it was one of the few Labour Party organs and was cherished by the TUC, was explicitly exempted from the deal and for a brief period flourished, or rather subsisted independently, as the *Sun*, with much the same content and format as the old *Daily Herald*. At the end of 1976 the *Observer* declared itself open to the embraces of a sufficiently well-endowed suitor.

The *Sunday Times*, under its new management, made an innovation in 1962 by launching a colour supplement and procured a gifted photographer in the person of Lord Snowdon to advise on artistic matters. The *Observer* soon followed suit, but the *Sunday*

Telegraph judging that many people preferred their Sunday papers in one piece, contented itself with a weekly colour magazine to support the *Daily Telegraph* and only switched its supplement to Sunday in the autumn of 1976.

Also in 1962, members of the group which had so successfully produced 'Beyond the Fringe' on the London stage, and had been encouraged by Sir Hugh Carlton Green's BBC venture, 'That Was the Week that Was', sensed that there was a growing public demand for satire, especially if not too much attention was paid to the law of libel and a sufficient amount of gossip, which other newspapers were too timid or too respectable to print, could be included. They launched *Private Eye*. It held no bars, it titillated and it titivated, it was sued by dozens of prominent men, it spared neither right nor left, it was as vile to Trade Unionists and left-wing militants as to financiers, industrialists, film stars, writers, social celebrities, the Royal Family, Mr Heath ('the Grocer') and Mr Wilson ('Wislon'). It was often uproariously funny, and just as often cruel and guilty of deplorably bad taste. Its circulation soared, even though W. H. Smith (which in revenge it christened W. H. Smug) and some other distributors declined to sell copies, and it was soon as widely read as the *Economist, Spectator* and *New Statesman* combined. There were those who thought it went too far and in 1976 Sir James Goldsmith, recently knighted in Sir Harold Wilson's list, sued it for criminal libel. Many of its readers rushed to subscribe to the cost of defence, and there were some, including Goldsmith, who alleged that they had no wish to destroy it provided its tone was moderated and its libels diminished.

The general desire to respect the freedom of the Press, but to discourage its more scandalous infiltrations into the lives of private citizens, led to the creation in 1963 of a new Press Council, based on one established in 1953, with an independent Chairman and a number of members who were not connected with the newspapers. Its membership was increased to thirty in 1973 and although it includes representatives of the newspaper publishers as well as the Institute of Journalists and National Union of Journalists, ten of its members have no connection at all with the Press. Lord Shawcross, a distinguished lawyer and former Labour Cabinet Minister, who subsequently renounced Socialism, is the Chairman, and the Council has the right of access not only to the Government but to the United Nations. Its primary functions are to preserve the freedom of the Press and, at the same time, to do its utmost to police journalistic activities.

In the late 1960s the influence of Canadians in controlling British newspapers was matched by the arrival on the scene of a brilliant Australian, Mr Rupert Murdoch. For reasons best known to themselves, *Private Eye* at once named him 'The Dirty Digger'. He is a man of shrewd judgement and a well-illuminated flair for business. He bought the *News of the World* and in 1969 the *Sun* which, while professing to retain its sympathy for the Labour Party and the Trade Unions, was converted into a tabloid putting sex and sport alongside politics and industrial relations. It acquired many new readers, some of them lured from the *Daily Mirror* which Sir Harold Wilson compensated by ennobling much of its senior management. Meanwhile, in 1966, another stalwart Sunday supporter of the Labour Party, *Reynolds News,* had ceased publication, preceded some years earlier by the *Daily Mail's* stable companion, the *Sunday Despatch.* In 1971 the *Daily Sketch,* long Lord Kemsley's pride, also closed its doors.

The *Times,* the famous Thunderer which all foreigners used to believe to be the mouthpiece of the British Government, was in serious financial trouble in the early sixties. After the First World War, Major John Astor had bought it, not for profit but because it was a national institution and he wished to be sure it did not fall into the wrong hands. Although the Proprietors, who included Mr John Walter as well as Major Astor, had the right to decide the policy of the *Times* in consultation with the Editor, they did in practice leave the decisions to the Editor whom they appointed; and in pursuance of his original objective in buying control of the paper, Major Astor provided that it should not be sold without approval of the new purchaser by a body of illustrious trustees. Its quality did not fall; and for a time after the Second World War its circulation rose in the wake of heavy marketing expenditure and such modernising devices as changing the masthead, altering the print, shortening the obituaries and replacing births, deaths and marriages on the front page by the main news. Nevertheless by the early 1960s it was faced by financial difficulties until Lord Thomson of Fleet, with motives as honourable as Major Astor's, came to the rescue in 1966. He bought the *Times* and ran it in double harness with the *Sunday Times*, employing the experienced Sir Denis Hamilton as the Coachman to drive them both. Its circulation made little headway, but its regular contributors were of constantly high standard and when Lord Thomson died in August, 1976, he left among his monuments a national institution which even those who prefer the *Daily Telegraph* the *Guardian* or the *Financial Times* would admit to being an integral part of Britain's life and heritage.

Thus, as the twenty five years drew to their close, the British national newspapers were reduced in number and were of uncertain profitability, while the British public relied increasingly on television and radio for their daily news. Some, such as the *Daily Telegraph*, had increased in popularity and consequently in circulation, but were bedevilled by rising costs and the intermittent strikes by printers who, being afraid of a few redundancies, illogically followed courses which might end by making them all redundant. Others rose and fell in their fight for circulation and advertising revenue. By the mid-70s, the *Daily Mail*, long believed to be in danger of collapse, was rising; and the *Daily Express*, deprived of Lord Beaverbrook's wayward genius, was falling, although the *Sunday Express*, well and imaginatively edited, seemed to be holding its own. Mr Murdoch's pair, the *News of the World* and the *Sun*, were galloping gaily ahead. The rise of the *Sun*, under outstanding Editorial direction, was the success story of Fleet Street in the 1970s; but the demand of its working journalists in October, 1976, that membership of the National Union of Journalists should be formally accepted as a condition of employment was seen by some commentators to be the first step towards a total elimination of freedom of choice emanating from the new Trades Union and Labour Relations Act. The most profitable sector of all is the large galaxy of small local papers, partly owned by independent companies but also containing many belonging to the Thomson Group and many others controlled by Lord Cowdray's Westminster Press. There is doubt how long some of the national papers can survive, but also a growing realisation that, whatever the merits, efficiency and impartiality of broadcast news and comment, a free society much depends for its survival on the continued publication of the written word, uninspired and uncensored by any of the other ancient or modern Estates of the Realm.

*

The third new Estate of the Realm, the Trades Union Congress, celebrated its centenary in 1968 by occupying the Guildhall in the City of London (with, it must be admitted, the connivance of the City Corporation) and by inviting both the Queen and the Lord Mayor to luncheon. They had come far in a hundred years. They had in large measure achieved their original objective of safe-guarding the rights and conditions of employment of their members, many of whom were by now also members of the new Affluent Society. They were already looking at broader horizons. In 1952 the Trade Unions, of which there were 183, had eight million members. By their Centenary year, the numbers had scarcely increased, but they were on the verge of a recruiting drive, to which the Trade Union and Labour Relations Act of 1974 and the Employment Protection Act of 1975, with its 'closed shop' provision, made a large, if to some extent 'press-ganged', contribution. It was estimated that by the beginning of 1977, the total membership would exceed eleven million.

In 1952 there was comparative industrial peace. The working days lost by strike action were 1,792,000 against nearly 3,000,000 in 1965, 14,750,000 in 1974 and over 6,000,000 in 1975. Arthur Deakin, Thomas Williamson, Will Lawther and Lincoln Evans, were personal friends of the Prime Minister, Winston Churchill, who invited one or more of them to every dinner party he gave at 10 Downing Street, partly because he thought they should be associated with affairs of State and partly because he liked them as individuals. They, for their part, admired the great war hero and statesman and bore no grudge against the man who in 1926 had fought the General Strike fiercely in the columns of the *British Gazette*, and had been Home Secretary at the time of Tonypandy. They probably knew that deeply though the Tonypandy incident was enshrined in Labour Party mythology, holding a status equal to the Tolpuddle Martyrs and the Great Betrayal of 1931, the then Home Secretary had in historic fact been guilty of no more than ultimate parliamentary responsibility for a charge against the strikers, who had taken to looting, by policemen with truncheons and rolled-up mackintoshes. Be that as it may, the Trade Union leaders bore no grudge against Mr Churchill's Conservative Government.

Mr Churchill (for he was not then Sir Winston) returned this sentiment of admiration and good-will. He was proud in the war to receive back from the Bricklayer's Union, which had by then acquired a longer and more impressive name, the Union Card he had held before 1926 but which had been removed on account of his belligerent opposition to the General Strike. Thus when the railwaymen, who were miserably under-paid, threatened to strike during the Christmas holiday period of 1953, Mr Churchill sent for the Minister of Labour, Sir Walter Monckton, and having calculated that the immediate cost of meeting the railwaymen's demand could easily be born by the Exchequer, if not by the Railway Board, persuaded Sir Walter to contrive that the railwaymen's demand be met and that the strike be averted. Sir Walter who, apart from being a delightful man was also a peaceable one, agreed with the Prime Minister, but there were many shaken heads and not a few commentators declared, with hindsight, that this surrender to Union demands was the beginning of an unstoppable rot.

In 1959 there was a public scandal involving an important Union, the Electrical Trade Union, which had fallen under Communist influence. It was a Union with 700 branches and 240,000 members, of whom fewer than 40,000 normally troubled to vote in the elections of officers of the Union and members of the Executive Council. This Council, chaired by Mr Frank Foulkes, the General President, had hit on a number of apparently fool-proof expedients to ensure the election of a Communist, Frank Haxell, as General Secretary in the face of a challenge by Mr John Byrne. Acting by the precept of Lenin that it is necessary for Communists 'to resort to all sorts of stratagems, manoeuvres and illegal methods, to evasions and subterfuges, in order to penetrate the Trade Unions and to remain in them' (Lenin, like Hitler, was often engagingly frank about the immorality of the methods he advocated), the ETU Executive Council perpetrated what a future Lord Chancellor, Gerald Gardiner, called 'the biggest fraud in the history of Trade Unionism'. Determined to defeat Byrne by foul means if fair would not suffice, they arranged for Haxell to be nominated by as many Union branches as possible, they trumped up charges against Mr Frank Chapple, one of Byrne's supporters, they had 26,000 extra ballot papers printed and fraudulently supplied to Communist supporters, and they altered some of the branch returns unfavourable to their candidate. To their horror, in spite of their precautions, Byrne won. So they disqualified the returns of most of the non-Communist branches and announced Haxell the victor.

There were in the ETU honourable men, such as Mr Chapple and Mr Leslie Cannon, whose political views were far to the left of centre, but who had the courage to stand up for the principle of honest elections. It was they who supported Mr Byrne in bringing a High Court action against Haxell, Foulkes and seven other Communist members of the Executive Council. They won their case, to the entire satisfaction of the moderate majority in the ETU, long deprived of a say in the Union's policy, and in elections for a new Executive Council the Communists were totally defeated. As for the TUC, they were so embarrassed by the charges levelled against one of their leading members that they kept silent on the whole matter until the Court pronounced its verdict. Then, as a mark of august disapproval, they briefly expelled the ETU, but reinstated it as soon as the new Executive, under the leadership of Mr Byrne, Mr Cannon and Mr Chapple, had made a thorough spring-clean of the Augean Stables.

Apart from this unsavoury episode, the affairs of the TUC in the 1950s followed an even course with only spasmodic interruption. Tory Government succeeded Tory Government for thirteen years. The TUC were not, indeed, working on the principle that their policy must be related to the economic situation, and they much resented Mr Selwyn Lloyd's proposal, as Chancellor of the Exchequer in 1961, to kindle a 'guiding light' by which increases in wages and salaries should be measured. But their policy was not yet dependent on their own political inclinations or the transitory, personal aspect of their relationship with an individual Chancellor or Minister of Labour. This was not at all the view of the militant members of the Parliamentary Labour Party, nor of the still more militant representatives of the Labour parliamentary constituencies; but the TUC stood firm by its policy of securing the best attainable wage-rates without trespassing deeper into the field of politics than their general allegiance to the Labour Party required. They celebrated their Centenary in apparent peace and quiet, despite the alarming growth of 'wild-cat' strikes, called without their consent or approval, and the fact that the largest of all their members, the Transport and General Workers Union, had renounced the moderate policies of Ernest Bevin and Arthur Deakin in favour of the more advanced views propagated by Mr Frank Cousins, the new General Secretary appointed in 1956. Dedicated, if unrepresentative, men were already aware of the opportunities offered by wide-spread apathy, and there was much political writing on the industrial wall.

In 1964 a Labour Government was returned by the electorate and it remained in power, with one intervening General Election, until 1970. Mr Harold Wilson shrewdly subscribed for an insurance policy by persuading Frank Cousins to join the Cabinet. The left-wing intellectuals in Parliament were pained by the evident conservatism of most of the Trade Unions, the representatives of which had almost always voted for moderation at Labour Party Conferences. The Trade Union leaders, for their part, believed that deep in his heart Mr Aneurin Bevan had held the Trade Unions in contempt: for some years to come his successors in the militant wing of the Labour Party were even more strongly suspected of so doing.

Members of the Government, whatever the views they had expressed when in Opposition, now felt obliged to take account of the realities of the industrial situation. First Mr Ray Gunter, Minister of Labour from 1964 to 1968, and then Mrs Barbara Castle, whose designation was improved to that of Secretary of State for Employment and Productivity, in accordance with the prevalent inflation of ministerial titles, were confronted by a growing series of 'wild-cat' unofficial strikes gravely injurious to industrial production. From the safely irresponsible Opposition benches, many members of the Government had spoken harsh words about Mr Selwyn Lloyd's 'guiding light' policy, but it soon became clear to them that in the interest of the national economy a Prices and Incomes policy was essential. The best of all possible worlds would be to inaugurate such a policy on a voluntary basis with the whole-hearted support of the Trade Unions and the Employers. So Mr George Brown, second-in-command to Mr Wilson, took the initiative in promoting a tri-partite Declaration of Intent. Unfortunately it was soon clear that the Declaration carried no weight at all and so after much heart-searching, the Cabinet agreed to a statutory Incomes Policy which would, however, only be applied in the event of indisputable economic necessity and then by means of a special Order in Council which must, of course, be subject to subsequent debate in Parliament.

In 1966 the Prime Minister, Mr Wilson, watched with alarm and foreboding the struggles of industry to raise production and improve productivity in the face of continuous trouble in the plants and factories. The loss of almost three million working days in 1965 as the result of strikes, most of which were unofficial, could not be regarded with equanimity at a time when the country was endeavouring to rectify a balance of payments deficit which had approached £800 million. He addressed one of the leading Unions with forthright courage, suggesting that they set their internal house in order and 'consign their rule book to the Industrial Museum'. The position deteriorated gravely in the early summer. The seamen were undoubtedly underpaid and they were disenchanted with their own leaders whom, rightly or wrongly, they considered too disposed to accept their employers' point of view. So they fell beneath the spell of more militant spokesmen, members of the Communist Party, and went on strike for seven weeks at the behest of a handful of their newly-selected leaders, whom the Prime Minister condemned as 'politically motivated men'. The serious dislocation of trade led to a sterling crisis and indirectly to the devaluation of the pound, as well as to a rise in the rate of inflation. It also did much to propagate an exaggerated belief that not just the seamen, but the Trade Union movement as a whole was dominated by militant Communists dedicated to the destruction of the economy as an essential preliminary to social revolution.

In July, 1966, when the seamen's strike was over, it was strongly argued in Whitehall that a Prices and Incomes policy was vital to the defence of the pound and the economy, for inflation was beginning, for the first time in modern history, to become noticeable to the British public as incomes rose faster than productivity. A six months' freeze on wages and salaries was proposed, perhaps to the grim amusement of the maligned Mr Selwyn Lloyd, although the

Conservative Party in the House of Commons decided to vote against the bill. The Transport and General Workers Union also at first declined to accept the policy and Mr Frank Cousins resigned from the Government, doubtless to Mr Wilson's relief. This, the biggest of all the Unions, proposed cuts in defence expenditure as an alternative. Thenceforward reduction in military expenditure, at whatever risk to national security, became the standard cry of all who were unwilling to contemplate a halt to inflationary wage-rises. It demonstrated an escapism only matched by those who invariably suggested that any embarrassing attack on British interests abroad be referred for solution to the United Nations. Finally the opposition of the TGWU was overcome and the Trades Union Congress agreed to the proposed freeze. Perhaps it was partly in consequence of their acquiescence that when, a year later, there was a dock strike almost as damaging to the economy as the seamen's strike of 1966, the TGWU lost all control of its members working in the docks.

In 1965 a Royal Commission had been appointed under the chairmanship of Lord Donovan to examine both the Trade Unions and the Employers' Associations. Its report, presented in 1968, minced no words. There was, it said, indecision and anarchy in industrial relations and it pointed out that nine tenths of the working days lost, which in 1967 were 2,787,000, had been on account of 'wild-cat' strikes. The Government could not fail to take both notice and action, however amiable and gratifying the TUC Centenary celebrations that summer had been; for the Donovan Report made it startlingly clear that the Trade Union leaders had little control over their members. Thus in January, 1969 Mrs Castle produced a document called 'In Place of Strife'. It foreshadowed a legislative measure which would among many other proposals, including revised negotiating procedures and the registration of agreements, provide power, backed by penal sanctions, to require the suspension of unofficial strikes while the issue in dispute was examined. In the summer she laid before the House of Commons her Industrial Relations Bill incorporating the proposals of 'In Place of Strife'.

The TUC were appalled. Here was a proposal, from a Labour Government, to regulate industrial affairs by legislation and to fine those who broke the law. Freedom, they declared, was at stake. Faced by a torrent of Trade Union disapproval, the Prime Minister and Mrs Castle fought hard for the principles of the new bill, but they were not supported by the majority of their Cabinet colleagues and they had to capitulate. Being, perhaps, admirers of Napoleon Bonaparte, they chose 18th June, Waterloo Day, for their surrender. The Government's legislative plans were replaced by a 'solemn and binding' Voluntary Agreement which the TUC would undoubtedly do its best to honour, but which they were in no position to guarantee their members would obey. They did, however, introduce measures to reduce inter-Union squabbles and the demarcation disputes which had so often sprung from them, particularly in the shipbuilding industry.

In 1970 the Conservatives returned to office and the new Prime Minister, Mr Heath, selected a man of integrity and known political sensitivity, Mr Robert Carr, to be Secretary of State for Employment, Mrs Castle's still more grandiose title having been slightly toned down. His appointment followed another Waterloo for Mr Wilson, whose defeat in the General Election took place, by some quirk of history, on 18th June, 1970. The following year Mr Carr introduced a new Industrial Relations bill, which contained many of the features, outlawing unofficial strikes, that Mrs Castle had wished to introduce. It went further: it decreed that Unions must be registered if they wished to retain the fiscal advantages by which they had long benefited and at the same time it conferred new benefits, with statutory backing, on those which did register. It outlawed the 'closed shop', and it sought to remove all compulsion on workers, formal or informal, to join a Union unless they voluntarily decided to do so. It was not, Mr Carr asserted with genuine conviction, intended to be hostile to the Unions. It was aimed solely at restoring order in an undisciplined industrial community. The TUC were no less appalled than they had been by Mrs Castle's proposed measure.

The General Council of the Trade Unions was composed of responsible men. They saw no advantage for the country or for the Unions in a confrontation with a democratically elected Government, blue though its colour might be. Mr Carr had issued a Consultative Document which he invited the TUC and the Employers to discuss with him. The TUC accepted the invitation in the genuine hope of removing the stress in industrial relations and finding a solution acceptable to all. The Government insisted that they alone be judges of certain principles in which they had declared their belief before the General Election and which they had stressed in their Manifesto. The TUC complained that they were only invited to comment on matters of detail. This was no solace to them, for they considered themselves to be intimately concerned with the principles as well as with the details. Unless this was agreed they would, they said, fight. As an alternative they offered the old and ineffective formula of consultation about the reform of industrial relations, provided the Government agreed to abandon all legal sanctions.

Discussions continued, for the leaders of the TUC held Mr Heath in high personal esteem. They recognised his intelligence and his integrity; for the time being they disregarded his obstinacy. They were hoping not only for consultation, but for a joint agreement. Whatever the colour of the Government, they were prepared to accept a partnership and a Social Contract. They would not, however, agree to decisions imposed by a parliamentary majority for, whether the Government knew it or not, they believed they were now speaking with authority. They had become an Estate of the Realm.

Though the Conservatives had voted against a Prices and Incomes policy in 1967, just as the Labour progenitors of that policy had opposed a comparable Conservative measure five years previously, Mr Heath now decided that restraint was essential. He hoped to reach an agreement with the Unions and some thirty items were tabled for discussion. Now the faces of Jones and Scanlon, as well as Vic Feather, became daily familiar on the television screens. As the negotiations went on, the Trade Union leaders learned with increasing disquiet of the surging threat of inflation. They well realised that fatter pay-packets, crammed with pound notes of ever decreasing value, had nothing to recommend them; but although from 1968 onwards the general public had grown uneasily aware that the pounds in their pockets were not what they used to be, the lesson, as yet untaught in all its stark reality by anything but serious articles in the newspapers, and equally serious speeches by Ministers (none of which percolated as deep as the Union branches, let alone the members), was not one the Trade Union leaders themselves had any success in teaching their members. Therefore they received Mr Heath's proposals for voluntary pay restraint and subsequently for a pay-pause, with cold, or at the best tepid, acquiescence. They were too conscious of the realities to say no; they were too uncertain of support by their own rank and file to say yes. The Opposition in Parliament had no such inhibitions: their duty, and their pleasure, was to oppose; and oppose they did, without carrying much conviction until Mr Heath had the misfortune to fall out with the miners, first in the winter of 1971/72 and again, still more seriously, two years later.

In his praiseworthy determination to do battle with inflation before the rise in prices was out of control, Mr Heath would perhaps have been supported by the mass of his countrymen in a struggle with any Union except the miners'. There has always been sympathy and admiration for a body of men who produce a commodity essential to the national welfare in conditions of dirt, danger and discomfort unknown to any other section of the community. There was no doubt that the miners, particularly those working at the coal-face, were under-paid; but they were not under-esteemed and however difficult it might be to make one exception in the pay-pause without also being obliged to bow to other demands, many who would have supported Mr Heath in a contest with electricians, boiler-makers or car-factory workers, were in sympathy with the miners.

In the first miners' strike the difference between the pay rise for which the miners asked and that the Government were ready to concede was small; but to the horror of the Government and the delight of extremists in other Unions, a Commission of Enquiry, established under the Chairmanship of Lord Justice Wilberforce, proposed an increase in pay of more than 20%, whereas other settlements were being made on a 7% or 8% basis. 'Let it,' said the Government and the TUC with one accord, 'be an exception.' This was nothing but a pious hope. The Government had been forced to settle on terms which made it impossible for them to keep the flood-gates closed against a torrent of claims from other quarters. These now began to be settled on highly inflationary terms. The TUC once again offered voluntary restraint, but in return for statutory price control. Such a deal would have been seriously damaging to industry and the Government refused. So in November, 1972, they imposed a temporary wages standstill and followed it with a stringent pay-pause, to be consummated in three successive phases. Initially this policy seemed set on a fair course. At the end of 1973, however, the miners, instigated by extremists in some of the coalfields, were persuaded to disregard the unexpected generosity of the Wilberforce award and to come back for more. They asked for a rise far in excess of what the Coal Board could afford or the national economy prudently sustain. The TUC said that if this claim were treated as a special case, they would undertake not to support any other claims for exclusion from the Incomes Policy. The Government declined and they received no support at all from the Opposition benches in their desperate efforts to avoid a settlement which would let loose the dogs of inflation on a scale never before conceived. The Opposition chose to cry havoc and to seize an opportunity of returning to power. There was a strike, but the violence, illegal picketing and ugly scenes recorded on the television screens during the first miners' strike were not repeated; for the extremist leaders of the miners knew these would be bad electoral propaganda. Mr Heath stood firm and he introduced a three-day working week to reduce the consumption of fuel.

Finally, in February, 1974, despairing of a reasonable settlement with the miners, Mr Heath submitted the dispute to the judgement of the electorate. The Labour Party made little headway at the polls, but the Conservatives, who received more votes than the Labour Party, won fewer seats and failed to contrive a coalition with the Liberals. Mr Wilson again became Prime Minister, but he had no parliamentary majority. He went to the country once again in October and although the Labour Party only polled 39% of the votes cast, they had an overall majority of five in the House of Commons. Meanwhile Wilson gave way to all the miners' demands and they received a larger pay rise than they had in fact expected. Industrial peace was temporarily restored, but inflation was out of control. In 1974 retail prices rose by 15.9% and in 1975 by 25% as against a mere 1% in 1960 and 6.4% in 1970. As the wiser Trade Union leaders had known, almost as well as Mr Heath himself, a pay-pause was vital. A breach of it, even in the exceptional case of the miners, would have presented the embarrassment of establishing a precedent. Perhaps, on a less generous scale than that finally granted, it would have averted the extravagant solution and disastrous price-rise that followed.

The Pay Board which the Conservatives had established was abolished and the statutory Incomes Policy was brought to an end on 18th July, 1974; but when Mr Wilson's Government had only been a year in office, and had agreed to a number of dangerously high wage settlements, they were obliged to adopt Mr Heath's strategy of an Incomes Policy in a different form. They performed the old political trick of stealing the other Party's clothes while bathing. With the support of the TUC they slammed shut the trap-door which they had opened with such extravagant alacrity when they took office in March. They did so by means of a Social Contract with the TUC. This contained much that was irrelevant to the economic situation, and was in essence a surrender to the political, not the industrial, demands of the extremist Trade Union leaders. It was sufficiently permeated with egalitarian sentiment to enable the Trades Union Congress, in September, 1975, to persuade its more militant members to endorse an agreement to limit pay rises to £6 a week. In 1976 this counter-inflation policy, approved by the TUC, supported by Mr Jones of the Transport and General Workers Union and eventually accepted by Mr Scanlon of the Engineers, was made more stringent by a further reduction of the increase to £4 a week. The strength of the Union Leaders and the acceptability of the pay policy were increased by the readiness of the Government to honour their own part of the Social Contract bargain. In fact they had no choice, for without it their anti-inflation policies would have crumbled to dust. They had become the vassals of the Trade Unions, whose leaders dictated a legislative programme acceptable to them but not, by any stretch of imagination, endorsed by the country as a whole.

In his anxiety to ensure the co-operation of the Unions, Mr Michael Foot, the Secretary of State for Employment, introduced a Trade Union and Labour Relations Act, followed in 1975 by an Employment Protection Act. The 'closed shop' received the sanction of law, and a worker was only permitted to refuse membership of a Union on religious grounds. The Union leaders were concerned that none of their members should be in a position to break ranks if they decided on Industrial Action. They also sincerely believed that those who work in a firm or factory where Trade Unionists are employed, and are able to receive the benefits offered by a Union, should be obliged to contribute to the funds of that Union. This was evidently not a belief shared by the work-force as a whole. For instance of the 46,000 employees in the Trust Houses Forte organisation, only 7% were voluntarily members of a Trade Union. Indeed it was clear that many non-Union workers strongly disputed the policy paternalistically adopted on their behalf, objecting to compulsion and still more to victimisation. It seemed, indeed, that those refusing to join a Union might even be persecuted by the State itself, for a librarian in Sheffield who was dismissed on account of her refusal was told that the reason for her removal might be given as 'professional misconduct' and she might therefore be deprived of six weeks' unemployment benefit. But the Government, fearing the rejection of their Incomes Policy, carried the day, even to the extent of accepting a provision that Editors of newspapers and writers who were not members of the National Union of Journalists might be prevented from publishing articles. This *diktat*, which was thought by many to threaten freedom of expression, was only carried against strong opposition, voiced in the House of Lords by Lord Goodman and supported by men and women of all parties. It encouraged the National Union of Journalists to aim at monopolist control of the Press and of the news services on television and radio. When, in the late summer of 1976, one of their own members dared to criticise an official of the Union, she was summarily ejected and would, if the monopoly could be enforced, be debarred from pursuing her professional career.

It is indisputable that Mr Foot's Employment Protection Act, despite some provisions menacing the future liberty of the subject, contained others which were generally held to be advantageous and combined some of the less contentious reforms in both Mrs Castle's 'In Place of Strife' and Mr Robert Carr's Industrial Relations Act. It can at least be recorded that at whatever cost to the economy in terms of inflation, and heavy though the load of social Danegeld that the Government were constrained to pay, labour relations did for a time show a marked improvement. No doubt the alarming growth of unemployment, the fear of losing jobs, and the fact that since the new incomes policy was generally accepted, no group of workers felt that another was stealing a march, were important factors. Certainly in the first half of 1976 there were fewer strikes than at any time since 1953 and the number of working days lost was 60% less than a year previously. During the annual conference of the TUC at Brighton in September, 1976, their concerted disapproval and support for the substitution of ingeniously contrived fringe benefits for the wage increases demanded, sufficed to avert an official strike proclaimed by the executive of the National Union of Seamen which would have placed in grave jeopardy the recovery of the country's fragile economy.

Many of the Trade Union leaders are well aware that their newly asserted power must be matched by responsibility. The first requisite has been to reach the individual members, to ensure that they are consulted on appointments within the Union as well as on policy, and to dispel the widely held belief, in which there has certainly been much truth, that the affairs of many Unions are controlled by a small group of dedicated, usually left-wing, militant officials whose policies do not reflect the opinions of the members. The members themselves had long been both complacent and disinterested; and there was danger in the fact, for they had allowed their votes to be wielded, without their authority and usually without their knowledge, sometimes by wise men who were the guardians of their best interests, but sometimes by scheming manipulators who cared more for some minority political cause than for the welfare and working conditions of the men and women they represented. As Lord Feather, former General Secretary of the TUC, said: 'Apathy is the midwife of totalitarianism.'

In 1975 the militants on the National Executive Committee of the Amalgamated Union of Engineering Workers, the second largest in the country, came within an ace of abolishing the postal ballot and thus ensuring that since it was mainly their own supporters who would bother to attend local meetings, and would vote by show of hands, control would remain permanently in their grasp. There was a tie in the vote of the executive, whereupon Mr Hugh Scanlon gave his casting vote in favour of abolition, although there was nothing in the Union rules which gave him the power to do so. However, the moderate members of the Committee appealed to the High Court which ruled that the executive had acted *ultra vires*. So the postal vote was retained and even applied to the Union's national leadership elections. Thus, Communist candidates, sure of election when as few as 10% of the members voted by show of hands, were defeated in ballots in which as many as half the members of the Union took part and made explicit the moderation of their views. No doubt still more would vote, in the AUEW and in other Unions as well, were it not for the high cost of postage both for a Union itself and for its members.

Thus, in the course of a few years the Trade Unions have assumed an importance, indeed a decisive influence, in the life of the country such as they have never known before. In the process they have not made themselves generally popular and opinion polls have indicated that a majority, including many Trade Union members, believe their power to be excessive. This unpopularity, stimulated by newspaper reports of extravagant statements and noisy disturbances, which overshadow wide-spread but unpublished activities of a constructive nature, is to a great extent unjust. The Unions have continued to fulfil their primary function, which is to promote the welfare and safety of their members. They have, by amalgamation, brought down their total number from 183 in 1952 to 116 in 1977, though still more rationalisation and new mergers would increase their efficiency and further reduce the clashes and the competition between them. The notorious demarcation disputes, which at one time caused the loss of many days' work because one Union would accuse another of trespassing on its preserves, have become rare events. Restrictive practices, much reported in the newspapers, are a disease which still thrives in some Unions and is particularly rampant in Fleet Street itself, where industrial relations are the worst in the country and where the endless squabbles of journalists, printers, warehouse-workers and type-setters are a threat to the survival of a free Press.

A wholesome aspect of the sudden, startling increase in the power of the Unions is the fact that at their best they represent the independence of the British working man, an independence which is a powerful bulwark against the dictatorship of right or left and, however Socialist the Unions may profess to be, against the encroachment of the State on the rights of the individual. Thanks to the growing power of the Executive, Governments are now more dominant than they have ever been in peace-time. Parliament has surrendered much of its authority to the Executive; the Sovereign may still advise but can no longer insist; the Churches can protest but are scarcely likely to make much headway by excommunicating Ministers, particularly those who prefer to 'affirm' than to swear by Almighty God; the Press and television may rouse opinion but are impotent to stimulate action. By a strange turn of the wheel, the Trade Unions, at their best embodying the sturdy common sense of the average Briton, and therefore essentially conservative (if not, indeed, sometimes reactionary) in their basic attitudes, have become in the 1970s a powerful counter-weight to the authoritarianism of the modern state.

The Trade Union leaders can only persuade their members, and this is one explanation of the ineffectiveness which they have too often shown in circumstances, particularly those relating to the economic health of the country, where it was apparent they themselves knew the course which good sense demanded they should follow. Men who are obliged to shoulder heavy responsibilities must win the support of branch secretaries and of local organisations which look no further than their own factory walls; and it has long been the case that men and women of extremist political views are more inclined to dedicate time, thought and effort to branch or regional Union activities than are those with an instinct for moderation who tend to prefer a more entertaining use of their leisure. If shop stewards must be taught the economic facts of life, which neither their school-teachers in the past nor their Management in the present have succeeded in teaching them, it must be conceded that it is not an easy task for the Trade Union leaders to perform. Moreover, it has been proved, even to the moderate-minded, that militancy wins financial rewards and that Governments, when resolutely confronted, find Ethelred the Unready a more acceptable father-figure than Sir Francis Drake. Neither directives from a distant Union headquarters nor complicated Acts of Parliament will suffice. Gradual persuasion is the only road to success. Since sticks are of no avail, carrots must be offered. They are often juicier than the wellbeing of the Community can justify. Statements are made which, whether or not they attract the good-will of Union members, arouse the antagonism of the country as a whole; for there is no shortage even of basically moderate Union leaders who, conscious that they are now a part of the national 'Establishment', nevertheless think it only decent, for the sake of auld lang syne, to maintain an outwardly ferocious and revolutionary mien.

The growth of the postal ballot, the gradual awakening of the ordinary Trade Union member to his responsibilities, and the realisation by the TUC that they have a duty to the nation and not solely to the welfare of their members, are among the healthier developments of the reign. That Governments, whether Labour or Conservative, are fully conscious of this strong new force in politics is obvious. It was perhaps significant that when, in July, 1976, the Prime Minister, Mr Callaghan, and his Chancellor of the Exchequer, Mr Healey, felt it necessary to convince their followers that cuts in public spending, however unpalatable, were economically unavoidable, they explained the fact first to the General Council of the Trade Unions and only when that had been done to their own supporters in the House of Commons.

The three traditional Estates, Crown, Lords and Commons, were locked in strife during the course of many centuries. Gradually all three found a distinct role to which they usually adhere with amiable tolerance. It may not be too fanciful to see, as the second Elizabethan age reaches its quarter-centenary, an area of conflict between the three new Estates, which if less formidable than the old, is none the less difficult to resolve in a democratic society.

The first, the Executive, effectively controls Parliament. It can rely on the force of law, which it can sometimes manipulate or even create to suit its requirements, although from time to time the Judiciary administers a wholesome corrective. The second, the Media, enjoying an independence of which they are rightly jealous, can influence public opinion by the selection both of news and opinions, and no less by their omission. This is frequently displeasing to the Executive. Successive Prime Ministers have claimed that they were deliberately denigrated and traduced. That the Media, are in fact, reasonably objective is proved by the conviction of most Conservatives that Fleet Street, the BBC and ITV are hot-beds of revolution, and the equally strong conviction of Socialists that they are controlled and directed by dyed-in-the-wool Tories.

The third Estate, the Trade Unions, having won for themselves in the middle seventies a power of which they never dreamed, are unlikely to relinquish it or to brook either competition by the Executive or attack by the Media. By enforcing the 'closed shop' and demanding under the Social Contract not a pound of flesh but a kilogram, their leaders have made the dangerous experiment of forcing a mass of citizens, whatever their wishes, to do what a group of well-intentioned men decree to be for their good. They have not modernised their outlook, as the changing conditions of life require, and they have not co-operated with the employers (themselves far from blameless in these matters) in devising a means to improve the productivity of British labour in comparison with the Europeans and the Americans. Nor have they contributed to making British industry more efficient. They have failed to realise, as the Americans, the French and the Germans have realised, that higher wages and a better standard of living follow industrial efficiency, but do not cause it and cannot therefore precede it. Efficiency necessarily involves redundancy when there is over-manning. It also involves a willingness to accept new methods of production and new means of transport, and an understanding that funds available for investment are the life-blood of a successful industrial society. The Unions have insisted on placing the pay-packets' cart before the productive horse. They have, it is true, recognised that their duty is now to the community as a whole and not just to improve the pay and working conditions of their members. What they have not recognised, or at least have not impressed on their members, is that at the end of the 20th century the attitude of Trade Unionists, no less than of Management, must be adjusted to the competitive changes that have taken place in international trade, and that higher productivity is as much their concern as that of Management. Of all the three, their instincts are the most conservative and their knowledge of the world outside Britain the most restricted.

Yet none of the three new Estates can be accused of inertia or complacency. There have been many periods in the history of Great Britain, especially after victorious wars, when the national institutions drifted into careless inefficiency and the people, in high places as well as in low, relaxed. In 1977 neither the Executive nor the Media nor the TUC allow them to do so, and it is likely to be many years before they can afford that luxury.

CHAPTER 6

Local Aspirations

It is evident that a majority in these islands prefer listening to their local radio than tuning in to a national programme, and that however acute the financial worries of Fleet Street, the local newspapers thrive. If the British were a logical people, a misfortune from which they have never suffered, they would be equally concerned with the affairs of the town or county in which they live. This is not the case, although local patriotism is by no means dead when it comes to supporting a football or cricket team, and patriotism has evolved, or deteriorated, into nationalism in the wider regions of Northern Ireland, Scotland and Wales.

The inhabitants showed little interest in local affairs, but the matter was taken out of their hands between 1957 and 1972. Local government was reviewed in detail and substantially reconstructed. Since 1888 when County Councils were first established, and were reinforced a few years later by the creation of District and Parish Councils, local government in England and Wales had remained shrouded in its late Victorian garments, its Councillors elected by a small fraction of those with the right to vote, its decision normally accepted by the rate-payers but only languidly reported in the Press, its deliberations closed to the public, and its structure unaffected by the changing scenes of life. At the accession of Queen Elizabeth II the boundaries were out of date and much of the system was out of tune with modern society.

The limits of the County Boroughs were fixed, but many of their inhabitants had overflowed into territory jealously retained by the County Councils, thus confusing and exasperating those whose function it was to provide fire and ambulance services, mend the roads, educate the children and attend to the sewers. The wires had become crossed. Indeed they were often more than crossed; they were inextricably tangled, and it had not yet been admitted that the advent of the motor car and the rise of the 'commuter' had blurred the distinction between town and country. Those whom the local authorities existed to serve grumbled about the rates, traditionally voted in local elections against the Party in power at Westminster, and were uninterested in the machinery which was supposed to be operating for their benefit. By 1957 it was clear to Mr Harold Macmillan's Administration that reform was essential. Under the provisions of a 1958 Act of Parliament a Local Government Commission for England was established to review the boundaries of local authorities in the provinces, and a serious effort was made to reform the local government of metropolitan London.

Sir Edwin Herbert was appointed Chairman of a Royal Commission which spent three fruitful years not only examining the working of the London County Council, with its twenty eight metropolitan boroughs, which sought to serve three million citizens in the central area of the capital, but also considering the much wider spread of greater London. For years the population had been steadily drifting away to suburbia and the countryside. A two-tier system was now proposed by which planning and other major functions would be allotted to a Greater London Council, enfolding eight million citizens in its ample bosom, and those most nearly affecting the lives of the citizens would be the responsibility of 52 new London boroughs. In 1963, a year before the Conservatives lost office, the London Government Act was passed. The basic recommendations of the Herbert Commission were accepted, but the number of London boroughs beneath the GLC canopy was reduced by Parliament from the 52 proposed by the Commission to 32, and the responsibility for education in inner London was given to a new authority called ILEA, covering the central area and catching three million people in its net. The old London County Council, which fought the creation of the GLC with might and main, was not the only battle casualty. Kent and Essex, Surrey and Hertfordshire were all condemned to forfeit some of their possessions to the new Colossus, and poor little Middlesex vanished from the map altogether, although it valiantly persisted in fielding a County cricket team and the Middlesex Hospital remained a lasting monument to its name. There can be no doubt that the steps taken to modernise the government of London were sensible and opportune.

A still further-reaching reform followed. Hard on the heels of the

Herbert Commission, Lord Redcliffe Maud, one of a band of exceptionally able Civil Servants from whom Britain benefited in the mid-20th century, was invited to preside over a Royal Commission with still wider scope. In 1966, when a Labour Government was in office, he and his colleagues began the examination of the whole structure of local government throughout England. Encouraged to make use of experts, statisticians and research organisations on a scale to which the Herbert Commission had had no access, Lord Redcliffe Maud produced his comprehensive, deeply considered report in 1969, just before Mr Heath became Prime Minister. It thus fell to a Conservative Government to give legal effect to the plan which their Socialist predecessors had commissioned and approved. They did so with speed and a new Local Government Act received the Royal Assent in 1972.

If it was not quite such a revolutionary measure as the Royal Commission recommended, it did none the less change the administrative face of England and in many places it changed the map. An obvious, indeed, essential, objective was to create units of local government large enough to finance and maintain the services required by the community, and to erase as many as possible of the blotched areas of divided or indeterminate control. The Act of 1972 did not accept all the recommendations in the Commission's report, but it did both rationalise and simplify a system which had rejoiced, or rather become enmeshed, in no less than nine different types of elected body with intermingled populations and illogical boundaries of authority. There had been over 1,300 local Councils or districts, mostly containing less than 20,000 inhabitants, in addition to 10,000 parishes, some of which elected Councils while others did not.

In broad outline the new system which emerged in 1972 was this. In addition to London, six new Metropolitan Counties were created, all in the North of England and the Midlands. Each of these contained a number of Metropolitan Districts which, like the London boroughs, are responsible for the main services such as education, welfare and housing, while the Counties plan the wider strategy, maintain the major roads, provide public transport and control the fire brigades and the police. Outside these thickly-populated town areas, unattractively called Conurbations by a generation which eschews a classical education but favours long Latin words, all County Boroughs were abolished. Thirty nine new Counties took the place of the old Counties and County Boroughs, few catering for less than 260,000 people; and in each County a second tier of District Councils was made responsible for various duties. Brand new Counties emerged: Cleveland, Avon, Humberside and Cumbria. Some old, time-honoured names vanished. Cumberland and Westmorland are no more; Herefordshire is united with Worcestershire; Rutland, wishing to remain England's smallest County, had earlier made a gallant, if obscurantist, struggle at the Church door to resist the amorous advances of Leicestershire, but was finally vanquished in 1972 and walked, by no means uncomplaining, to the altar. Within the surviving Counties there were additions and subtractions. For instance, Surrey was robbed of Gatwick Airport to the greater glory of the West Sussex rate-payers. Many of these changes evoked sentimental sighs and historical groans, but the compensating social, economic and administrative advantages were irresistible.

Still more important was the disappearance of the County Boroughs. They had been tightly defined since the end of the 19th century and had provided services which took no account of those living a few hundred yards beyond their boundaries and obliged to rely on the good offices of an entirely separate authority. They were now usefully combined with the surrounding territory to serve a far larger population. Size is far from being synonymous with efficiency, but in the provision of such amenities as education, public health, housing and welfare, experience had conclusively shown that a better service could be offered at less cost to the rate-payer in a large unit. This was one good reason for giving to the Counties, rather than to their subordinate Districts, many of the responsibilities which in the new Metropolitan Areas were attached to the thickly-populated Districts.

The smaller towns lost their Urban District Councils, and groups of villages lost their Rural District Councils. All were merged in wider areas, usually uniting town and country, so that some 300 new districts replaced 930 old ones and the population which each must serve was raised to an average of 90,000. A Local Government Boundary Commission was established with the task of recommending such changes in boundaries as may become fitting when populations increase or decrease and local conditions change with the ebb and flow of industry and commerce.

Until 1974 elections to one or other of the nine different kinds of Local Authority were held on scattered and easily forgotten days in April and May. It was gratifying if much more than a quarter of the electorate cast a vote and those who did so were probably more interested in voicing their censure of the Party in power at Westminster, or objecting to the latest rate increase, than in expressing their views about the local policies of the Councillors. Under the new dispensation it was decreed that all local elections should take place on the same day, thus attracting more concentrated attention from the media and increasing the citizens' awareness of the choice before them. However, local elections are more often than not conducted on a party political basis. Indeed one result of the 1974 Act has been to diminish the strength of the independent candidates for election, especially in the rural areas where independents were formerly strong. Thus, beneficent as the changes have been in many respects, party politics have become the rule in local government and nothing has been done to encourage the people to vote on a local issue without regard to their national and traditional Party prejudices. This means the introduction of a change in the relationship between elected members of a Council and its permanent officials, for local policy may in some cases be subordinated to political considerations which are not of strictly local relevance, while there are not, on the other hand, any traditional links between local electors and the Councillors whom they have chosen to serve them.

Local authorities cannot move far against the wishes of the Central Government or the dictates of Whitehall. Since much of the money at their disposal comes not from the rate-payer but, in the form of Exchequer Grants, from the tax-payer, it has always been accepted that the Central Government must exercise substantial influence on Local Authorities; nor would any other course be reasonable, for the power of local government to raise the rates is bestowed by Parliament, and the expansion or contraction of local expenditure is one of the principal methods of controlling the economy of the country.

However, in 1965 the Labour Government proposed to introduce universal Comprehensive Education and though under the then existing law they could not force recalcitrant authorities to put forward such a scheme, they asked them to do so. A long-drawn-out battle ensued, for many towns and Counties wished to retain their Grammar Schools. In 1976 a local election was fought on this issue at Tameside in Lancashire and the opponents of the Comprehensive system won a decisive victory. The policy of the Central Government in a matter which had little or nothing to do with the control of expenditure was thus brought into direct conflict with the wishes of the people expressed in the local ballot box. There had, for once, been a vote given on a specific local issue rather than solely on the basis of party political loyalty. Nevertheless, the Secretary of State for Education, Mr Mulley, unhesitatingly over-rode the wishes of the local electors, until he in turn was over-ridden by a decision of the High Court.

In other ways, too, Whitehall, making such a contribution to the piper's wages, feels free to express a view about the tune. The Departments of the Environment, of National Health and Social Security and of Education and Science cannot be accused of neglecting opportunities to interfere; and although this interference is normally by consultation rather than by direction, it is as true in 1977 as it was in 1952 that greater freedom in local government is an aspiration to which the Government pays pious lip service but gives no practical encouragement. The structure has been radically revised, but the source of power remains the same.

Effect was given to the recommendations of the Herbert and Redcliffe Maud reports, or to such parts of them as Parliament approved, with laudable speed. The report of a third Royal Commission touched on deeper, more sensitive nerve-centres. In 1969 Geoffrey Crowther, well-known for many years as Editor of the *Economist*, was invited to lead an investigation of the advantages and practicability of regional government, involving the devolution of power from the Central Government in Whitehall and from the British Parliament to locally-elected bodies which would exercise powers of a different kind from those of local authorities. On Crowther's death, Lord Kilbrandon succeeded him and the Commission presented its report in 1975.

The delicacy of this enquiry, and the long reluctance of the

Central Government to declare its hand, arose from the agitation of Scottish and Welsh Nationalists, and indirectly from the gravity of events in Northern Ireland.

At first the Welsh seemed to concentrate their discontented feelings on the use of their native language, with which the majority of Welshmen have neither the wish nor the energy to become familiar. However, the Celtic nostalgia for ancient, almost prehistoric romance expressed by reverence for Bards, Eistedfodds, beautiful singing and melancholy poems, was combined with a growing conviction that even the Labour Party which, with a few Liberal relics of David Lloyd George's Welsh wizardry, represented the constituencies of the Principality, was paying undue attention to the United Kingdom as a whole and failing to concentrate on the peculiar problems of Wales. The innovation of a Secretary of State for Wales in 1964, and the creation of a Welsh Office, were regarded as palliatives inadequate to satisfy the demand, comparatively small though it might be, for greater self-determination.

Thus, while in the 1960s, wild young men and women demonstrated about the language, letting off an occasional home-made bomb in order to attract attention, a more serious body of Welsh Nationalists took to the hustings in 1974 and succeeded in winning two seats in Parliament. They assert no desire to break up the United Kingdom, but they do demand a Welsh Parliament responsible for the Principality's internal affairs. They propose, in addition, to retain full representation at Westminster, and it would be a disaster for the Labour Party if they did not. Their attitude, except on the wider fringes, has been reasonable and though the degree of independent authority likely to be thought appropriate for a Welsh Parliament and Executive is sure to be debated with acrimony, the principle has found some sympathy in England. The initiative of the Prince of Wales in going to a Welsh university and learning to speak the language proved that, at any rate at the very summit, the value of Wales was neither underestimated nor forgotten.

Scottish Nationalism, long latent and not generally believed to have strong support, became militant just before the reign began. The Stone of Scone, on which British Monarchs had been crowned for three hundred and fifty years, was stolen from Westminster Abbey and transported to Dunfermline Abbey whence Edward I, the Hammer of the Scots, had removed it in 1296. The Nationalists also objected to the new Royal title. The Queen was not, they declared, Elizabeth II, for Elizabeth I had never been Queen of Scotland; and for a week or two they blew up all the pillar-boxes they could find with E II R inscribed upon them. The Cabinet settled this vexed problem by advising the Queen that future Sovereigns should always adopt the higher royal numeral, whether of English or Scottish origin, so that if a new King James were to ascend the Throne he would not be styled James III but James VIII. Fortunately Charles I and II were Kings of both England and Scotland, so that the Prince of Wales, born four years before this pillar-box revolt occurred, was unaffected by the decision.

Whether or not they were mollified by this polite compromise, the Scottish Nationalists stopped blowing up pillar-boxes and for a good many years their electoral support seemed negligible. However, in 1967 Mrs Ewing, whose good looks were only surpassed by her extreme nationalist views, won a by-election at Hamilton. The movement nourished itself on the belief that Scotland had always been treated as a poor relation, a belief which had little or no foundation in recent history. For instance, Scottish rate-payers receive substantially higher relief from the national budget than do their English equivalents. Bitterness was also fostered by a rate of unemployment higher than in England, which was due to the impact of world recession on the general pattern of Scottish industry, and on the Clyde shipyards in particular. The movement gathered so much strength that in a 1974 General Election eleven Scottish Nationalist Candidates were elected.

The Labour and Conservative Parties, already working out their own schemes of devolution, were now impressed by the urgency of the situation and decided that Scottish Nationalism must be taken seriously. In 1975 the Labour Government produced a White Paper proposing a measure of devolution which the Nationalists immediately dismissed with disdain and which, during 1976, split the Labour Party in Scotland. Nevertheless, by the end of 1976 the majority of the House of Commons was committed to devolution for Scotland and it was necessary to discover what degree of independence, short of leaving the United Kingdom, would be acceptable to the majority, not indeed of Scottish Nationalists, but of Scots. Avarice has never been conducive to moderation, and the discovery of oil off the coasts of Scotland in greater quantity than off the coasts of England has sharpened the tongues, though not, it may be hoped, the knives of the Scottish Nationalist negotiators waiting impatiently for serious talks to begin.

The devolution to which Scotland and Wales were looking as the Silver Jubilee approached with, in the case of Scotland, a variegated interpretation of the word, had collapsed in tragedy, hatred and bloodshed in Northern Ireland. The Ulster Parliament at Stormont, with its own Ministers and Government Departments, should have been the model of all future regional government; but because the provincial elections were fought on a religious rather than a party platform, the predominant Protestants ruled almost unopposed for the fifty years of Stormont's placid existence. The division was in fact less one of religion than of historic antipathy, for as Mr Terence O'Neill, the one Northern Irish Prime Minister who made a genuine effort to heal the wounds of centuries, said in his resignation speech: 'We could have enriched our politics with our Christianity; but far too often we have debased our Christianity with our politics.' He also said, with tragically prophetic foresight: 'Either we live together or we have no life worth living.'

The Ulster experiment had been a compromise. The Protestant majority would have been content to be an integral part of the United Kingdom, thus underlining their total distinction from the republican South. The Roman Catholic minority wished to be united with the Irish Free State or, as it became in 1948, the Irish Republic. Power in the hands of a permanent Protestant majority was misused: jobs and houses were allocated to Protestants in preference to Roman Catholics; and by a strange anomaly the universal suffrage which applied at parliamentary elections was denied in local elections. The hot-heads among the Roman Catholic minority, looking across the border for inspiration, fell beneath the malign spell of the Irish Republican Army.

All the same, in spite of a bout of IRA outrages in the 1930s, and the refusal of Southern Ireland to join forces against the Nazis in the war, the waters of the Irish Sea were calm when the Queen came to the throne and there were grounds for hope that a saner mood might prevail in North and South. The IRA, doubtless alarmed by such a possibility, murdered a few policemen in the late 1950s and blew up quite a lot of buildings; but prosperity was returning to Ulster; British and foreign companies, encouraged by low rents, large grants and a plentiful supply of labour, were establishing factories, and the old dependence of the labour force on the Belfast shipyards and the linen industry was being relieved by new and diverse opportunities. Indeed Ulster's retraining schemes were more advanced than those introduced anywhere else in the United Kingdom. Unemployment was still high, but it was falling and it was surmised that quite a lot of ingenious citizens were contriving both to earn wages and to draw unemployment benefits.

Early in 1965 Mr Terence O'Neill made the unprecedented gesture of inviting the Southern Irish Prime Minister, Mr Lemass, to luncheon at Stormont and paying a return visit to Dublin a month later. The Ulster Unionists gasped but temporarily restrained themselves; and when O'Neill continued these exchanges of visits with Lemass's successor, Mr Jack Lynch, there was a glimmer of hope that the frank discussion of problems at the top, and the sincere wish of both Prime Ministers to discover a road leading to peace and compromise, might infect their Protestant and Roman Catholic followers. O'Neill went further and forced through his own Cabinet, and through Stormont, a measure to give universal suffrage in local as well as parliamentary elections.

In the newly-built housing estates, Protestants and Roman Catholics were beginning to live side by side; and the poorer Catholics, impressed by the thrift, hard work and resultant prosperity of their Protestant neighbours, were tending to become less feckless. They even dared to defy their priests to the extent of restricting the size of their previously unbirth-controlled families. The mixed areas offered a short-lived hope of communal understanding. The sun seldom shines in Northern Ireland, but the barometer was rising, and it really did seem that the clouds were about to break.

These hopes were shattered. The long knives of the obscurantist Protestants led by the Reverend Ian Paisley, whose Holy Orders stemmed from no Protestant sect known to man (and almost certainly not to God either), were sharpened to attack O'Neill. The bigoted Protestant masses were marshalled against him. The Roman

Catholics and the Socialists, led for the most part by well-meaning idealists who little knew what a terrible Djinn lurked in the bottle they were unscrewing, organised Civil Rights Marches which led to riot and disorder. The British Army was sent in to quell the disturbances; the IRA fanned the flames; Anarchists, Marxists, Trotskyites and International Socialists saw a fertile field in which to sow; and for two long years the Protestants sat back and suffered in silence while the odium for murder, outrage and destruction fell on the IRA. Tribal instincts revived. Tens of thousands who had been adapting themselves to a new and broader outlook in the mixed areas, were forced to revert to their atavistic hatred and moved physically back to the ghettoes of religious intolerance whence they had sprung.

The United Kingdom Government took direct control. Stormont closed its doors and successive British Administrations, Labour, Conservative and once again Labour, used every ounce of negotiating power and all the diplomatic skill they could muster to bring about a political solution. It eluded them entirely. The Protestants in their turn took to the streets with bombs and guns. Sectarian outrages were daily events; and, in spite of all the security forces could do, there were twice as many political murders in the first half of 1976 as in that of 1975. Shops and public houses trapped women and children as they collapsed in flames. Catholics ambushed Protestants and Protestants murdered Catholics in a religious war which was a direct negation of the Christianity they affected to profess. Both of them, in their blind, barbaric hatred, turned their guns on the British troops.

There is, however, a limit to what human beings will stand, no matter how deeply their emotions are stirred. Amid the encircling gloom of Ulster, a kindly light was kindled in the autumn of 1976 when a few brave women, sickened by the ceaseless violence, started a peace movement which soon attracted thousands of supporters, Protestant and Catholic alike, who marched through the towns in solemn protest against bombing, burning and murder. It must, in the end, be the people of Northern Ireland themselves who extinguish the blaze of civil war.

Meanwhile, the British Army, reinforced step by step, stood its ground in the grim streets of Belfast, and ventured along booby-trapped roads on the border with the Irish Republic, while assassins shot young service-men dead on patrol and gangs of Southern accomplices crossed the border to plant land-mines. The old words of the Wearing of the Green – "Tis the most distressful country that I have ever seen' – were truer of Northern Ireland in the 1970s than they had ever been of the South in the 1790s. The two rays of light in the dismal scene were supplied by the women of the Peace Movement and by the imperturbable courage of the British troops who, in spite of a constantly mounting casualty list, showed a patience and a discipline at which their fathers and grandfathers, veterans of two world wars, stood in proud amazement.

It is not an auspicious prelude to the performances in Scotland and Wales on which the curtain is about to rise; but the grievances of the Scots and Welsh, real or imaginary, whether stimulated by genuine desire for self-government or by the lure of oil, are not comparable in either bitterness or historic tradition with those of the Irish. While the politicians pirouette in anxious, but painfully obvious, manoeuvres to satisfy Scotland and Wales without weakening their own parliamentary strength at Westminster, it may yet be seen that the Parliament at Stormont was a pace-setter in regional self-government from which other parts of the United Kingdom, untrammelled by pseudo-religious strife, will eventually decide there are lessons to be absorbed and precedents to follow.

CHAPTER 7

Seven Men

When Queen Victoria, sixty years on the throne, celebrated her Diamond Jubilee in 1897, there had been eleven different Prime Ministers in Downing Street. Queen Elizabeth II's score is already seven by the time of her Silver Jubilee.

All seven were men of virtue and most of them were men of valour. With one exception they received, as the virtuous must expect, their full and unfair share of mud slung by opponents and commentators. The exception was Sir Winston Churchill, on whom more abuse had been heaped during his long political career than on all the other six combined; but by 1952 the abusers had left the auditorium and this Victorian-turned-Elizabethan was acknowledged, by foes across the floor of the House as much as by countless friends, to be the most revered statesman alive. So the slinging of supplementary mud was reserved for future historians.

The Churchill who kissed the new Queen's hand as she stepped from the aeroplane on her return from Nairobi had mellowed with age and experience. He was 77 years old. Triumph, which is not always the impostor Rudyard Kipling claims, had not corrupted him. His personal ambitions were long since satisfied and he surveyed the world, in particular the British Isles, with a benevolence which was returned in full measure. No longer the wayward genius of 1915, or the thunderer of 1940, he could still on occasions hold the House of Commons spell-bound; and his capacity for speaking to the country in terms that people understood was undimmed.

His gifts and achievements, and also his misjudgements, are the subject of countless volumes. What the new Queen found in 1952 was a Prime Minister not only hallowed in the eyes of the public by his legendary war-time leadership, but genuinely devoted to her service and the historic continuity she represented. His errors were forgotten: he was, as he had always been, a man quick to rise either to an occasion or to a challenge, but incapable of bearing a personal grudge, devoted to the already fading image of a Great and Greater Britain, and more affected by human distress or by any suggestion of injustice to an individual than by indices of production or terms of trade. Churchill, Leader of the Conservative Party with a Parliamentary majority of 18, was then, as he had always been, a Liberal at heart, long disenchanted by the political activities of the Party to which he had once belonged ('So few,' he called them, 'and so futile'), but still inspired by the ideals, most of them long realised, which were the mainspring of what had been, perhaps, the greatest of all British peace-time Administrations, the Liberal Government of 1906.

Before Sir Anthony Eden, subsequently Earl of Avon, became Prime Minister, he had spent almost his entire political career at the Foreign Office. He was, as Churchill complained, Foreign Officissisimus. Yet there was, in 1955, nobody in the House of Commons with a longer experience of Government or the vicissitudes of political life, and he conducted the 1955 General Election with brilliant acumen, winning more votes than the Labour Party and the Liberals combined. His integrity shone like a star, and his courage, in peace as in war, was acknowledged by all. He was not a speaker comparable with either his predecessor or his successor, and he was capable of an impatient irritability which could estrange both his supporters in the Conservative Party and the Civil Servants who worked for him. Nevertheless, his personal qualities were well proved, he was a brilliant negotiator at the conference table, and when he was at ease there was no statesman whose charming smile, ready wit and attractive personality won more friends and admirers. His misfortune was to become Prime Minister, after a long period as heir apparent, when ill-health had damaged his constitution and exacerbated his temper, as well as temporarily distorting his judgement. Churchill, who was devoted to him, said when he appointed him Foreign Secretary at the end of 1940: 'Anthony has courage, and courage is what is needed in war. He would always charge a battery – although, of course, he might charge it at the wrong time and from the wrong angle.' At Suez, in 1956, he fulfilled Churchill's prophecy; but he acted from motives which he and, at the time, most of his fellow-countrymen believed to be just; and if what he did was impetuous, it was certainly courageous. Being an honourable man, as well as an honest one, he blamed none but himself and accepted the consequences with humility. He was, in the best sense of the old-fashioned word, a great gentleman.

Few British Prime Ministers have taken office in conditions more politically strained, and indeed personally invidious, than Mr Harold Macmillan. In January, 1957, the Suez disaster was but two months old and Macmillan, known to have been Sir Anthony Eden's active supporter in preparing the adventure, was the Minister whose words of dire warning on the mortal damage sanctions would inflict on the economy led to the ignominious withdrawal from the Canal Zone. Like Churchill in 1940, Macmillan, faithful supporter of his predecessor, had stepped into that fallen predecessor's shoes. He remained Prime Minister for more than six years and was, by common consent, a powerful, original and imaginative holder of the office.

It is arguable that successful statesmen must be good actors. Churchill was, Wilson was, and Eden, Home and Heath were not. Macmillan was a superb performer in an age which could boast of Olivier, Gielgud and Alec Guinness. He was scarcely their inferior in the art, but he was not an actor in the sense that he played a part in which he disbelieved. On the contrary he chose the role and he performed it with style and professional polish.

Macmillan, like R. A. Butler, his rival for the leadership, was a man who always drove in the middle of the road. Prime Ministers, facing realities of which they had little need to take notice when they were in Opposition or on the back benches, almost inevitably do so in the event; but Macmillan, unlike Harold Wilson and unlike Churchill in his earlier days, had throughout his political career thought it wise to keep as far as possible from the curb and the ditch. In so deciding he aligned himself with the feelings of the great majority of his countrymen, and his judgement was proved correct by the speed with which he restored the self-confidence of the people after the humiliation of Suez.

Perhaps he was lucky, for the last few years of his Premiership coincided with a period of prosperity; but it would be unjust to deny most of the credit to a pilot who kept so firm and experienced a hand on the tiller. In the early days of his Administration he faced waves of great unpopularity for his Party. In 1958 even the safe

Conservative seat of Tonbridge came within an ace of being lost at a
by-election, but in 1959 his leadership was vindicated by a General
Election in which his Party won a majority of 100 seats. He was the
first Prime Minister to master the new political technique of television. There were some who laughed at his style, and there were
others who delighted to parody and caricature; but there were few
who denied his unusual capacity for leadership. Nor, in retrospect,
should his success in mending the bridge across the Atlantic, severely
strained by the Suez affair, be underestimated or forgotten, even if
one of the declared reasons for General de Gaulle's determination to
exclude Britain from the European Community was Macmillan's
close personal alliance with Presidents Eisenhower and Kennedy.

He will be remembered as the Prime Minister who opened the
Imperial door to the Wind of Change, who sorrowfully but sternly
excluded South Africa from the counsels of the Commonwealth,
but who restored Britain's waning influence in many other parts of
the world. Like Sir Anthony Eden, his last months in office were
clouded by illness, and he handled the unhappy Profumo affair with
unaccustomed ineptitude. At a by-election in 1962 the Conservatives lost one of their safest seats, Orpington, to a Liberal. The
popularity of the Government began to wane and Macmillan himself was increasingly in physical distress. It was not, however, his
fault that the timing and manner of his going brought the Conservative Party into a disarray such as it had seldom experienced.

He declined the Earldom and the Garter which he richly deserved,
preferring to scatter smaller honours, like confetti, on his loyal, able
and devoted staff; but in 1976 he emerged briefly from his long
retirement to urge on the country the necessity of a National
Government and in so doing proved himself, once again, a brilliant
virtuoso in the art of political television performances.

When the 14th Earl of Home was selected as Prime Minister in
1963, most of his friends and opponents were astonished. A few
were not. Two years previously, at the end of a convivial dinner
party, the author of this book asked the Secretary of the Cabinet,
Sir Norman Brook, who could conceivably succeed Mr Harold
Macmillan in the unhappy event of his being run over by a tram. Sir
Norman looked down the table, at which both Mr Macmillan and
Lord Home were present, and pointing to the latter, said: 'That

would be the only possible choice.' The choice was made in unfortunate circumstances, for the life of the Parliament had but a year to run and a number of important Conservatives, such as Mr Ian Macleod, were opposed to it. After winning three successive General Elections, it was improbable that the Conservatives could win a fourth. They considered themselves the natural Government of the country, a claim which the Labour Party in their turn made in the mid-1970s; and in both cases there was nothing better calculated to persuade a high proportion of the undecided members of the Electorate to cast their votes the other way. Lord Home, or Sir Alec Douglas Home as he rapidly became, using the facilities successfully demanded by Mr Wedgwood Benn to renounce his peerage, therefore succeeded to an uneasy inheritance. It was, as Sir Winston Churchill had told Sir Anthony Eden in 1955, dangerous to succeed a well-established Prime Minister towards the end of a Parliament: remember, Churchill had said, Rosebery after Gladstone and Balfour after Salisbury.

Nevertheless, apart from the disadvantage of being a bad screen performer in the new television age, Douglas Home had high qualities. He had won golden opinions at both the Commonwealth Relations Office and the Foreign Office. His good nature, ease of manner, true simplicity, transparent goodness and oratorical wit (except on the television screen) won the affection of all who came into contact with him and the sympathetic support of many who did not. His attractive modesty was emphasised by his good manners and reinforced by the sub-conscious certainty that he had no need at all to worry about his social position, family happiness, personal popularity or financial solvency.

He lost the 1964 General Election by four seats. It is by no means impossible that any other Conservative Prime Minister might have lost it by a wider margin. In defeat he made way gracefully for Mr Edward Heath with whom, to the credit of them both, he retained an excellent relationship which culminated in his glad agreement to serve as Foreign Secretary once again in Heath's 1970 Government.

Mr Harold Wilson, who became Sir Harold in 1976, was invited to form a Government in 1964. He did so with a majority of five in the House of Commons (for the Conservative Speaker was, by convention, neutral), and less than 45% of the recorded popular vote.

It was, however, a moment of ecstatic fulfilment for the Labour Party which had been so long in the wilderness of Opposition that few of its leading members, apart from Harold Wilson himself, had any experience at all of Government. During the long years of waiting his old men had dreamed dreams and his young men (and young women too) had seen visions. Being lofty idealists rather than experienced administrators, many of them supposed that a Socialist Utopia would be created by a few strokes of the legislative brush and the fiscal sword. Mr Wilson was fond of describing himself as a pragmatist and he was certainly far too intelligent to share these views; but his people had seen the Promised Land and it would have required a Moses to restrain them from their excited determination to enter it without delay.

Mr Wilson was no Moses. He was faced, throughout all his long years as Prime Minister, with a situation no Conservative Prime Minister ever had to face: a Party so divided by its honest differences of opinion that one half was always ready to fall on the other with sharp tooth and pointed nail. He saw at once that it was necessary to throw a bone to the traditional theorists whose shibboleths were mainly outworn but still tenaciously held. So he offered a deliberate insult to the Spanish Government, which had been labouring quietly and successfully to restore the country's shattered economy ever since the end of their civil war, twenty five years previously. The Spanish Government's immediate rejoinder was to make things exceedingly difficult for the inhabitants of Gibraltar; but honour was satisfied and the traditionalists of the Labour Party were temporarily content. The pattern was thus set for future Government, with special reference thenceforward to internal affairs: bones, some juicy and some with their leanness camouflaged by oratory, were thrown to the left-wing at regular intervals in order to keep the Party united and intact.

Mr Wilson and his Government were so sincerely convinced that the Labour Movement stood for everything that was noble and compassionate that they made the mistake of confusing it with the country. They never won a majority of the popular vote, even in 1966, but they believed that what the Labour Movement, or a part of it, decreed to be right must actually be so. They spoke of their Movement with the reverence that a Roman Catholic reserves for the

Real Presence. In consequence the sin against the Holy Ghost was to risk splitting the Party and Mr Wilson was himself so obsessed by this article of the Creed that he did from time to time, though by no means always, prefer Party unity to the national good; or rather, he equated the two in his mind. The most damaging example was in March, 1974 when, having formed a Government without any majority at all, he threw wide open the floodgates of inflation by a surrender to wage demands larger than the Trade Unions expected. He did so to the almost unanimous applause of his, for once, united supporters. He proceeded to win another General Election in the autumn of the same year, with the positive support of 28% of those with a right to vote, and he made no move to correct a statement by his Chancellor of the Exchequer during the Election Campaign that the rate of inflation had been reduced to 8% per annum. It was in reality running at twice that figure.

Much of this was discreditable, and it gave rise to a belief by many who were by no means traditional Conservatives that Mr Wilson was devious. In fact he had many compensating virtues which the people as a whole, who continued to show in the Opinion Polls that he personally stood high in their esteem, perceived with greater clarity than most of the political commentators. He tried consistently, in years filled with intractable difficulties, to do what he sincerely believed best for a storm-tossed Britain. He sometimes said divisive words, but his actions were aimed at reaching and maintaining a consensus of opinion. Vital though he believed the unity of his Party to be, there were times, as in the Rhodesian imbroglio and the Communist machinations which led to the seamen's strike of 1966, when he spoke unequivocally in the national interest at the cost of antagonising many of his supporters. Like Mr R. A. Butler, he knew politics to be the art of the possible, but for him, as for most of his colleagues, that art was circumscribed by the sectional, though devoutly held, belief that keeping the Party together was the supreme obligation of a Labour Prime Minister.

Wilson, whose mastery of the television screen was among his foremost assets, had others which will be recognised by the historians. However firm his personal belief in the rightness of a policy, such as entry into the Common Market, he was not prepared to force it through reluctant colleagues in the Cabinet or Parliament till the matter had been fully debated; for there was nothing of the dictator or the unscrupulous hustler in his make-up. He would go to great lengths for his Party, torn as it was by internecine strife and riddled by intrigue, while the left-wing militant minority jockeyed for position in the Constituency Associations and the Party's own National Executive Committee; but in the last analysis he would never contemplate sacrificing the safety or interests of his country if, according to his own lights, those interests seemed to be at risk. The method and the timing of his departure from 10 Downing Street in 1976 were among the least becoming of his decisions, for he left an unenviable inheritance to his successor; but he had been Prime Minister for nearly eight years in all and he had, in the broad perspectives, deserved well of his countrymen in circumstances which would have overwhelmed a man who did not have exceptional patience, will-power and resilience.

Edward Heath, chosen to succeed Douglas Home by the Conservative Party under a new elective procedure, had five years to wait before he could form a Government. He was the first Conservative Prime Minister of humble origin and there were many of his followers to whom this fact was by no means unwelcome. His musical talent had secured him an Organ Scholarship at Balliol where he made the best use of his opportunities, not only academically and artistically, but also in the famous political training-school of the Oxford Union. He had a high intellectual capacity, absolute integrity and a resolve, from which nothing would at any time deflect him, to pursue the political and economic objectives he judged best for his country. Firmness of purpose is the substance of which leadership is made, but it is still more efficacious when seasoned with flexibility. Heath lacked that seasoning, at any rate in the early years, but he believed it could be replaced by the qualities of a modern political technocrat, sensitive to the hard, practical realities of the time. In that he was the antithesis to Home: jointly they might have formed a well-balanced synthesis.

Heath had the ability of a trained advocate (which he was not) to master a complex brief, store the facts in his retentive memory and present his conclusions with compelling conviction to a small and intelligent audience. He carried less conviction on a wider stage, for although he never failed to put the interests of his country before his own or those of his Party, he found it difficult to master several defects which contributed to his defeat as a political leader. The first was obstinacy which, when the results happen to be propitious, is sometimes called courage. He had an honest, but in the event fatal inability, skilled yachtsman though he was, to set his sails in any way but that which a true, unchanging wind demanded. It was his misfortune that when he was Prime Minister the wind changed at a crucial time and, precisely because of his honesty, he could not bring himself to trim the canvas. A second and disastrous failing, stemming both from innate shyness and a certain intellectual arrogance, was his refusal to suffer fools gladly or make allowance for those who, whatever the adequacy of their intentions and their intellects, did not choose to express views which he found congenial.

Finally, he shared with Home a failure to win public esteem on that new, discomposing, but vital measure of political acceptability, the television set. Heath's qualities were admirable; his technical qualifications in Government were greater than those of Harold Wilson; his intentions were wholly disinterested; the logic of his actions could hardly be faulted; but as Prime Minister he lacked, or was unable to project, that essential gift in a parliamentary leader: public charm.

In 1975 the Conservative Party declined to re-elect him as their leader. He retired, like a wounded Achilles, to his tent, but he emerged refreshed in the autumn of 1976; his public performances were better received than in the years gone by, he shook hands publicly with his successor, and it was generally assumed that his last political bolts had not been shot.

On becoming Prime Minister in the spring of 1976, Mr James Callaghan succeeded to an economic disaster, a divided Party and a parliamentary majority dependent on Scottish and Welsh nationalists for survival. His bland good humour and a calm refusal to be ruffled, worthy of Mr Macmillan himself, won him tolerant esteem even from his opponents. The Parliament was at least half-way through its term and many held that, with no majority and an uneasy truce between the opposing forces in the Labour Party, his Government could not run its course. Coming after Sir Harold Wilson, Mr Callaghan was thought by some likely to share Sir

Alec Douglas Home's fate of being Rosebery after Gladstone or Balfour after Salisbury. In the first few months of his Administration he did, however, show a laudable refusal to be deterred from pursuing the unpopular policies he believed essential to economic regeneration, and he was applauded for declining to be put off his stride by the irresponsible resolutions with which his wilder supporters bombarded him. As unperturbed as Lord Cardigan, Callaghan cantered at the head of his Light and progressively Lighter Brigade, disregarding the volleys to right of him and the still louder volleys to left of him. In November, 1976, his Party lost two by-elections in seats which had always returned Labour Members with overwhelming popular support, and his majority in the House of Commons was reduced to one. With no less *sang froid* than Lord Cardigan, he announced his determination to continue the Charge, but there were many who declared that they now understood Sir Harold Wilson's unexpected decision to resign in the previous March. The survival of the Labour Party, and the avoidance of its fragmentation, mattered deeply to Callaghan; but few believed him to be a man who would put sectional interests before those of Britain.

As winter closed in, and the uncertainties persisted, it remained to be seen whether Mr Callaghan had the ability to translate into action intentions which were certainly good and words which had won approval both at home and abroad. If he could not, there was at least a possibility that the seven men might be succeeded by a woman.

Part III

THE WEALTH OF
BRITAIN

CHAPTER 8

The City

Those who have no connexion with the City of London usually regard it with awe tempered by suspicion. On the one hand its proceedings seem wrapped in mystery and shrouded by technical jargon; on the other it is commonly supposed to be a place where the quick-witted, not to mention the unscrupulous, make vast fortunes by juggling with figures, mesmerising the unsuspecting and the uninitiated, and using to their own advantage money which they control but do not own. There is, or has been some truth in these suppositions, but they represent a small and decreasing element in a hive of complex financial business which, taken as a whole, is one of the most professional and productive centres of activity in the world today.

The City does create wealth by using the savings of the community, and it creates that wealth for the purchasers of life insurance, for the beneficiaries of pension funds and for the British economy, as well as for private and institutional investors. In the Bankers' Clearing House the cheques of the entire community, reaching the City from several thousand branches of the large Clearing Banks, are settled in an orderly manner. The transactions of Arabs, South Americans and rich Europeans, as well as of countless Trust Funds and investment companies, are handled in every foreign currency and in the Eurobond and Eurodollar markets. Funds, almost unlimited in amount, are raised for British Industry. Intricate mergers of companies, or take-over bids of one company for another, are arranged and effected. Insurance and re-insurance is accepted or placed in all parts of the world; and apart from the purely financial dealings, there are countless commercial operations, including the sale and purchase of metals, raw materials and ships.

Those who work in the City cannot operate in any but the restricted circle of their own experience, and there are many trades or skills practised in neighbouring offices of which they have no knowledge at all. Yet this whole diversified activity is concentrated in one square mile, with intense competition, but no crossing of wires, little friction and a huge contribution to the British balance of payments. It is self-governing; it has its own Court and its own police force; and it covers the area of Roman and medieval London, once the crowded dormitory of all the citizens and now practically uninhabited when the last office door has closed.

If the City had not changed in recent years, both in its outlook and its procedures, it would have lost its position as the most important financial centre in Europe and, in some respects, the entire world. In contrast to British industry during the same period, it did, in the event, adapt itself to new circumstances and thereby held its international pre-eminence. It did so partly by ingenuity and flexibility, partly because as an entity, and despite rare but much publicised lapses from grace by individual banks or companies, it kept its reputation for honest and efficient dealing; and partly because it suffered no interference at all from labour disputes, and less than industry or commerce from Government intervention and restrictive legislation. Citizens of the United Kingdom had little freedom to invest abroad, and none to transfer their wealth unless they chose to emigrate; but the City was not hampered in its foreign dealings, and its institutions were free to employ as many foreign experts as they chose, on a permanent or temporary basis.

It is convenient, first of all, to record what did not change. The Bank of England, brooding with maternal care and an occasional touch of maternal asperity over the square mile crammed with banks, discount houses, the Stock Exchange, insurance companies and every other kind of financial organism conceived by man, continues to rule by precept rather than by legal enforcement of its wishes. The big four Clearing Banks, two of them larger than any bank in Europe, remain free of State control in spite of threats by the National Executive of the Labour Party, which were recognised to have no backing from the general public. They have increased and diversified the scope of their activities, but resisted the temptation to copy the German banks in seeking to perform all the functions known to financial man (there remains in 1977, as in 1952, a notable shortage of financial women). In 1952, British overseas banks held a virtual monopoly of banking in India, the Middle East and British

Africa. Twenty five years later they are still the largest overseas bankers, with more than 5,000 branches in territories abroad; but they are meeting growing competition from the Americans, the French and even the Japanese, and in some countries their traditional predominance is being challenged by local ambitions to control the banking system if not yet, in most cases, by nationalisation. The Discount Houses, treated with a mixture of special indulgence and sharp severity by the Bank of England, are, as always, a unique feature of London. The Merchant Banks, at least those which are members of the Accepting Houses Committee, are also fostered and, when appropriate, guided by the Governor of the Bank of England. They merge with each other, welcome with varying degrees of warmth newcomers into their midst, continue to offer financial advice; and sometimes Chairmen and Directors too, to British and foreign industrial companies, tailor their activities to changing international patterns, and still contain in their ranks names which have been famous for generations.

Throughout these years, the Insurance Companies, reinforced by the resources of the steadily growing Pension Funds, were generating the money necessary to ensure that when commerce or industry required fresh long-term capital, it would be forthcoming. However, from the early 1970s onwards, rates of interest were so high that industrial companies were more often than not obliged to raise additional capital by rights issues to their shareholders, rather than by the long-term debenture or loan issues that had formerly been so readily available. Some compensation was provided by the new readiness of the banks, which had traditionally made only short-term loans, to lend money for five or even ten years at flexible interest rates, so that bank lending to provide capital funds for industry and commerce rose from 11% of the total in 1971 to 30% in 1974.

Meanwhile, Lloyds retains its strength as the largest, best known and, above all, universally trusted group of insurance brokers and underwriters in the world. The Commodity Markets, though no longer, as in 1952, assured of a near monopoly in buying and selling almost the entire produce of the British Empire, still deal extensively in metals, food-stuffs and raw materials; and when in 1968 gold ceased to be traded at an unalterable fixed price, London nevertheless remained in the centre of a two-tier gold market. The Baltic

Exchange continues to offer ships and aircraft for charter or for sale and to provide a market for grain. The Stock Exchange, dealing in ten times as many quoted securities as the second largest European Stock Market, Paris, houses itself in a vast new building which dominates Threadneedle Street. It has seen many of its members merge and a few go under, is increasingly discouraged from dealing in foreign stocks and shares, is politely indignant with the banks and Insurance Companies for evolving a method of exchanging securities without using a stockbroker, but maintains its traditional, if internationally unfashionable, structure of jobbers and brokers, and manages to conduct a brisk business in foul weather as well as in fair. Its profits have benefited from the proliferation of Unit Trusts which were a feature of the 1960s, as well as from the massive investment needs of the life assurance and pension funds.

The City preserves some of the best traditions on which its renown was founded. When one or two of the smaller and less cautious Insurance Companies foundered, the entire Insurance industry closed its ranks, took stock of its position and did what it could, with the help of the Board of Trade, to rescue the uncovered policy-holders. When several of the so-called 'Fringe Banks' succumbed to extravagant property speculation in the early 1970s, their depositors were helped, under the auspices of the Bank of England, to salvage all their money. Whenever it is practical to do so, the Stock Exchange takes steps to help investors faced with loss because of the ill-advised speculation of a broker with whom they had placed their trust and their savings. Some British and American banks risked serious loss when the doors of a German bank were closed during market hours. It was unable to meet its commitments and the foreign banks were forced to take legal action against the German Central Bank itself. It was universally accepted that had such a misfortune occurred in Britain, the Bank of England would in no circumstances have allowed the name of the City of London to be tarnished or foreign bankers to be denied immediate repayment.

Above all, the City remains a place where business, often involving millions of pounds, can be done by word of mouth and where it is unthinkable that any respectable institution would evade an undertaking given by an authorised member of its staff. The firms of City Solicitors are never short of business, but their services are not required, as they would be in New York, Paris or Frankfurt, to ensure that agreements between bankers or brokers, however well they know each other, are sanctioned in accordance with every legal nicety. The professional skill of the Chartered Accountants is universally respected, so that firms such as Price Waterhouse, Peat Markwick, Deloitte and Coopers and Lybrand are known throughout the world and their offices established in dozens of countries in all the continents.

To this important extent the City has not changed. In other respects its appearance and activities in 1977 would not have been recognisable in 1952. The large Clearing Banks have grown in size by mergers and acquisitions. The National Provincial joined forces with the Westminster, and Barclays bought Martins. There have been many other such significant changes in the financial world, and the Insurance Companies were scarcely less active in this respect than the banks. In consequence the City institutions are much larger than before, and their power to generate and provide funds is correspondingly increased. When the Queen came to the throne sterling was one of the world's two reserve currencies, in more general use than the dollar for the settlement of international payments and the conduct of trade. It had, indeed, recently been devalued, in terms of the dollar, from $4.60 to $2.80 to the pound, creating some alarm among the holders of Sterling Balances; but as many of these were members of the Sterling Area, which included the whole British Empire, apart from Canada, and many Middle Eastern countries as well, the shock was not unbearably great.

At that time, too, citizens of the United Kingdom could, as is still the case twenty five years later, buy foreign securities only by making use of the dollar premium pool. It was, however, less of a hardship then, for the dollar premium was often low and none of it was forfeit to the Treasury when the shares were sold. In practice it only meant that shares in American and Canadian companies were a trifle more expensive than would otherwise have been the case. None but a crank would have considered buying European or Japanese shares, and those of Australian or South African companies were freely traded in the London market. Buying South African gold shares was popular, because in the 1950s South Africa seemed to be a stable, prosperous British Dominion and gold was thought to be among the safer and more profitable speculations.

In the 1960s sterling, passing shakily through a series of balance of payments crises, lost favour in international circles; and the dollar, as the only other reserve currency, became almost the universal instrument of international financial transactions, outside the United States as well as within its frontiers. The City was nevertheless prosperous, for there was much investment at home, both personal and industrial, and companies were constantly seeking to raise money or to merge with their competitors. However, the Americans, intent on shielding the dollar from the strains that its increasing use as a world currency induced, imposed in 1963 an Interest Equalisation Tax which effectively closed the New York Stock Market to foreign borrowers. The City of London gave full rein to its skill in improvisation. One of the banks took the intelligent initiative of offering to a European borrower, barred from New York, dollars which the bank knew to be available in Europe. Others followed suit and the Eurobond and Eurodollar markets were thus created. European banks, and later the American banks themselves, leaped on to the bandwaggon, but London was established as the unchallenged centre of this new market, which grew rapidly in the size and scope of its operation. Despite the eventual abolition of the American tax, the Eurodollar has remained a main and growing instrument of European and, indeed, of international finance.

Since Britain must export to feed and equip a population of 56 million people, it has been necessary to encourage British industrialists to sell their products in countries where large risks would, by normal standards of commercial prudence, be likely to deter them. Even before the war, the Government had established an Export Credits Guarantee Department which guaranteed, on receipt of a commission, the short-term loans required by the British suppliers of goods for export. It was left to another of the Merchant Banks, assisted by the enthusiasm and ingenuity of an Under Secretary in the ECGD itself, to devise a system of 'buyer credits', whereby a medium- or long-term loan was made to the foreign purchaser, thus enabling him to buy capital goods for which he could not otherwise have paid. For many years, until the Bank of England was authorised to offer rediscount facilities, loans were provided by the Clearing Banks at artificially low rates of interest and as a contribution to the export trade which their detractors and would-be nationalisers seldom acknowledge. Other European countries were quick to follow this example, although in their cases it was sometimes the State rather than the banks which provided the low-interest money.

The standing of Britain in international banking, and particularly in the Eurodollar market, was recognised by the stampede of foreign banks to open in London. In 1952 there were 63; by the end of 1975, 244 had branches or representative offices, and as many as 331 had established a presence in one way or another. In consequence of this the City, and the British banks in particular, have become more cosmopolitan both in outlook and in practice. Methods and systems which would have been considered outlandish as late as 1960 were in common use ten years later, and the change was assisted by the rise to power and fame of the Computer, a miracle of which few had even heard in 1952.

The amateur, with his nose for a profit, his sensitive fingertips and his contempt for detail, dominated many financial institutions in the 1950s. He was often a man of wide and useful experience in business matters; but his hours were short, his desk was gratifyingly free of paper, he spent much of the day in general conversation about the state of the market, and he could call on an army of reliable but not very well remunerated clerks to cope with all but the decisions of policy. If he was in the right firm and knew the right people he might well retire with a fortune. In 1977 he is a rare bird, verging on extinction. The professional is in charge and the 'insider' dealings which, while legally permissible in the 1950s, were thought to be socially undesirable in the 1960s, are eliminated in all respectable City institutions.

There are still in the City important family firms controlled by the descendants of their founder. The best known are included among the Acceptance Houses and it is gratifying to those who set store by hereditary talent that banks such as Rothschilds and Barings, Hambros and Kleinwort Benson have not only survived, but have produced Directors and Partners of ability from the families which established and own them. They are, however, the exception. The City in the 1970s has been chary of recruiting young men who are not already professionally trained or prepared to devote time and energy to increasing their skill by courses and instruction. Business schools, conceived on the lines of the famous prototype at Harvard, opened in London and Manchester; and intensive management courses were provided at Henley and Cranfield as well as in the universities. The Computer may store the knowledge, but the man who applies it is required to be an expert who can successfully stand comparison with his competitors in New York, Frankfurt and Zurich. He has one great advantage in that, because New York and London have remained the two pre-eminent financial centres, English is universally accepted as the language of business and finance. Even the celebrated gnomes of Zurich address a London banker or broker in his own tongue; and it is usually helpful, in dealing or negotiating, to have the upper linguistic hand.

In addition to modernising its attitude to business, the City has taken some steps to police its activities. The simple and commendable expedient of moral disapproval prevailed with sufficient force in 1952 to deter any of the well-known firms and institutions, whose good name was important to them, from stepping at all far over the boundary dividing what was generally agreed to be permissible from what was not. By the end of the 1960s this unwritten code of good behaviour was no longer adequate to curb the enthusiasm of new, aggressive men and companies, who were tempted to disregard it in the hope of outstripping their competitors and making quick profits. This was particularly so when, in the late 1950s, the era of take-over bids began. It was clear that unless the City itself took preventive action, the State would feel justified in so doing, and the freedom of action which so rewardingly distinguished London from New York and other cities would be severely trammelled.

Thus, a Panel was established to lay down rules for the issue of securities to the public and to pronounce on any disputes which arose. The British Insurance Association and the Council of the Stock Exchange took careful note of their members' activities, and did not hesitate to remonstrate if there was occasion to do so. The Bank of England looked searchingly at the balance sheets and liquidity ratios of the Acceptance Houses and Commercial Banks, some of which had certainly been guilty of excessive lending during the short-lived and over-speculative property boom of the early 1970s. It was, unfortunately, less zealous in examining the affairs of the 'Fringe Banks', which were more dangerously implicated in property transactions. The Government produced proposals, in 1976, for licensing banks and establishing a fund for the protection of small depositors. It became clear that it would also be necessary to consider how the practice of British banking might be harmonised with the laws by which banks in the other Common Market countries were bound.

In addition to all this, and despite the comparative rarity of scandal, (for it was not to the City that Mr Heath addressed his remarks about the 'ugly and unacceptable face of capitalism'), there were by the mid-1970s many who believed, and some who feared, that a regulatory body, comparable to the American Securities and Exchange Commission, would in due course be imposed on London. The chances of such a development seemed likely to be increased when the City's good name was temporarily injured, first, by the failure of some of the 'Fringe Banks' and still more, in September, 1976, by the publication of an enquiry into the affairs of Slater Walker. This was a new star in the financial constellation, an investment company with a dynamic policy which shone for some years with unusual brightness, and compared favourably with the longer established and more cautious Merchant Banks and Finance Houses. Slater Walker had not, however, been in the first rank of City institutions; it was not a member of the Accepting Houses Committee, nor had its Directors been invited to join the boards of Clearing Banks, leading Insurance Companies or large Industrial Corporations. It was rescued from total disaster by the timely intervention of the Bank of England and the willingness of several well-known men to be elected to its board and to scrutinise its activities. Its fall from grace was proclaimed by the Press in large headlines, and welcomed by political opponents of the whole financial system as a grave blow to the reputation of the City. In fact the Slater Walker crash, like the earlier demise of the 'Fringe Banks', may be judged to have proved the strength of the City; for there was no financial panic and the only boats seriously rocked were those of incautious investors and property speculators.

Well though the Merchant Banks attuned themselves to fresh

opportunities in international banking, and skilfully though they continued to advise on the capital and loan requirements of British industrial companies, they were not equipped to examine in depth the wider activities and needs of their customers. It is doubtful whether a banker, and still less a Civil Servant, who has not himself worked in industry is capable of giving anything but financial or perhaps administrative advice on a company's problems. In 1966, Mr Harold Wilson created an Industrial Reorganisation Corporation with the task of enquiring into the detailed affairs of certain sections of industry, and making proposals for mergers or measures of nationalisation. These were to be put into effect, not by action in Whitehall but by Merchant Banks or whatever other instrument in the private sector the IRC might deem appropriate. The new Corporation proposed and arranged for the professional execution of a number of mergers which were of benefit to industry and significance to the economy as well as for some which were not. It was also supplied with public funds with which it could itself buy holdings of shares in industrial companies.

The latter function was thought by many to be an insidious method of introducing State interest, and perhaps State control, into private industry by the back-stairs. When a Conservative Government took office in 1970, the IRC was abolished. Nothing daunted, Mr Harold Wilson replaced it in 1975 by a National Enterprise Board which was promised still more money, and given still greater powers, to acquire a Government stake in the world of free enterprise. It remained to be seen whether it would be competent to provide the professional advice and quasi-medical services which the banks were accused of failing to give their customers. Some industrialists, impressed by the unquestioned abilities of its members, and their determination to make a positive contribution to re-establishing the fortunes of those companies in which the NEB had taken shares, believed it might perform a useful service. They had no such cheerful expectations of another State enterprise, the British National Oil Corporation. The Conservatives announced their intention of dissolving both when next they returned to office.

Among the City's worthiest (and least acknowledged or applauded) achievements is the growth of its foreign earnings. They have increased year by year, and they supply a high proportion of those Invisible Exports without which the United Kingdom would have long since been bankrupt. During the whole twenty five years of Queen Elizabeth II's reign there have only been three in which the visible balance of trade has been favourable. Sometimes, on account of a seamen's strike, or a dock strike, or a recession in world trade, the adverse balance has been little short of catastrophic and the only comfort has been in the Invisible Surplus. Thus in 1974, when the visible trade balance showed a deficit of £5,264 million, by far the worst in the history of the United Kingdom, there was a net surplus of £2,877 million on Invisible Exports in the private sector and, even after the deduction of a deficit of more than £1,200 million in the public sector, there was a contribution of £1,614 million from Invisible Exports to reduce the disastrous results. In other years, such as 1970, the invisible earnings turned an overall loss on visible trade into a national surplus for the year.

While France, Germany and Japan surged ahead of Britain in the contest for exports, and Britain's share of the world trade, although increasing in volume, dropped in percentage from 23% in 1955 to a mere 7.5% in 1973, there was a strikingly different order of merit in the league table of Invisible Exporters. Britain, consistently second to the United States alone, has held her long lead over Germany, France and Japan, while the Common Market countries as a whole have been in deficit. Between 1965 and 1970 Britain's earnings from this source doubled, and they did so again between 1970 and 1975. In the latter year receipts exceeded £10,000 million from the private sector, and these, after the deduction of invisible imports, more than compensated for the cost of the Government's foreign expenditure and were equal to 35% of the country's total foreign income.

For this story, so different from many others that must be told in these years, the City can claim much of the credit. It has generated one third of the nation's *net* invisible earnings, achieving a total of approximately £1,000 million in 1975. There are, of course, many other sources of invisible income, among which shipping is of special importance, while the tourist trade, construction firms, entertainment, consulting engineers, doctors, lawyers and account-ants all contribute their share. The City, for its part, earns foreign exchange through the insurance industry, the banks, the merchants, the Baltic Exchange and many other financial institutions. Those earnings have been substantially increased by the expansion in foreign exchange dealings and London's domination of the Euro-dollar market, both of which are due to a neo-Elizabethan confirmation of the City's status as the financial capital of Europe. The invisible exporters have received but little official encouragement by comparison with the visible exporters of manufactured goods: and they have even been reviled as parasites. They have proved themselves a parasitic infestation of remarkable value to the health of the body politic; and by contrast with this vast and vital contribution to the nation's economic survival, the scandals and the bankruptcies, so advertised by the media and so relished by the self-righteous, can be regarded in their proper perspective.

CHAPTER 9

Industry and the Economy

A mystery more apparent than real is the failure of British Industry, and in consequence the British economy, to profit from the opportunities which lay wide open before it in the years immediately after the war. It had indeed suffered from bombing and from direction to war production for six long years, but although Britain received a massive loan from the United States shortly after the war ended, the proceeds were used more for consumption than for capital investment, whereas Japan, Germany and the formerly occupied countries of Europe were lavishly assisted in their own energetic efforts to build new factories and recreate their shattered economies. British manufactured exports faced virtually no competition from any country except the United States. The failure to seize this great, but short-lived, opportunity was broadly due to the structure of industry, to the featherbedding of those who owned, managed and worked in it, to the out-dated equipment of the factories, and to a lack of resources to exploit ingenious inventions and initiatives. As the years passed there were other causes, not least the failure of management and workers to co-operate, and the denial by successive Governments of incentives to hard-working managers with imaginative ideas and a modern outlook.

In 1952 both industry and the trade unions were unprofitably fragmented. The Craft Unions were jealously intent on defending their own membership against the depredations of other Unions in search of more subscribers, and on ensuring that the jobs of which they believed they should have a monopoly were protected from the hammers, chisels and picks of their rivals. Employers conducted the affairs of thousands of small companies, often family-owned and directed, by methods which their grandparents had found effective. There were, indeed, a handful of well-run giants, like ICI, Shell and Unilever; but even the comparatively large companies in the steel, electrical and engineering industries were too small, and often too conservative, to face the challenges about to be offered. The owners of a myriad of smaller firms saw no reason why life should not always continue as placidly and unalterably as it always had, and averted their minds from the stress, strain and family disturbances which an effort to increase profits and profitability seemed likely to entail. The structure of British industry was as archaic as the philosophy of those who controlled it.

There was, in any case, no great need for the small industrialists to bestir themselves. The textile trade might be damaged by competition from India and Hong Kong, and Imperial Preference did seem to offer greater advantages to exporters from the Dominions and Colonies than to their opposite numbers in Britain; but there was no shortage of markets, at home and abroad, labour was cheap and during the fifties the terms of trade were, on the whole, favourable. There was then a change in the pattern of world trade, and in the sixties, by which time there had also been a few, but not enough, changes in the structure of British industry, the alarmingly successful competition of foreign countries wakened both the Government and industrialists to the dangers of complacency.

Often solely to avoid a surtax assessment on private companies with a handful of shareholders, boards and proprietors became resigned to selling some of their family shares to the general public; and there were many companies which either succumbed to take-over bids or saw the advantage of agreeing to mergers whereby large units would be created to face the new competitors. One result was the so-called 'managerial revolution'. This did not mean that the new managements were necessarily modern in outlook or effective in method. What it did mean was that control of a company's affairs and decisions on its future policy passed from a tightly-knit band of shareholders to the management; for the new owners, a scattered and heterogeneous collection of individuals and institutions, were never invited to take more than a passing interest in a company's activities and were, in large majority, unanxious to be concerned with anything but the rate of dividend. They became still less interested as the taxes on unearned income and the restrictions on dividend payments removed the rewards of risk capital. Thus, by the seventies policy decisions in all but the smallest companies were firmly in the hands of the management, who tended to pay less deference to the interest of their shareholders than to that of employees and customers.

The Kennedy rounds of tariff cuts, which took place between 1962 and 1967, further lowered the barriers by which British manufacturers had been comfortably protected, making them more vulnerable to foreign imports in the home market, and alerting them to the necessity of being more competitive. Mr Edward Heath, at the Board of Trade in 1963, brought in a measure to ban resale price maintenance, thus removing a barrier to competition at home. Finally, in 1973, Britain's entry into the Common Market removed the last of the featherbeds and replaced them with hard spring-mattresses from which, thenceforward, British industrialists might be expected to rise earlier and more energetically in the mornings. A long period of protected, but decreasingly affluent, complacency was ended in 1975, at a time when British industrial production had remained static for a whole five years. It is too early, at the beginning of 1977, to judge whether British industry has in fact been wholesomely invigorated by the Common Market challenge; but it is not too early to conclude that the previous measures and exhortations aimed at inducing a livelier and more competitive spirit had been fruitless exercises.

The new plants and factories erected in Europe and Japan on the ashes of war-time destruction were equipped with the most modern machinery available. Those in Britain were operating contentedly with machinery decades, if not half a century, old; and it was not always because the cash flow was insufficient to provide renewals. British industrialists took years to learn how to make the best use of their assets; they suffered from the national disinclination to face up to realities except in times of emergency; and they had an inherited conviction that what was old, whether clothes, motor-cars, or machinery, was, for that reason, good. There was resistance to the new managerial methods, which the Americans developed with well-proved results, and there was a tendency to confuse the introduction of bureaucratic control with sound managerial practice. Planning and analysis are essential, but an excess of information dulls the brain, a mound of paperwork obstructs efficiency, and committees are often a device to delay decision. In Industry, as in Government, it is all too often the modern technique of management to face a new problem by establishing a new department.

There was no shortage of funds available for new capital investment, except when gigantic amounts of money were required to launch an expensive new development as, for instance, in the aircraft industry. Even the immense sums required for the exploitation of North Sea Oil and Gas were provided by the City. Governments provided help in the form of Investment Grants and Initial or Capital Allowances; but the steady decrease in the return on investment, due partly to higher costs unmatched by proportionately higher prices and profits, and partly to fiscal and other disincentives, did nothing to encourage adventurous investment decisions. However, in 1974, in the trough of a bad recession, industrial and commercial companies spent £2,700 million on fixed investments, and in the following year the total exceeded £3,000 million. Much of this was for North Sea oil equipment, and it is questionable whether the balance of these large sums was used to the best advantage or spent on the purchase of British goods. The disastrous record of the British Machine Tool Industry over many years indicates that much of the new equipment installed in the factories had to be imported from abroad.

It must not be supposed that British industry in its entirety lay in the grip of old-fashioned management and out of date methods. There were many bright exceptions. Britain still laid claim to a high proportion of the fifty largest companies in Europe, and none of these could be accused of sloth or inefficiency. The Electronics industry produced and sold abroad components of fine precision and original design; Pilkington's discovery of float glass was of universal interest and significance; British telecommunications and structural engineering won tenders against the strongest challengers. There were, indeed, many new British products which had little to fear from foreign competition; but there were several instances of inventions and initiatives failing simply because the company was too small to provide the resources necessary to fight off foreign predators. One example is the Vickers 1000, which would almost certainly have retained for Britain the lead in Civil Aviation if only Vickers had had, or had received, the vast sums required to develop it. Another is the razor-blade of revolutionary excellence produced by the Wilkinson Sword Company, but soon rivalled by the mighty American Gillette, which had both the money and the marketing strength to outsell its small British competitor in the American market.

If the Second Elizabethans lacked, at least in industrial affairs, the dash and enterprise of the First, it may be because Sir Walter Raleigh was prepared to accept any risk and undergo every discomfort in his search for El Dorado, whereas his 20th century successors know full well that if they find El Dorado, the Chancellor of the Exchequer will confiscate it. The personal taxation of senior management is so much higher than that of their opposite numbers in the industrially successful countries, such as the United States, Canada, France and Germany, that they have no incentive to work harder or take greater risks in order to earn more. To seek to be rich is a social misdemeanour and Conservative Governments have been scarcely less assiduous than the Socialists in ensuring that it is in any event an unattainable objective. There is the best possible authority for favouring the weak at the expense of the strong, but there are also limits beyond which it is neither wise nor just to proceed; and over-soaking the rich can be counterproductive. The American belief, shared by managers and workers alike, that profit is a desirable motive and that its achievement brings rewards to all concerned, is unfashionable in the United Kingdom.

Equally, although almost 80% of the profits of industry is used to pay wages and salaries, whereas in Japan the figure is only 50%, there were many industries in which payment was low by comparison with others, and it was late in the day that managers began to reason that if the workers produced more, they should be paid more. It only occurred to a few that the boredom of modern industrial work, accepted in years gone by because no alternative was recognised, was likely to cause discontent in days when the knowledge of better things was made daily apparent by improved communications and in particular by the television programmes. Most British companies have been dilatory in providing for their workers those amenities which are taken for granted in the United States.

The workers for their part have displayed little ambition to improve their own lot by harder and more productive work, and although they have been understandably keen, in inflationary times, to receive higher wages, they have as often as not coupled the demand with one for shorter hours and longer holidays. They have, on the whole, wanted less for themselves and their families than their American and European counterparts, so that the calls for higher productivity in return for more pay have tended to fall on deaf ears. Half the working population are women, whose aim is to earn some extra money, usually on a piece-work basis. In relative terms the workers are now richer than the middle-classes by comparison with pre-war standards. Taking account of inflation, for each pound a university professor would have received before the war he was paid 75p. in 1975, and a doctor was paid 93p; but a factory worker received £1.90, an agricultural worker £2.04 and a miner £2.63. If attitudes in industry had been different, and the Gross National Product had continued to rise in step with that of other developed countries, there was no reason why the factory worker, and the miner too, should not have earned still more. Nor need they have done so at the expense of the university professor and the doctor.

Governmental interference in the working of industry, and even in its structure, was intensified during these years. Some of the measures enacted by Parliament, such as the Restrictive Practices Laws, were intended to remove obstacles to efficiency, and there were many which were benevolently aimed at improving the welfare and security of employees. The gospel was spread, no less by Mr Macmillan's Government than by Mr Wilson's (though not, at least initially, by Mr Heath's), that Government is a cornucopia from which all good things flow. Some of those responsible for directing the Nationalised Industries, and in particular Sir Richard Marsh when he was Chairman of British Railways, seemed doubtful whether this belief was justified; and indeed almost all the Chairmen of the Nationalised Industries complained of ill-judged and frequently ill-informed interference with both the short- and long-term policies of the Boards and Corporations.

This was still more the case in the private sector where Ministers were suspected of wishing to impose their will and, by one means or another, to gather more and more industrial plums into the Whitehall basket. When, for sound business reasons, the three large electrical companies, Associated Electrical Industries, English

Electric and the General Electric Company were merged by normal commercial processes in one giant company, under progressive and imaginative management, the national economy and Britain's competitive power in foreign markets were greatly improved. British Leyland, originating from a merger between Leyland and the British Motor Corporation (itself the result of a series of mergers) presented an entirely different picture. Its component parts were badly managed; its workforce found striking more congenial than production. The Government encouraged the final merger which, at any rate initially, brought neither success nor contentment to the motor industry. Equally, governmental efforts to rationalise the ship-building industry, in particular the yards on the Upper Clyde, were frustrated by short-term political considerations and were a dismal failure. The decision in 1976 to nationalise the Shipbuilding and Aircraft industries was regarded with dismay by those with ex-perience of such previous initiatives, especially as, apart from the motor industry, the private sector's record of days lost by strikes is remarkably favourable by comparison with the Nationalised Industries. Confidence in the Measure laid before Parliament was not increased by the discovery, when the bill reached the House of Lords in November, 1976, that four fifths of its clauses had not been debated or conscientiously scrutinised in the House of Commons.

The disputes between management and labour increased as the years went by. In the 1950s they were, by later standards, moderate in extent and caused but little loss of production. It was, for a few years, an age of golden affluence. The Gross National Product was rising steeply and the purchasing power of the pound was falling only gradually, indeed, to most people imperceptibly; while the income per head of the population almost doubled between 1952 and 1960. In the 1960s industrial relations worsened. There were stoppages in the motor industry, with constant and much publicised strikes in the Ford Motor Works at Dagenham; there were dock strikes and a seamen's strike; there were 'wild-cat' strikes all over the country which neither a Labour Government nor the TUC had any power to control. The loud and painful climax was reached in the 1970s, when first the electricians and then the miners brought chaos and darkness to the community, and pickets, sometimes recruited by political extremists from outside the areas in which they arrived to operate, asserted their claims to obstruction by violence.

If in some cases the workers were to blame, it must at least be said that in others unsympathetic management was culpable. As far as the employees were concerned, there was certainly over-manning to a degree which became financially intolerable, but which neither the Government nor the Unions did anything to discourage. There were too many Unions, too many restrictive practices, too many indifferent and gullible workers influenced by well-trained and, as Mr Harold Wilson put it, 'motivated' militants. It must, however, be remembered that while the Europeans feared inflation, of which they have long and distressing experience, the British workers, who have incorporated memories of the dole queues of the 1930s in their folk-lore, feared unemployment. On the other side of the fence (and the fence itself was often too high), little was done to explain the reasons for managerial decisions; not enough trouble was taken to dispel fears of redundancy, or alternatively to find new jobs for those who had to be made redundant; information was either withheld or disseminated in unintelligible form; and the paternalism of the small family firms, which had been their principal surviving merit, was often replaced by the official coldness of a managerial representative, who might excel as a technician or an accountant but was expected to communicate with a larger body of workers than he could handle with close, personal understanding, and was often unskilled in the old military accomplishment called 'man-management'. It seems that this quality, well understood by officers in the armed forces during two world wars, has been less successfully taught to a new, professionally trained body known as 'Personnel Officers'.

The trials and tribulations of British industry thus increased rather than diminished. The apposite text for a sermon on the subject would be 'Both Sides of Industry', a phrase used with depressing frequency in Parliament and the newspapers, and one which illustrates the basic truth that neither industrial peace nor higher productivity will be achieved until managers and workers look upon themselves as a unit dedicated to the same objective. There was much talk of worker participation; Lord Blake presided over a Commission to make recommendations about the representation of workers on Boards of Directors; and in spite of British Leyland's chequered history of industrial strife, the new management established in 1975, under the Chairmanship of Sir Ronald Edwards and then, on his sudden death, of Sir Richard Dobson, introduced participation committees which include managers and shop stewards. All the same a consensus of opinion does not seem much nearer in 1977 than it was in 1952: the cleavage is deeper to the extent that it has become more clearly defined by constant political wrangling, but there is a glimmer of light visible in the growing realisation of both management and Unions that the road to improvement lies in collaboration rather than conflict.

A happier account can be given, and more immediately cheerful prospects seen, in the largest of all British industries, Agriculture. There are those who declare that it is not so much an industry as a way of life. Whichever it be, the story of its development includes the progressive virtues missing in that of the manufacturing and extractive industries. With a minimum reliance on manpower, and an intelligent use of both mechanisation and new scientific methods, British farmers have a more successful record of efficiency than the agricultural communities anywhere else, in the Old World or the New. This is the more remarkable in that for a hundred and fifty years the British considered themselves the foremost industrial nation, at once progenitors and heirs of the Industrial Revolution, and nonchalantly disregarded agriculture.

In the First World War there was a brief realisation, in the face of a U-Boat blockade which brought the country within three weeks of starvation, that it was of urgent importance to plough the fields and scatter. With the return of peace the urge quickly subsided, so that between the wars the price of land fell, cheap food was easily imported and the farming community was regarded as a picturesque but largely irrelevant survival of the olden days. It was the Second World War which changed both the face of England and the status of the farmers.

The exigencies of war restored farming and the farmers to their proper position in the list of national priorities, and provided the impetus which made the post-war achievements possible. But digging up or grassing down the acres was not in itself sufficient: what transformed farming into the most productive of British industries was the modernisation of the farmer's methods and outlook. A community renowned for hide-bound conservatism adapted itself to changed circumstances and seized new opportunities more readily than manufacturing industry, so that between 1952 and 1977 agricultural productivity rose each year by more than twice the national average.

The Combine Harvester was an innovation much coveted but rarely seen when the reign began. Twenty five years later those huge machines are familiar features of the later summer landscape, and many other previously unknown mechanical devices are in common use. In consequence the 870,000 workers employed on agricultural holdings in 1952 shrunk to 380,000 in 1975, and there was at least one British industry which could not be accused of over-manning. Many of the hedges, so long a feature of the countryside, were replaced by wire fences requiring no annual attention; helicopters hovered to spray the crops in spring; fire consumed the stubbles in autumn; and for twenty years the rabbits, beloved of children but the bane of farmers, seemed to vanish. They were all but exterminated in 1953 and 1954 by the man-made plague of myxomatosis, and the farmers rejoiced in larger crops unravaged by hordes of attractive, furry invaders. However, the rabbit is a strong and wily antagonist. By the mid-1970s he was once again as productive as the farming industry itself and a great deal more so than the rest of the British economy.

There are still a lot of small farms, uneconomic in cost and effort, but many of them have been aggregated with their neighbours, and elsewhere arrangements have been made for the sharing or hiring of expensive machinery. Large rationalised farming units have been created and small labour forces carefully deployed with an eye to productivity. Methods were devised to educate the practical farmer in new techniques, a process to which the Government contributed by its Agricultural Advisory Service and the large manufacturers of equipment and fertilisers by the expert advice their representatives were trained to offer. By the seventies the farming community, with all its ancillary suppliers, accounted for more than 15% of the Gross National Product while employing a labour force, including the farmers and their families, which comprised little more than 2% of the population.

The modernisation of farming methods was as important as the mechanical aids and the mental adaptation. New technology was readily accepted: weed-killers, insecticides and fungicides of startling effectiveness (and, as some thought, environmental danger) were invented by the chemists and applied by the farmers. Artificial insemination, which only became generally available for cattle in 1950, was applied to 25 million cows in 1965. The plant breeders and the geneticists exercised their ingenuity for the revolutionary increase of yields in crops, cattle, eggs and poultry. Pigs and chickens were produced, fattened, graded and killed by processes of vertical integration hitherto unexplored.

On top of all this, business methods which a previous generation of farmers would have neither welcomed nor understood were introduced to the agricultural community. Profit forecasts were made, cash flows were calculated and, since farming is among the most capital intensive of all industries and also that on which the return is slowest, an Agricultural Mortgage Corporation was established to provide long-term finance for the farmers. Loans for as long as thirty years were provided, but even they could not be insulated from the rapid upward swing in interest rates which rose like a tidal wave in the seventies. The rate of 4.75% asked for such loans on the day of the Queen's accession had reached 15.75% at the end of 1974 and was 16.5% at the end of 1976.

The farmer's time was saved and his efficiency improved by new marketing arrangements. The old Corn Exchanges closed their doors, often remaining considerable architectural adornments to the market towns, and the farm produce was collected by large agricultural companies or by the Marketing Boards, of which the Milk Marketing Board was notably important. Finally the Chancellors of the Exchequer were not unhelpful in the subsidies and tax incentives to which they gave their reluctant approval throughout the period. The effect of this reforming influence and modernising zeal is well illustrated by the statistics. Despite the absorption of good farming land by housing estates, industry and motorways, and the consequent fall in total agricultural acreage (which was over 31 million in 1952), by half a million acres ten years later and, by one and a half million before 1976, the twenty five million tons of crops harvested in 1952/53 had risen to 35.5 million in 1975/76. The annual yield of the wheat fields increased steadily at the rate of 2% over each preceding year, and that of barley at 1.5%. Sugarbeet was the only crop to fall. There were no more dairy cows in 1976 than in 1952, but nearly 3,000 million gallons of milk were produced against 2,200 million, and the cows gave an average 917 gallons against 700. The amount of beef and veal doubled; so did lamb, (which the statisticians, unlike the butchers and the restaurateurs, are honest enough to call 'sheep-meat'); and so did eggs. The introduction of the broiler and deep-litter systems resulted in seven times as much poultry being sold in 1975/76 as in 1952, and hens were cajoled into laying an average of 234 eggs each year against a mere 150.

Thus agriculture, so long neglected and starved of capital in a self-consciously industrial society, rose to the top of the productivity league-table, helped not only by scientific ingenuity and the rare blessing of good labour relations, but also by a growing awareness of a threatening world food shortage, by the incentive which farmers derived from the knowledge that they were profiting from their own unrestricted efforts, and by the national urge to save expensive food imports. Not to grumble would be a breach of farming tradition and etiquette, whether the climate or the meanness of the Annual Farm Price Review be the chosen target; and none can deny that the hours of work on the land, as well as the small and slow return on capital, are a strain on the farmer's patience. However if, in 1977, all British industry could boast of the pro-gressive outlook and solid achievements in productivity to which the farming community can indisputably lay claim, the brief account of the British economy which follows would be a more cheerful tale.

The story of Civil Aviation in this period is one of misfortune abetted by mismanagement. In 1952 more than half the aircraft in the entire world were powered by Rolls-Royce engines and this was still true in 1960. British air frame designs were no less famous and successful. The *Spitfire* and the *Hurricane*, the *Mosquito*, the *Lancaster* and the *Halifax* were only heroic memories; but they were recent ones which had made a deep impression in every quarter of the world. Group Captain Sir Frank Whittle was the original inventor of the jet engine, and though muddle and delay in London had enabled the Germans to produce a jet-propelled fighter and the V1 pilotless aircraft well ahead of the British, reparation had since been made and the first jet-airliner, the *Comet*, had already arrived at the production line. Meanwhile, Britain established a long lead over her competitors with the new turbo-propeller aircraft. The Vickers *Viscount* dominated the short and medium distance air routes of the 1950s, so that it was bought by every air line, European, American or Asian, which set store on winning its share of a passenger traffic market expanding by leaps and bounds every year. The *Viscount*, still flying on some of the remoter routes in the 1970s, was followed by the *Vanguard* and the long-distance *Britannia*; but the turbo-propeller was only a half-way landing on the huge development stairway which now stretched upwards. The day of the jet-airliner was at hand.

It was, however, at the earliest stage that misfortune struck. The *Comet* made its first commercial flight in 1952. The eyes of the world were on it and all the airlines, or the governments supporting them, were preparing to untie the purse strings. It seemed that Britain had a lucrative export market at her feet, even though the capacity to meet the expected order was sure to be inadequate and there would be plenty of opportunities for the giant American Corporations, Boeing, Douglas and Lockheed, when their late-starting jet passenger aircraft were ready to fly. On 3rd March, 1953, a *Comet* crashed without any obvious explanation. Two months later another followed suit and then, early in 1954, a third and a fourth. All *Comets* were grounded. Divers searched the bed of the Mediterranean to salvage fragments for scientific analysis, and although it was discovered with remarkable speed that the cause of the crashes had been metal fatigue in a few, but by no means all, of the *Comets* which had been built, it was too late. Alterations were made; new *Comets* were built; they continued to fly for years without one further disaster; but confidence had been lost and so had Britain's undoubted lead in Civil Aviation.

Mismanagement coupled with pernicious parsimony lost the next opportunity. The firm of Vickers, celebrated for more than half a century as the first of British munitions manufacturers, and shortly to join the Bristol Aircraft Company in forming the British Aircraft Corporation, was far advanced in the design and prototype production of a jet-airliner called the Vickers 1000. Full production was beyond the financial means of the company and it had not the resources to borrow the huge sums required. So Vickers asked the Government for help. With short-sighted folly the Treasury declined. Doubtless the amount needed was inconveniently large at a time when retrenchment, as almost always in the history of the 20th century, was a foremost consideration. All the same, the Vickers 1000 could have been in service before the American Boeing 707 and there is little doubt that it would have replaced the *Comet* as Britain's winning entry for the Jet-Aircraft Stakes.

The American aircraft companies, subsidised by their Government on account of their contribution to national defence, and supported by access to financial resources incomparably greater than those available to Vickers, swept into the lead. The new British Aircraft Corporation struggled on and produced, too late in the competitive day, the VC10, lineal descendant of the rejected Vickers 1000. It made its maiden flight in June, 1962, and once it was in commercial service it won universal esteem. Every seat was booked on its trans-Atlantic flights. It took off and landed in half the distance necessary to its Boeing and Douglas competitors, thus offering a safety margin which might be held to compensate for the fact that it was slightly more expensive to operate. But it was too late, and so for export purposes, was the admirable Hawker Siddeley *Trident*, a medium-range airliner which, like the VC10, first flew in 1962. The ill-judged decision to cancel the Vickers 1000 had cost Britain her lead in the subsonic race.

In 1972 Rolls-Royce, bearing the name best known in the whole world for its aircraft engines as well as for its motor cars, the very hallmark of excellence and perfectionism, one of Britain's proudest monuments, announced that it faced bankruptcy. It was as if the Tower of London had fallen down, or Blackpool had been shattered by an earthquake, or the Brigade of Guards had mutinied. A shudder of incredulous horror shook the population of the British Isles and distant lands as well. It was particularly embarrassing for Mr Heath's Government which had firmly stated that British industry must learn to stand on its own legs, that Government subsidy and support were inherently unhealthy and that 'lame ducks' must be left to their unhappy fate. To desert Rolls-Royce at such a crisis was unthinkable, and so the Government went to the rescue, severed the motor car manufacturing unit from that making aircraft engines, and formed a new nationalised company, Rolls-Royce (1974) Ltd., of which they invited Sir Kenneth Keith to be Chairman. They also provided the company with the means to complete its undertaking to the American Lockheed Company by producing an expensive engine called the RB 211 for installation in the Lockheed *Tristar*. Rolls-Royce engines, after their brief and almost fatal illness, were soon re-established in the markets of the world.

In spite of the Government's short-sighted refusal to participate, the firm of Hawker-Siddeley contributed to the design of a new European Air Bus, combining the skills of several European countries; but the principal and most expensive venture in Civil Aviation, after the *Comet* and Vickers 1000 disasters, was the Anglo-French *Concorde*. Mr Julian Amery, Minister of Aviation in Mr Harold Macmillan's Government, negotiated the proposal with the French Government. It was not only important as a joint Anglo-French pioneering project but, since two industrial companies, the British Aircraft Corporation and Sud-Aviation, were also parties to the agreement, it was an early example of combining the skills of private industry with the resources of the State. It could at least be expected to avoid the financial starvation which had killed the Vickers 1000; and as the Anglo-French governmental participation was sanctified by a treaty, it would be difficult for one Government to withdraw its support without offending the other, although this consideration did not, in the event, deter the British Government in 1975 from declining to proceed with another Anglo-French enterprise, the Channel Tunnel, on which a treaty with France had been signed.

There were times during the fifteen years of gestation which divided the conception of *Concorde* from its birth, when the British Government, harassed by financial anxiety, was tempted to abandon the project. Mr Wilson had his doubts and Mr Heath had his doubts; but just as the collapse of Rolls-Royce would have brought in its train massive unemployment in Derby, so the abandonment of *Concorde* would have thrown thousands out of work in Bristol and Toulouse. The costs exceeded the budget year after year; the eventual profitability of the super-sonic aircraft and the likely effects of rejecting it were submitted for study by Civil Servants, economists, scientific advisers and finally by the Think Tank; and the wrath of the French Government and Britain's entry into the Common Market were weighed in the balance. After many governmental nails had been bitten to the quick, the huge sums required were provided and, to propitiate the prophets of financial doom, alternative ritual sacrifices were found in the Channel Tunnel and the proposed new deep-sea port and air-terminal at Maplin. In the spring of 1976 *Concorde* became a commercial aircraft in the face of environmentalist antagonism and prophecies of insupportable decibels. If the glory was shared with the French so, too, was the expenditure. By the end of the year thoughts were turning to a larger *Concorde* which, by carrying more passengers, might turn a remarkable engineering achievement into one that was profitable too; for the initial cost of regaining a lead in commercial aviation had proved much higher than expected. The question to be answered was whether by further expensive development the original losses might be recouped.

Just as the increasing popularity of psychiatry and psychiatrists led to no apparent fall in the numbers of the mentally deranged, so the proliferation of economists had no beneficial effect on the economy. This was partly because the economists, however correct their analysis of the problems, differed profoundly in their prescriptions for the remedies, and partly because their most sensible remedies were more often than not inapplicable for political reasons. In so far as the study of economics relates to the future, it is a still less exact science than psychiatry or, as some might even assert, meteorology; for while the behaviour of a single human being and the vagaries of cloud formations are, with a little bit of luck, predictable in the short run, political diversions, by which the logical deductions of economists are so easily contradicted, are inscrutable in both the short and the long run. The economists have, however, provided explanations of what went wrong, and why, in the past twenty five years. They are more credible as historians than as prophets.

It is necessary to distinguish the external factors which made an impact on the United Kingdom, providing its Government with little scope for influencing them, from the internal factors which can be identified with conflicts of interest, deliberate choice, self-indulgence and lack of foresight. The external factors can be simply stated. They were the changes in the terms of trade, of constant significance to a country which must buy its raw materials as cheaply and sell its manufactured goods as dearly as possible; the loss of captive markets overseas combined with rising competition in the world markets from the newly-recovered industrial countries in Europe and from Japan; the effect of inflation throughout the world in the late 1960s and above all in the 1970s; the periodic onset of small world recessions culminating in a deep and damaging one between 1973 and 1975; and the strain on the pound due to Britain remaining banker to the Sterling area.

Until the first devaluation in 1949, a fifth of the entire monetary reserves of the world were kept in sterling. By the early 1960s this figure had halved and in 1975 the original fifth had become a twentieth. Whereas half the world's trade accounts had formerly been settled in sterling, the dollar to a large extent now replaced the pound, and the fact that in 1976 nearly a fifth of world trade was still on sterling invoices was due to Britain's own importance as a trading country, and to the remarkable increase of her invisible exports. In spite of these facts, the sterling balances, held by their owners as London deposits, rose from £4,000 million in 1965 to £7,500 million in 1974. A third of this vast sum was owned not by Central Banks and Governments, who might be expected to retain their deposits in London as part of a concerted effort to support the pound, but by foreign individuals and corporations. It was they, and not the gnomes of Zurich or the multi-national companies, on whose continued holding of sterling the fate of the pound depended; and if they had been anything approaching unanimous in their decision to sell their holdings, sterling would have crashed still further and faster than it did in the autumn of 1976.

From time to time all these external trends and developments struck blows at the British economy, and the wisest Administration could not have deflected them. The internal factors present an altogether different picture.

Throughout the entire period there were alternating Stops and Gos. Sometimes there was too much consumption of goods, too few workers for whose labour scores of employers were competing, and a rapidly rising import bill to meet the needs of the affluent community. Then the balance of payments would lurch into the danger zone and the Government would raise interest rates, and sometimes taxes, demand special deposits from the banks, and tamper with the Hire Purchase arrangements. A year or two later, with unemployment rising, wage claims nevertheless pending and industry demanding funds for investment, the Green light would be shown, and bread and circuses would be restored to the people. Governments tended to change just when it was necessary to turn the lights Red again. This provided the new incumbents with a convenient opportunity for blaming their predecessors.

Thus, in 1951 the Conservatives were elected at a time when the terms of trade were markedly unfavourable and there was a temporary recession. They were able to declaim against the spendthrift follies of the Socialists. They raised bank rate from the 2% at which it had been stationary for several years, they took certain other First Aid measures, they contemplated abolishing the fixed rate of the pound and allowing it to float to its own level, and in eighteen months the storm passed. There were further Stops and further Gos, usually at three- or four-yearly intervals, and there was an interlude of sustained prosperity, when all seemed to be for the best in the best of worlds, between 1958 and 1962. In that year the balance of payments showed ominous signs of plunging once again. As the standard purge, raising the bank rate, did not seem to be relieving the patient, Mr Selwyn Lloyd tried the device of an incomes policy, to be imposed by persuasion rather than by edict. He hoped that the imposition of a Capital Gains Tax would make the tonic of less extravagant wage-rises palatable to the Trade Unions. It did not, because the Trade Unions were looking inwards at their own pay-packets and were not as yet alive to the threat of inflation. The economic situation deteriorated sharply in 1963 and 1964, so that when the Socialists took office they were able to repay the Tories for what had been said in 1951 and 1952, and to announce that the calamitous state of affairs, demonstrated by a balance of payments deficit of nearly £800 million, was entirely due to thirteen years of Tory misrule. They imposed a 15% surcharge on imports, believing that it would, at the cost of annoying the European Free Trade Area and the country's other suppliers (as well as risking retaliation), prove a successful temporary restorative.

In 1966 there was another sterling crisis and this time there was no outgoing Government to accuse, so the blame was laid, with some justice, at the door of the seamen who went on strike for seven weeks; and in November, 1967, after the closing of the Suez Canal at the end of the Israeli-Egyptian Six Days War and further serious strikes by the dockers and the railwaymen, sterling was devalued from $2.80 to $2.40 to the pound. There was a favourable movement in the terms of trade and by 1970, when Mr Heath became Prime Minister, the balance of payments was again in surplus. Go replaced Stop. It did not last long, for the rapid rise in incomes, bearing no relation to productivity, which Mr Wilson and Mrs Castle had foreseen but been unable to forestall, opened the inflationary door. Mr Heath now tried the experiment which Mr R. A. Butler and the Governor of the Bank of England had favoured in 1953 and Mr Wilson had seriously considered in the 1960s: he allowed the pound to float. In the early stages of so doing it remained gratifyingly buoyant.

The worst economic crisis Britain had to face came in 1973 and 1974, when the deepest world recession since 1931 synchronised with Mr Heath's losing battle against the miners and with Mr Wilson's decision, on becoming Prime Minister again in March, 1974, to meet the miners' claims in full, giving them indeed more than they expected, and to abandon all pretensions to a statutory incomes policy in favour of a Social Contract with the Unions. The world depression continued, unemployment surged upwards and inflation became a raging torrent. Government borrowing requirements rose from £1.7 thousand million in 1970 to £11 thousand million in 1976. By the time the Social Contract, with its voluntary pay-pause, began to take effect, the British balance of payments was in overwhelming deficit. A loan of $5000 million had to be raised from foreign Central Banks, the pound plummeted below $1.70; and in the autumn of 1976 Mr Callaghan's Government was obliged to repeat a previous experiment, made in 1968, by putting the country's financial fate in the hands of the International Monetary Fund and implicitly accepting whatever restrictions on its social policy this might entail. The alternative was bankruptcy.

This was the unedifying sequence of events. The internal causes, as opposed to the external factors, were manifold. First was the determination (entirely laudable when the country could afford it) to establish a basic social wage, in addition to an increasing personal wage, and to maintain a standard of living and rate of consumption greater than the nation earned. In 1952 Mr R. A. Butler, as Chancellor of the Exchequer, prophesied that the standard of living would double in twenty five years and, making due allowance for inflation, his prophecy came true. In many other European countries it trebled. But although the Gross National Product in Britain rose from £14,000 million in 1952 to £93,000 million in 1975 (both figures being calculated at 1975 prices), domestic consumption ran so close to it that the margin for saving and investment, let alone Government expenditure, was small indeed. The British lived consistently beyond their means and it was a severe shock when in 1975, for the first time, the standard of living actually declined.

In order to finance the heavy public expenditure, which the country expected and the Trade Unions demanded, successive Governments resorted to the printing press and there was an unending expansion of the money supply. The figures tell their own sad story. In 1952 the total money supply was £8,447 thousand million. In 1960 the 8,447 had only risen to 10,077 but by 1970 it was 18,175 and in June, 1976, the horrifying figure was £42,184 thousand million. Thus, the money supply increased five-fold while the Gross Domestic Product did not, in real terms, even double. The alternative to printing money was, in conditions of such low productivity, to reduce public expenditure, for taxation was already as high as the community could bear. This meant the deprivation of schools, hospitals and social services, even after dangerous reductions in defence expenditure and the gradual reduction of food subsidies; and it was more than successive Governments had found politically expedient.

Year after year industrialists were exhorted to export more. They were told that the country's survival depended on their success. They were successful in so doing because the outside world bought and consumed more than ever before; but their success did not bear comparison with that of other developed industrial countries. Thus, Britain, which in 1952 had been near the top of the export table, was bumping along on the floor twenty five years later.

Meanwhile, industrial profits represented a steadily falling share of the national income and there was a steep decline in the real rate of return on capital employed. In 1974 this return, which had been 13% in 1960, fell as low as 4% before tax and nothing at all after tax.

The pattern of the country's trade changed drastically. Whereas she had formerly sold half her exports to the Commonwealth and only a fifth to Europe, the figures were almost exactly reversed by the mid-seventies. The Commonwealth countries were more selective in their suppliers and had Britain not joined the Common Market, thereby obtaining duty-free or special preference terms for her sales to Europe, it would have been a hard task to find alternative outlets for her trade. The exporters themselves were as much to blame as the Government; they were less astute than the French, Germans or Italians in adapting the design of their goods to the foreign customers' requirements; they often quoted excessively long delivery dates, which even then they failed to fulfil; and their after-sales service was widely criticised. The Conservative Government did not help matters in 1972 by their decision to abolish the British National Export Council which had been remarkably successful in combining governmental facilities with the enthusiasm of businessmen prepared to give up much of their time to visiting foreign countries, organising trade fairs abroad and entertaining potential customers at home. The dissolution of this body of unpaid salesmen was an act of bureaucratic folly.

The greater success of Britain's trading competitors was partly due to the incentives they were allowed to receive. In Germany the highest rate of tax on earned income was 56%, in France 49% and in the United States the top Federal tax was 50%. In Britain, on the other hand, successful industrialists were taxed at the rate of 83% on their earnings, and if they owned shares in the companies they directed, they paid 98% tax on the restricted dividends they received. The only reasons for working harder were patriotism, sorely tried by increasingly suspicious taxmen, or a keen interest in the work. Both may be incentives, but neither suffices for all men, and it was largely because young men and women of drive and ambition saw so little chance of making their fortune in Britain, that by the end of 1976 there was a slowly swelling tide of emigrants.

Nor was incentive denied to the managerial class alone, for doctors, nurses and teachers were beginning to recognise that there were other societies in which they could work and also retain a larger part of their reward. The country suffered from a fiscal system adopted for political rather than economic purposes.

There were, of course, other causes of Britain's economic decline, not the least being the task of converting an Imperial emporium into a medium-sized industrial economy. There was the sudden quadrupling of oil prices by the producers in 1973. There was the factor of waste: in 1971 corrosion alone is estimated to have cost the country £1,365 million. There was, also, a misuse of the tax-payer's money, and of the nation's resources, by faulty planning and forecasting. Thus, for instance, in the 1960s the Central Electricity Generating Board, misled by the estimate that an 8% growth in electricity demand was assured, financed an expensive nuclear power programme, only to discover that the actual increase in demand was 3%. The huge expansion in universities and polytechnics was founded on the belief that a steady 4% increase in the Gross National Product could be confidently assumed. The M4 motorway was built with two double carriageways, and bridges of the right width to span them, but within a year or so it had to be expanded to three double carriageways which could only, with the utmost difficulty, be fitted beneath the bridges.

Government expenditure overseas soared from £50 million to £1,500 million a year. As the exchange rate of the pound fell and inflation galloped ahead, so the cost of defence expenditure, the upkeep of Embassies, aid to under-developed countries and the servicing of foreign debt grew inordinately. At the same time British multi-national companies increased their overseas investments, thereby also increasing their overseas earnings; and an influx of American companies, establishing factories and offices in England, Scotland and North Ireland, brought a welcome and much needed contribution to employment and to the balance of payments. Most important of all was the unfaltering rise in invisible exports without which Britain could not have met her overseas commitments or paid the interest on her debts.

In a White Paper issued in 1944, the Coalition Government pledged itself to the maintenance of full employment. This was a pledge which all the Governments in Queen Elizabeth's reign have done their utmost to keep. The fact that it implied over-manning, particularly in the Nationalised Industries, and meant that money had to be poured into the economy at times when it would have been more prudent to withhold it, was immaterial. The memory of over two million unemployed in the early 1930s was impressed on the minds of the TUC and of the politicians. Even the suggestion that in a healthy, competitive economy an unemployment rate of 2.5% provided a reasonable reservoir of labour, and would be sufficient to prevent a wage spiral, was regarded as political suicide. For some twenty years the pledge was more or less maintained, at a high cost to the economy; but the world recession of 1974, coupled with an uncontainable rate of inflation, was a strain too great to bear. Unemployment passed the million mark in 1975, and by the end of 1976 the figure was approaching one and a half million. School-leavers and the immigrant community were among the worst sufferers, and the cost to the Exchequer of Social Security payments rose to unexampled heights.

The purchasing power of the pound had already halved between 1938 and 1952. It continued to fall until, in 1974, £16.20 was all that £100 at the 1938 value was worth. Such had been the effect of inflation. It began slowly. In 1952 itself prices rose by 8.7%, but the following year the rise was only 2.2% and in 1960 1.1%. The yearly increase was well below 5% until 1969, in spite of the devaluation of the pound, but in 1971 the percentage rise jumped to 9.5%. This was in part due to the decimalisation of the coinage, an attempt to modernise the currency, using the wrong basic units, which was mildly beneficial to those who were bad at arithmetic, but had an immediate inflationary effect out of all proportion to its advantages.

The British peoples, long shielded from the inflationary agony so familiar to the French, Germans and Italians between the wars, suddenly felt the pain. There was a temporary improvement in 1972 and 1973; but in 1974 a combination of imported inflation from abroad and a total surrender to the wage claims of the miners and other industrial workers at home resulted in a 15.9% rate of inflation, followed by 25% in 1975. The rise in the rate between April, 1974 and April, 1976 was 45%. The Social Contract steadied matters a little, but they nevertheless reached such a pass that for 1976 the Government used self-congratulatory tones in setting a target for a mere 12% increase, even though that was in the event unattainable and both the Americans and the Germans were proving much more successful in restoring their inflationary boats to an even keel. It may be that inflation will provide its own homoeopathic cure, for if it exceeds the rise in earnings, the high prices can no longer be paid and they are bound in due course to fall. There is thus a thermostat on the boiler, provided it is not overheated by fresh fuel and the setting of the thermostat is not thoughtlessly raised.

Prices which had increased by only 2.5% in 1965 rose by over 24% in 1975. Wages more than kept pace until 1976 when there were signs of their being overtaken; for although wages had risen by 30% in 1975, the real standard of living, which year by year had increased by 3%, and even in 1974 by 2%, showed the first signs of decline. The average earnings of all employees were two and a half times greater in 1976 than in 1970, and manual workers' wages more than doubled in the same six years; but the rise in the retail price index was also more than twice that of the other industrial countries. In the autumn of 1976, the continuing fall in the value of the pound on the foreign exchange markets meant that the cost of imports was rising by 1.5% each month, and in consequence further price rises could scarcely be avoided. There were many who doubted whether the Social Contract would bear the strain.

The British public disliked facing the facts. They bought as many television sets as the greater population of Germany and five million a year more than the French. They owned just slightly fewer cars, but their hire purchase arrangements were so much better developed that they were tempted to invest in more modern domestic appliances than any of their richer neighbours. They still believed, wrongly, that their standard of living matched that of other developed countries. Such savings as they had once had were eroded, and most of them did not even know the meaning of that word which used to be included in the Boy Scout's Promise, thrift. It was clear well before the Jubilee that the Ship of State was sailing in rough and dangerous waters; but there was some comfort in the fact that beneath the waves lay the riches of North Sea Oil and Gas. By the end of 1976, the first year of exploitation, more than 15 million tons of oil had been brought ashore. The question was whether enough could be extracted to pay off the mounting debts and, at the same time, to continue financing the Rake's remarkably profligate Progress.

CHAPTER 10

Energy and the Environment

The word environment assumed a new significance when mankind awoke to the fact that the science and technology in which such giant strides have been made in this century were responsible for by-products of a pernicious kind. The natural beauty and the resources of the Earth are in process of erosion. The air we breathe, the water we drink, the food we eat and the very oceans themselves are contaminated. Governments and their advisers became so conscious of the danger signals that in 1970 Mr Heath created a Secretary of State for the Environment, whose duties covered a wide range, but who included high in his list of priorities the task enjoined on his Sovereign in the Coronation Service of 'restoring the things that are gone to decay, maintaining the things that are restored'. There can be no doubt that the demand for an ever-increasing supply of energy, different in form and origin but almost uniform in creating pollution, is the core of the problem. It is therefore logical to describe, in this chapter, the endeavours made both to combat environmental menaces and to discover new sources of energy, however contradictory the two aims may be.

In the conviction that nobody will believe them, the British think it good taste to speak deprecatingly of themselves and their possessions, although the degree of genuine humility which this habit reflects is sometimes questioned by suspicious foreigners. In particular, because they think it bad manners to open any conversation without talking about the weather, they have selected their climate as the primary object of abuse. For centuries they asserted that on the rare occasions when the British Isles were not wrapped in impenetrable fog, they were soaked by ceaseless rain. They even wrote books and produced Christmas cards which induced a general belief that the Feast of the Nativity was invariably celebrated in thick snow. They made these untruthful assertions so often that they ended by thinking they were true.

This was a slander on the British climate, especially the myth about endless drizzle. After 1969, when a series of almost unhealthily warm and, from the agricultural point of view, inconveniently dry winters began, and when most of the summers which followed them were bright and beautiful, it became an effort to support this traditional attitude. So in 1975 and 1976, as one hot summer's day succeeded another in apparently endless succession, and a drought necessitated serious water restrictions, the inhabitants changed tack and asserted that the Sahara Desert was moving northwards. Conversation was further restricted by the virtual elimination of fogs. When, for some inscrutable meteorological reason, a dense fog did strike London in the winter of 1975/76 the relieved sighs of long-deprived middle-aged grumblers were almost audible in the still thickness of the night.

It is, however, indisputable that the Industrial Revolution, Britain's historic contribution to man's material progress, bequeathed a legacy not only of dark satanic mills, but of pollution nourished by sulphureous smoke and industrial waste to which modern breeds of atmospheric, soil and water corruption were added throughout the first half of the 20th century. In the 1950s flights over England were made above a gloomy haze which even on the sunniest of summer days hung over the midland towns, obscured Manchester and spread its unhealthy incidence from the cities of the West Riding to Darlington, Durham and Newcastle. Nor was Edinburgh called 'Auld Reekie' without good cause.

On 6th December, 1952, exactly ten months after the Queen's accession, there descended on London a diabolical pea-soup fog of such opacity that a man could not see his own hand if he stretched out his arm into the encircling gloom. Sufferers from bronchitis died in scores and the cattle in Smithfield, where an agricultural show was being held, were asphyxiated. The Government took immediate action. A Royal Commission was established under the Chairmanship of Sir Hugh Beaver, Managing Director of Guinness, who diverted his unusual abilities from brewing to Clean Air and produced a report of so authoritative a nature that Parliament was enabled to pass a bill giving effect to his proposals through all its stages, in both Houses, in the space of a few months. Fifteen years later a further Royal Commission on Environmental Pollution was established with Sir Eric Ashby, Master of Clare College, Cambridge, as Chairman, and this Commission also produced reports of notable value to the community, emphasising amongst other things that the purification of rivers and water supplies was of supreme importance.

Measures to purify the atmosphere met with a success which was astonishingly rapid. In large cities domestic fires were restricted to the use of smokeless fuels, like coke and anthracite, and as central heating and the use of electric fires became more wide-spread many new flats and houses had no fireplaces at all. Smokeless zones were established by law so that countless small chimneys, from which for generations past the smoke emanating from Britain's cheapest natural product, coal, had poured into the skies, became unused monuments of a by-gone age. When clouds were low the black smoke, and the grit which had been wafted aloft with it, was no longer trapped beneath them until acrid fog, with the sour smell of an old-fashioned railway terminus, swirled through the streets of the cities to obscure men's vision, blacken their lungs, houses and gardens and shorten the lives of those afflicted with pulmonary weakness. At the same time the chimneys of the power stations were made taller so that fumes of sulphur dioxide were dissipated high above the roof tops; and since the cleansing of the fumes and the water in the modern power stations, such as that at Bankside on the Thames, was performed by a new, more efficient method, there was a substantial decrease of pollution in the air and in the rivers. Devices such as wind tunnels were used in the design of power stations to test, and thus help to restrict, the strength of the poisonous emissions reaching the ground; and for scenic reasons the North of Scotland Hydro Board went so far as to build some of their stations underground.

Thus, in twenty five years the air in London, Edinburgh and the other thickly-populated towns of the British Isles became cleaner than that of all the big European and American cities; whereas the inhabitants, who once prided themselves on the spotlessness of the parks and public thoroughfares, developed a slovenliness, and an imperviousness to exhortation about unsightly litter, which out-stripped that of almost any other country. London and Manchester sparkled in the sunshine, the buildings washed and cleansed of soot, so that the citizens of Paris, Madrid, Milan and New York had cause to be ashamed of the comparison; but the freshly-washed doorsteps, the streets free of waste-paper and empty cigarette cartons, the neatly lidded and frequently emptied dust-bins were memories of the past. The British who were once accustomed to equate Cleanliness with Godliness grew negligent of both, although perhaps this was only the case externally, for by the middle seventies they were using 8% of all the fuel consumed in the island to heat water with which to wash themselves, their clothes and their cooking utensils; and this was more than all the energy consumed by the private motorists.

The exhaust of motor-cars is a source of atmospheric pollution less noxious than the old-fashioned coal fire, but as the number of cars and lorries increased from 3,476,000 in 1952 to 15,443,000 in 1975, their influence on the problem became graver. As long ago as 1861, the Road Locomotive Act (for steam locomotives with tyre-less wheels had even then made their appearance on the roads) laid down that the new juggernauts must consume their own smoke; but by 1865 the country's legislators were thoroughly alarmed by the phenomenon and they restricted the speed of road locomotives to 2 m.p.h. in towns and 4 m.p.h. in the country. It was quicker to walk, and much quicker to ride, so that this early initiative to insist on smoke consumption, and the regulations to which it gave rise, were an important factor in delaying the development of the motor car in England a full thirty years.

The initiative was, however, revived to good purpose in the third quarter of the 20th century when factories were increasingly equipped to eliminate the smoke from their chimneys. Meanwhile, in the matter of road vehicles, the arrival of the internal combustion engine, and the use of petrol with a heavy lead content, had given rise to pollution of a potent, if invisible, kind. The tram and the trolley-bus, both electrically powered and thus in themselves harmless to the atmosphere, were replaced by faster but more noxious forms of public transport; but in the present reign there have been developments that more than compensate for this, namely the electrification of the railways and the increasing use of diesel fuel which, however disagreeable its smell, has no lead content and is less harmful precisely because it is more efficient.

The rivers have attracted as much intelligent attention as the atmosphere. In 1952 a would-be suicide, leaping into the Thames from Westminster Bridge, was liable to be poisoned before he was drowned. His fate would have been the same in the Tyne at Newcastle, in the Trent, the lower reaches of the Severn and almost all the great waterways. In 1977 it is safe, though not necessarily to be recommended, for a human being to swim across these rivers; and the arrival before the Houses of Parliament of the first salmon to risk its welfare in the Thames for over two hundred years is confidently, if a trifle optimistically, awaited. This transformation is due to the building of sewage plants which treat effluents with such chemical efficiency that they became an agricultural benefit instead of a noisome source of pollution. If there are exceptionally heavy rains, the sewage plants may be flooded and a mass of untreated effluent drained into the rivers, but this is a sufficiently rare event to be little more than an uninsurable hazard for the fish.

Industrial waste, an even greater polluter of rivers than sewage, has been less susceptible to treatment, but stringent regulations were imposed by Parliament and the local authorities, helpful advances were made in the mastery of detergents, and techniques were devised for the collection and disposal of the outflow from the factories. The unprecedented drought of 1976, reducing the flow of rivers far below their normal level, introduced new hazards which none can be blamed for failing to foresee. However, in general, Managers and Boards of Directors, long oblivious of the damaging aftermath of their manufacturing processes, have become aware of the problem as never before in Britain's industrial history, and the pricking of their consciences is an inoculation that provides, if not total immunity, certainly a gratifying measure of protection. A notable contribution to the general improvement has been made by the Central Electricity Generating Board. In its massive construction of power stations throughout the length and breadth of the land, the Board has built cooling towers that reduce the total demand for water, and induce new oxygen into that which is extracted for use in the generating plants before returning it, refreshed and revitalised, to the rivers.

The human race, at once attracted and alarmed by the unpredictable might of the sea, has used it as a dumping ground since time began and has found comfort in the belief that salt water purifies all things. It was thus a shock to the majority when they learned, and soon saw for themselves, that the sea-shores, and the very sea itself, had succumbed to the prevalent pollution. In contrast to the Mediterranean, in parts of which it has become dangerous to bathe, the seas round the coasts of Britain are fortunately moved by strong tides; and the purification of the rivers has meant that, unlike the coasts of Holland and Belgium, poisoned by the Rhine, or the north-west coast of France, scarcely less afflicted by the Seine, the in-shore waters of Britain have become cleaner.

No strength of tide or measures to purify the rivers has sufficed to remove the oil slicks that are increasingly blown on to the beaches, subjecting the sea-birds to a slow death and contaminating the spawning grounds of the fish. In March, 1967, the *Torrey Canyon*, a heavily laden oil-tanker, foundered off the south-west coast of England, and an impotent cry of distress was raised as the oil drifted in thick black masses on to the beaches of Devon and Cornwall. The necessity for urgent action challenged the inventive and, indeed, defensive skills of the scientists, so that the appropriate detergents were mobilised to disperse the oil and to decontaminate the beaches. Oil, however stringent the rules to which the captains and crews of tankers are subjected, remains a menacing threat to the environment of the British Isles and to the spawning grounds on the sea-beds.

Two disturbances to the peace and enjoyment of the people, the one aural and the other visual, here engaged increasing attention in the 1970s. Constant noise must be a cause of mental distress, although a growing predilection for background music, in shops and factories, in aeroplanes, in kitchens and in the early morning peace of the bedroom, may be thought to run counter to this argument. Some successful efforts at noise abatement have at least been made. Barricades have been built where motorways run through thickly-inhabited areas; double glazing is increasingly used to lessen noise as well as to conserve heat; and there has been much research into the methods of reducing the sound of aeroplanes. Early in the reign, the Rolls-Royce Conway engine, the first 'by-pass' engine and a pioneering success in the reduction of the noise produced by jet-aircraft, was installed by BOAC in its commercial aircraft. The British had already taken the lead in aircraft

engine design by manufacturing, first, turbo-jet engines for the
Viscounts, unrivalled in their quality and popularity in the 1950s,
and a jet engine for the ill-starred *Comet* which, among other
apparent virtues, emitted less black smoke and was quieter than its
American competitors. In the 1960s a new and costly initiative was
taken, jointly with the French, in the slow process of building
Concorde, the supersonic marvel of its time. When the first commercial flights began in the early summer of 1976, there were fears
of unbearable noise and of pollution in the stratosphere, but as the
months went by, and the noise was found to be little worse than
that of the earlier jet-aircraft, the cries of alarm and dissent were
replaced by pioneering pride, only tempered by doubt whether the
enterprise would prove to be a paying proposition.

The visual damage to the environment is to some extent unavoidable, for modern building materials such as concrete, glass
and structural steel are less pleasing to the eye than the traditional,
but prohibitively expensive, brick and stone. However, dogged
efforts have been made to reduce the eyesores. Transmission lines,
which for many years cut across the countryside like scars on the
face of a beautiful woman, were improved in design and appearance;
power stations were built with a taste putting to shame the architects
of the parallelograms on stilts and rectangular boxes which desecrated so many of the towns; and although the cost of burying
transmission lines underground is twenty times higher than that of
erecting them above the surface, as much was spent on the former
as on the latter. Conservation, not only of wildlife and the countryside, but also of fine buildings, which only a generation ago would
have been recklessly destroyed in the interest of commercial exploitation, became a cause proclaimed and led by the Duke of
Edinburgh, tirelessly advocated by the Poet Laureate and by
numerous societies and finally accepted by the Government at
national and increasingly at local level, so that in 1977 it is wholesomely embedded in the British conscience.

A development with the double virtue of being productive and of
removing excrescences which had offended the eye for generations,
was the conversion of solid waste into green and fertile hillocks. The
slag heaps of long disused coal-mines, the thirteen million tons of
ash produced every year by the coal-burning power stations alone;

those and other unsightly dumps began, by some miraculous scientific discovery, to be grassed over and to take an unobtrusive place in the green countryside. This restorative process is well begun as the Queen celebrates her Silver Jubilee, and it is clear that by the time of her Golden Jubilee much of Britain that was ugly, scarred and pitted when she came to the Throne will have received a gracefully successful face-lift.

There remains one potentially dangerous problem of pollution which has not been finally solved: that of radio-active waste from the nuclear power stations. It is a problem which did not exist in 1952 and even in 1977 it is less an actual worry than an over-hanging fear for the future. The disposal of such waste is achieved by methods entirely different from the treatment of that produced by fossil-fuelled power stations, which is released into the atmosphere and diluted to a level rendering it harmless to health, even if it remains a contribution to pollution. Nuclear waste is concentrated and placed in containers, so that the amount of radio-active material affecting the environment has hitherto been small and its effect on the health of the population negligible. The fear of a radio-active leak or accident has not been erased from the public mind, for a fire at the Windscale nuclear reactor in 1957 came close to a catastrophe; but the disposal of the waste is a problem distinct from the safety of the plants.

The treatment of low or medium radio-active waste presents no difficulty. The volume is large, but the toxic content low, and the policy of burying it deep in the ground or dumping it in the sea has led to no contamination of the environment in excess of the limit which the authorities, in their wisdom, consider acceptable; but an international movement against sea-dumping developed in the seventies so that this method of elimination may have to be discontinued. Anxiety is principally concentrated on the waste with a high radio-active level. This is small in quantity and thus easy to contain; but its toxic content is correspondingly high. Nevertheless, taking account of both the high and low radio-active waste material, it can be said that nuclear wastes as a whole have a poisonous potential which is modest by comparison with the other waste materials produced by an industrial society, such as those from chemicals, heavy metals and coal-fired power stations. What danger there is will reduce by half in thirty years as the result of radio-active decay, and after a century or two the waste from a nuclear power station will be less toxic than the uranium ore from which it was originally derived. It may well be an entirely different story if the fast-breeder reactors are built and it is necessary to dispose of plutonium waste; but that alarming hazard is not one which has affected the first twenty five years of the Queen's reign.

During the last few years of the quarter-century there was, however, one significant step in improving the provisions for handling nuclear waste. Stainless steel tanks have been used to store radio-active material in liquid form. No leaks have in fact occurred in the ground or under the sea; but it would be over-sanguine to suppose this will always be so. Therefore a prototype plant was constructed to solidify the waste so that it may become a form of glass. Whether this solidified waste would be buried in a suitably stable geological region, or beneath the ocean bed itself, is a matter for future decision; but if the waste material is successfully converted in this way, the fear of contamination felt in the sixties and seventies will be almost entirely allayed.

While the struggle to progress without damaging the environment was being waged, a search to provide new sources of energy, and to conserve those with which nature has provided us, was undertaken with unflagging diligence; for it was feared that as the population grew, as the standard of living was raised and as new methods of heating houses, driving machines and operating factories were evolved, demand would soon outstrip supply. The more efficient use of fuel, and in particular of gas, oil and electricity, made a useful contribution. Thus, from 1962 onwards the demand for 'net energy' by domestic users was actually less than it had been in 1952, despite the increased number of houses and the constantly rising standard of living. Yet it was thought certain that the total demand would increase. The mercury in the thermometer seemed to be rising dangerously.

The great national asset, coal, was for a time fecklessly disregarded. During the 1960s the annual investment in the mines was reduced from £100 million to £10 million and, while the use of oil doubled, electricity consumption went up two and a half times and gas nearly four times, the amount of coal sold to consumers fell by a half. Then the Government and Parliament awoke to the danger of neglecting so important and traditional a source of energy which, moreover, employed a huge, skilled labour force; and by a happy coincidence this renewed awareness synchronised with the discovery of a vast new coalfield near Selby in Yorkshire, and, later still, another in the Vale of Belvoir, and yet a third in Scotland. Before the end of 1976, the first shaft had been sunk in the new Selby mining area, but since it takes a full ten years to develop a coalfield, it was well that new sources of energy were literally in the pipe-line.

The most exciting discovery for Britain in the present reign was oil and natural gas beneath the turbulent waves of the North Sea. The mere fact of their turbulence meant that the task of extraction was a long and difficult process, perhaps the most difficult ever faced by off-shore oil engineers. The natural gas harvest was the first to be reaped and by the end of the sixties and early seventies it was already heating the kitchen stoves of British town dwellers. By 1973 13% of the total national fuel consumption was of North Sea Gas, by 1975 the figure was 15% and in 1976 the rate of consumption was already 18.5%, while the stoves of thirteen million customers of the Gas Board had been modified to receive it. This alone meant a valuable saving of imported oil, the price of which was raised to all but catastrophic heights by the Arab producers after a brief Israeli-Egyptian war in 1973.

North Sea Oil followed close on the heels of natural gas. The newspapers constantly reported the discovery of new fields; vast oil-rigs, which were encampments for the crews as well as drilling platforms, were towed far out into the inhospitable northern waters off the Shetlands and the Orkneys; and in spite of warnings not to be over-elated, or excessively expectant of a black El Dorado – for the oil might only last a decade or two – the British public comforted themselves in their perennial economic anxieties by the thought that not only self-sufficiency but an exportable surplus would shortly be theirs. The Scottish Nationalists found the prospect particularly alluring. The exploitation of North Sea Oil began in 1971 and early in 1976 the Queen turned the tap which brought the first oil ashore. In the first three months of that year 1.3 million tons of indigenous oil was extracted, and in spite of storms, stresses and wrangles about nationalisation, it was confidently predicted that by 1980 there would indeed be an exportable surplus.

Meanwhile, during the first twenty five years of the reign, the Central Electricity Generating Board had built the largest and most efficient closely controlled electrical power network in the world, with no less than 47 large steam turbines, every one of them capable of producing 650,000 horse power and thereby generating enough electricity for each station to meet the maximum demand of over half a million people. Into the national grid which the Board had established there had also began to flow in 1956 the first fruits of nuclear power.

The story of Britain's experiments with nuclear power is not dissimilar from her ventures in civil aviation. The early morning was bathed in sunshine but by noon the sky was overcast. In the case of civil aviation the clouds were formed by a combination of misfortune and ill-advised parsimony; in the case of nuclear energy, they were heavy with muddle and mismanagement. In the 1950s there was every reason to hope that Britain, the begetter of nuclear fission, and partner of the United States and Canada in the war-time developments, would for many years to come have none but America as her rival in the production of nuclear reactors and their sale as lucrative exports. Thus, when the Government established a United Kingdom Atomic Energy Authority in 1954, they declared that Britain's lead in this field of technology must not be allowed to falter and that they intended to approve the building of twelve nuclear power stations.

Two small, experimental power reactors, one in America and one in Russia, had begun to operate in 1954, but the first full-scale power station was British. The Queen opened it, at Calder Hall in Cumberland, in October, 1956, and Britain glowed with pride as, in a blaze of well-organised international publicity, the Queen pulled the lever which released the first nuclear electric power into the National Grid. Twenty years later there were 250 power reactors in the world, of which America had 53, Britain 29, Russia 16 and France 10; but that is far from presenting a full picture of what happened in those years of vigorous development. Three more reactors were built at Calder Hall and, for the gratification of the Scots, four at Chapelcross, a few miles north of the border. Eventually twenty eight reactors were built on the Calder Hall model, one being exported to Japan and one to Italy. The design was improved, pre-stressed concrete was introduced for safety purposes, and measures were taken to reduce the risk of radio-active escape in the event of an accident. Already in 1966 the power generated by these stations, and eight more which had started to operate, was such that Britain's nuclear contribution to the national electricity supply was greater than that of any other country, including the United States.

This was as far as Great Britain's aspiration to lead the world in these new devices was able to go. Muddle, misjudgement and mismanagement took charge. It was decided to switch from the improved Calder Hall design to Advanced Gas Cooled Reactors or AGRs. The first 'went critical', which is the nuclear jargon for becoming operative, in 1962. It was, alas, the only one to do so for the next fifteen years. Five more full-scale stations were started; yet by the Silver Jubilee none is completed. On the other hand, in 1972 a prototype Fast Breeder Reactor, which produces more fissile material than it consumes, and which had only been ordered in 1966, 'went critical' at Dounreay in the extreme north of Scotland. Its so doing was critical in more sense than one, for its American rival had suffered an accident which came close to necessitating the evacuation of the whole population of Detroit. Caithness and the Orkneys have fewer inhabitants, with more sanguine temperaments.

The AGRs faced competition from two American alternatives, a Pressurised Light Water Reactor and a Boiling Water Reactor. Three groups of companies placed tenders, and in 1965 the Government decided in favour of the British gas cooled design. The chosen contractors for the first plant at Dungeness were unable to deliver the goods; those who were given the contracts for the other stations plodded wearily on, hampered by engineering problems and afflicted by the effect of inflation on their fixed-price contracts. It was soon clear that completion would be seriously delayed, and that in all probability none of the plants, when they were finally delivered, would be capable of producing the output of power originally envisaged. Potential foreign purchasers transferred their contracts to the USA and to France. There was a cheerless awakening from the day-dreams of sustained British supremacy in the field of nuclear power.

In 1973 Parliament and the dispirited British nuclear industry were surprised to learn that the Central Electricity Generating Board, disenchanted by the unsatisfactory prospects for the AGRs, intended to place contracts based on the design of the American pressurised light water reactors, and that they hoped to install thirty two between 1974 and 1983. This proposal was made just as Mr Heath's Government had decided to consolidate all the British industrial interests concerned with the manufacture of nuclear reactors in one National Nuclear Corporation, managed by the General Electric-English Electric Company. The Board's announcement provoked a storm inside and outside Parliament, partly because the American reactors were untried and were believed by some to be unsafe, partly because they would not be British (and expensive components would have to be imported); and partly because the size of the programme was thought to be unrealistically large. On a previous occasion the Electricity Board had greatly over-estimated the future demand for power.

In spite of this, the Conservative Government might have decided to proceed; but the Labour Party, on their return to power in 1974, rejected the proposal and decided to build six plants of a totally different kind called Steam Generating Heavy Water Reactors, which were akin to an apparently successful model designed by the Canadians. Total confusion now reigned, although the original reactors at Calder Hall and elsewhere, built in the 1960s, were still safely and efficiently pouring their contribution of electricity into the National Grid. Public interest in the supply of energy was thenceforward directed more to North Sea Oil and the new Selby coalfield than to the distressing vagaries of British policy on nuclear power. Meanwhile the experts turned their by no means unanimous thoughts to the question whether more Fast Breeder Reactors, developed from the prototype at Dounreay, should be built and, if so, what should be done about the dangerous, highly radio-active and long-lasting plutonium waste which such plants might be expected to generate in intractable forms and quantities.

At least one important lesson has been learned. The wealth of Britain, as of every country in the modern world, depends almost as much on the availability of energy as on the skill of management and the efforts of labour. That wealth loses its entire value if nature is ravaged, and her gifts destroyed, in the process of creating it. For two whole centuries the British have fecklessly scarred, blackened and adulterated large parts of their country. They were, it seemed, well set on a journey leading to self-immolation when in the latter half of the twentieth century they perceived how close they were drawing to a point of no return. The production of more, and cheaper, energy was essential to them, but the elimination of its polluting effect on the British Isles was vital to health and happiness. Henceforward, energy and the environment must be regarded as Siamese Twins.

Part IV

BRITISH SOCIETY

CHAPTER 11

The Orb and the Cross

The Britain of 1952 contained cleavages between Canterbury and Rome, and between both of them and the Nonconformists, almost as deep as they had been a hundred years previously. In 1977 the Christian Churches are still separate and the differences significant; but instead of glowering at each other across a hostile and most un-Christian divide, as they did when the Queen first came to the throne, they now try to understand one another and explore the ways by which unity could become a reality.

In 1976 one of the first acts of the new Cardinal Archbishop of Westminster was to accept an invitation to preach in Westminster Abbey. But in 1953 when, by command of the Queen, the Earl Marshal of England, himself the premier Roman Catholic layman in the country, invited five Roman Catholic bishops to attend the Coronation, he was surprised and infuriated by a reply which expressed astonishment at his ignorance in supposing that any ordained Bishop of the Roman Church would be allowed to attend a service which it was implied, though not actually stated, was heretical. Five laymen were offered instead, but the suggestion was understandably ignored and the angry Earl Marshal was even heard to mutter the word 'Treason'.

It is to the Roman Catholics, and to the Vatican itself, that the main credit must be given for the first ray of light to illuminate this medieval miasma. Pope John XXIII, old when he was elected to the papacy, but a man whose eyes, undimmed by prejudice, were fixed on the future rather than the past, put the weight of his office behind a movement to heal the breaches in the Christian Church. For he knew it to be faced, as a whole and not just in part, by the growing strength of Communist atheism and, more dangerous still, by religious apathy.

The Vatican Council, inspired by Pope John and, after his death in 1963, brought to a triumphant conclusion by his successor, Pope

Paul VI, not only modernised the liturgy of the Roman Catholic Church, introducing the use of vernacular languages in place of Latin and simplifying the form of the Mass, but also instituted a new policy of co-operation with other Christian Churches, rejecting the unyielding traditions of the Counter Reformation. In 1976 there was a much publicised reaction against these reforms by a group of traditionalists led by a septuagenarian French Archbishop. This caused embarrassment to the Vatican, but did not halt the steady ecumenical progress approved and espoused by all denominations. As barriers were lowered and tensions reduced, mixed marriages between Roman Catholics and members of other Christian Churches, which ever since the Vatican Decrees of 1870 had been a fertile source of ill-will because of the rigid conditions on which Rome insisted, became less distressing for all concerned.

The Archbishop of Canterbury, Dr Geoffrey Fisher, and his successor, Dr Michael Ramsay, welcomed this liberal revolution with acclaim, and the Queen herself, as Supreme Governor of the Church of England, took the initiative of inviting members of all denominations, and indeed of all religions, to be present on special occasions in Anglican Churches. At a service in St Martin-in-the-Fields, which the Queen herself attends annually, Hindus and Moslems are included in a congregation of all religious faiths and sects.

The dark, lowering clouds of centuries, reflecting on the Christian Churches the very negation of their Founder's teaching, began to evaporate, and there was a public revulsion against the narrow institutionalism of religious factions. In the new towns and the spreading suburbs, Anglicans, Roman Catholics and Nonconformists agreed to share church buildings and even to hold joint services. It is still against the law of the land for Roman Catholics to use Churches belonging to the Established Church, but it is an ancient law which is sensibly disregarded. In new universities and colleges inter-denominational Chapels were built, and if the infallibility of the Pope in matters of doctrine remains, and is long likely to continue, an insuperable stumbling-block to the formal reunion of Rome and Canterbury, the association and understanding of the two Communions grows yearly closer. It has been one of the wholesome revolutions of the neo-Elizabethan age.

A less happy event was the refusal in 1972 of the Church of England, by a small majority, to agree to reunion with the Methodists who had, for their part, welcomed the proposal and were prepared to go far towards meeting the basic requirements of the Anglicans, even to the extent of recognising episcopacy. Archbishop Fisher had made a notable contribution to the *rapprochement* with Rome, and as early as 1946 had invited the Free Churches to 'take episcopacy into their systems' as a means of reuniting with the Church of England. Now he changed course and threw his weight against the proposed agreement with the Methodists. To the regret of many Anglicans, the scheme then foundered in the wake of a small adverse vote by the new General Synod of the Church of England. The Congregationalists and Presbyterians, however, set an example to the rest of Christendom by coming together a few months later in order to form a United Reformed Church, and recognition was given to the ecumenical spirit of the times by the decision to hold a service of inauguration in the Royal Peculiar of Westminster Abbey in the presence of both the Archbishop of Canterbury and the Cardinal Archbishop of Westminster. Cardinal Heenan, who was the head of the Roman Catholic Church in Britain from 1951 until his death in 1975, was as instrumental as any Churchman in propagating the new spirit of toleration which so rapidly spread far and wide throughout the Christian community.

The Established Church took steps to put its own house in order. In 1970 the Church Assembly, created shortly after the First World War, was replaced by a General Synod. This is divided into three houses, the Bishops, the Clergy and the Laity. They normally sit together, but they vote separately. It is now the Parliament of the Church of England, which in 1977 disposes of powers to regulate its own affairs such as it has never before possessed in the nearly four hundred and fifty years of its existence. Since a resolution of the Synod must be approved by all three houses, the Laity have an authority as great as that of the Bishops, or of the Convocations of Canterbury and York, in all matters of general importance to the Church, its liturgy and its discipline.

Ever since its foundation in the 16th century, under the Supreme Governorship of the King or Queen of England, the Church of

England has, precisely because of its origins, been an Erastian Church, its Bishops and many of its Deans and Canons appointed by the Sovereign on the recommendation of the Prime Minister, and any changes in its forms of worship requiring the approval of Parliament. Indeed, at her Coronation the Queen was required, like all her predecessors, to swear a solemn Oath that she would 'maintain and preserve inviolably the settlement of the Church of England and the doctrine, worship, discipline and government thereof, as by law established in England'. It was, by sensible courtesy to the Church of Scotland, the Moderator of that Church who placed in her hands the Bible, 'the most valuable thing that this world affords'; but it was the Archbishop of Canterbury, representing the Church of England 'as by law established', who presented the Orb with ancient words full of ancient meaning: 'Receive this Orb set under the Cross'. That part of the terrestrial Orb which the Queen governs is, at least in theory, set under the Cross, so that Orb and Cross are, by historic tradition, indissolubly linked.

This was, by the second half of the 20th century, an interpretation ignored by most of the Queen's subjects, and no longer acceptable to the Church of England itself. The fact that the Archbishop of Canterbury is the first subject of the Crown, taking precedence of the Lord Chancellor and the Prime Minister, and that the senior Bishops, with seats in the House of Lords, can vote on all bills submitted to Parliament, and can rise to express their views on any matter in which they choose to intervene, has not been held by churchmen of the present day to be adequate compensation for parliamentary control of the Prayer Book and political selection of the leading ecclesiastical dignitaries.

Dissatisfaction with an anachronistic state of affairs was voiced with persistence in the 1960s and a Commission was established, under the Chairmanship of Professor Owen Chadwick, Master of Selwyn College, Cambridge, to review the relationship of Church and State. The report of the Commission was published in 1970 and the reforms which it recommended were accepted by the Church. Immediate steps were taken to instigate changes in the two areas which caused concern: the control of the form of worship by Parliament and the appointment of Bishops by the Crown.

Neither Church nor State was so rash or revolutionary as to mention the topic of Disestablishment.

In 1928 the House of Commons had refused to approve a revised Prayer Book. In 1965, even before the report of Professor Chadwick's Commission and the establishment of the General Synod, Parliament sanctioned a Prayer Book (Alternative and other Services) Measure, which gave the Church authority to use experimental services for a limited period. This was followed, ten years later, by a further Measure, of permanent validity, introduced in the House of Lords by Dr Michael Ramsay on his last day as Archbishop of Canterbury. In spite of fears in some quarters that it might lead to Disestablishment, and in due course render obsolete the superb language of the existing Prayer Book, this second and more far-reaching innovation was accepted by Parliament with appropriate safeguards to prevent the total dethronement of the Prayer Book of 1662. The General Synod was empowered to define the Church's doctrine and decide its form of worship. One of the major issues on which many members of the Church of England felt so strongly had been resolved. The other, selection of Bishops by the Crown, seemed likely to be a stiffer hurdle.

The right of the Crown to choose the high ecclesiastical dignitaries of the Established Church is a legacy of the Reformation, although even in pre-Reformation England, and in France and Spain, the Kings had often claimed such a right and the Popes had sometimes found it expedient not to dispute it. The Dean and Canons of an English Cathedral can, in theory, elect their own Bishop, but under the Statute of Praemunire, which Henry VIII found indispensable, they were liable to hideous penalties, including disembowelling, if they were rash enough not to elect the Sovereign's nominee. It would have been a nice point whether, once capital punishment had been abolished for murder, the Queen would have felt justified in resorting to such an extreme measure against recalcitrant Canons; but all possible embarrassment to Her Majesty is avoided because the Cathedral Chapters never have rejected a Royal nominee, and also because Parliament, in its wisdom, has left the Statute in being but has removed tee gory punishment.

The patronage of the Crown has been exercised with dispassionate care. It was occasionally supposed that Prime Ministers made episcopal recommendations on political grounds; but this was an erroneous suspicion. Mr Ramsay Macdonald was believed to have promoted Dr Hewlett Johnson, 'The Red Dean', to the Deanery of Canterbury on account of his advanced socialist opinions. In fact, the suggestion was originally made by King George V, who had been impressed by the spiritual worth of Hewlett Johnson when, as Dean of Manchester, he dined, slept and preached the sermon at Windsor. Bishop Barnes and Bishop Hunkin, both prelates with advanced views, were appointed to Birmingham and Truro respectively, not because Ramsay Macdonald admired their politics but because the then Archbishop of Canterbury proposed them. Later Prime Ministers and their Secretaries were meticulous in seeking the advice and approval of the highest Church authorities before submitting names to Buckingham Palace, although it must be admitted that Sir Winston Churchill did, if there was a choice, show a preference for candidates who had won a DSO or MC as Chaplains to the Forces, and it was surmised that if a cleric with a Victoria Cross had been available, he would have gone straight to an Archbishopric.

In spite of the virtually stainless record of 10 Downing Street in these matters, those who had fought victoriously to win for the Church the right to decide its own worship and doctrine, were ill-content to rest on their laurels. This time they only won a partial victory. Praemunire, less its disembowelling clause, remains on the Statute Book; but in 1972 the General Synod asked the Archbishop of Canterbury and the Chairman of the House of Laity to discuss with the leaders of all three political Parties a new policy for administering the Ecclesiastical Patronage of the Crown. As a result of these consultations, the Prime Minister announced in July, 1976, that a Church Committee would in future submit to 10 Downing Street two names for a vacant Bishopric. The Prime Minister would in normal circumstances undertake to submit one of them to the Queen, so that no Bishop would in fact be appointed unless his name had, in the first place, been proposed by the Church Committee.

While the Church of England was reforming itself, those regularly profiting from its ministrations decreased. There was, however, no startling fall in the numbers giving formal and occasional acknowledgment of their membership. Thus, in 1952 there were some 1.9 million Anglican communicants on Easter Day; and in 1973 the number had only fallen to 1.5 million; while communicants at Christmas exceeded 1.7 million. Baptisms declined from some 420,000 to 300,000; but this was in the Church of England alone, and it may therefore be assumed that of the 540,000 children born during that year a considerable majority were baptised as Christians. Ordinations declined annually, so that there were fewer than 400 each year from 1971 onwards, and many parishes had to be amalgamated because of the shortage of clergy. However, as Oliver Cromwell put it: 'A few honest men are better than numbers'; and this was certainly the view of the early Christian Church. Forcible conversion, fines for non-attendance at Divine Service and rich, comfortable livings were later innovations.

What undoubtedly occurred in this period was a fall in the number of conventional church-goers. The Victorians of all classes, and particularly of the upper- and middle-classes, are accused of hypocrisy with varying degrees of injustice. It seems indisputable that they were in general a more God-fearing generation than our own, brought up, as they were, to regular church-going, Bible-reading and family prayers, and much less distracted by travelling to distant work, by alternative occupations and by exposure to the garish life now transmitted all day long on the radio and television. It may even be argued that if the majority were more credulous, and frequently disposed to fundamentalist beliefs about the Creation, the probability that God the Father had a long beard, and the nature of Heaven and Hell, they were in many ways less superstitious than their descendants.

It is none the less true that their religious observances were conventional. They went to Mattins every Sunday at 11.0 a.m. if they were well-to-do, and to Evensong at 6.0 if they belonged to the lower orders, merely because it was a socially expected act. In 1952 most of their grandchildren, who seldom gave religion a thought except at the required hour on Sunday and even then dozed comfortably throughout the sermon, were still subject to this inherited tradition. In 1977 the majority of their great-grandchildren find failure to go to Church on Sundays no burden on their conscience at all.

The fall in the numbers going regularly to church is, thus, partly a reflection of the change in convention, though it does not signal the end of conventional attitudes; for they are endemic in society and each generation creates its own. There are, as there have always been, many people who feel committed to the faith of their ancestors, and are intellectually convinced of the virtues of Christianity without being in the least devout; and there are still more, obedient to an instinct of folk religion, who are married and buried by the Church, and have their children baptised, partly in deference to inherited custom and partly by way of subscribing for an inexpensive insurance policy. These have been little affected by the changes in the Church of England, except for a vague awareness that the forms of Service are not what they used to be. In 1952 there were just under 350,000 marriages in England and Wales, and of these 173,000 were celebrated in the Church of England; nearly 70,000 by other Christian denominations; and only 106,000, or well under one third, in Registry Offices. By the end of 1976 there were many more divorces and many more illegitimate children; but there was no marked decline in the numbers electing to be married in church.

There is a third category who have fallen away from the Church but who, because there is in all men a spiritual element which distinguishes them from brute beasts (though not necessarily in the way the marriage service suggests), seek an outlet for their religious instincts in superstitious practices of varying kinds. It is in no way harmful to believe in the cure of physical ailments by the Box, even if there be no religious or scientific basis for such beliefs. Churchmen and scientists alike may, however, be forgiven for raising disapproving eyebrows at those who dabble in witchcraft, black magic and the occult. Astrology shows no sign of decreasing its hold on the credulous, and atavistic instincts keep a number of pre-Christian fetishes and taboos alive. Some who no longer find in the Christian Churches the spiritual uplift for which they yearn have transferred their allegiance to Buddhist and Hindu mysticism, sitting patiently at the feet of an Oriental Guru; others have migrated to wilder shores. On the other side of the balance sheet, the example of the Queen and the royal family in never omitting to go to Church wherever they may be, at home or abroad, cannot have failed to encourage many who might, but for that example, have found it easier to tread the idle path of non-attendance.

The Church of England, like the Roman Catholic Church, is healthier for the fall-away, just as a small army of trained soldiers usually fights better than an ill-disciplined horde. It is only when an untrained horde, such as the French Revolutionary Army of 1791, the American Colonists of 1780, or the Vietnamese in more recent days, is impassioned by fervour and genuine enthusiasm that it may hope to win the day. The hordes of the Christian world are no longer so impassioned, at any rate within the United Kingdom; and it is to the dedicated minority that the Church now turns for support. For these devout but not superstitious men and women, the liberation which the Church of England has achieved has real meaning, and it should not be assumed that they are few in number. They are certainly less beset by internal strife, for Protestant fanaticism is now a dying cult and the new forms of worship have done much to bring peace to the Church. Members of the congregation have been encouraged to take part in the services, and the fall in candidates for ordination as full-time Ministers of the Church has been compensated by an Auxiliary Pastoral Ministry. This, like the Territorial Army without which two world wars could scarcely have been won, recruits its volunteers from the ranks of those earning their living in secular occupations. The Lay Reader is an old established assistant to the Clergy: the new Auxiliary Ministers, sacrificing leisure hours after a full week's work, can, because of their ordination to the priesthood, give still greater help to the Parish Priest.

So the Church of England has become a much changed institution in twenty five years. The old Sunday routine in force throughout the land in 1952, has been replaced by Family Services and Parish Communion Services at whatever hour of the day is convenient to the congregation. Ancient shibboleths, such as objections to afternoon or evening Communion services, disagreement whether the Priest should look northwards or eastwards when standing at the altar, and many other trivial conflicts of external unimportance, have been almost forgotten in the concentration on providing a form of worship which satisfies those whose motive in going to church is more to worship God than to appease society.

The renewal of interest in the Bible and in biblical theology has been coupled with a deeper understanding of the significance of scientific discovery. The revelations of science and the triumphs of technology have neither disproved the existence of God nor diminished the relevance of the Gospels, except for those who wish to be relieved of their own residual anxieties on the subject. They have, however, dispelled vertical illusions about the whereabouts of Heaven and Hell, and drawn attention away from the physically superficial to the metaphysically essential. During these years some radical thinkers, like the Bishop of Woolwich (who wrote a book, *Honest to God*, which raised many hackles but produced no revelations), sought to express in words the changes in belief; but nothing that was written altered the basic reliance of Christians on the original books of their Faith and the later expositions of it by scholars down the centuries. Nor can the Bishop of Woolwich have wished it otherwise.

The new translations of the Bible and the alterations in the services of the Prayer Book are approved by many Church people, and have been adopted in a majority of parishes. It must therefore be presumed that they are beneficial. They do, however, represent a loss to the English language which can only be justified if there are compensations of spiritual value. The Church of England had the good fortune to inherit a Bible and a Prayer Book written or translated in the great age of English prose, an age in which Shakespeare wrote, an age in which the best prose was in itself poetry. The new translations provided in the 20th century are by comparison flat, dull and uninspiring.

It is true that certain passages of scripture are difficult to understand in the Authorised Version of the Old Testament and the Epistles of St Paul. It is vital that those who take their religion seriously should be able to interpret its meaning, but obscurity is seldom found in the Jacobean translation of the Gospels, and there are many other sublime passages in the Bible which are entirely comprehensible in the Authorised Version. It is a tragic, and many will say an outrageous, desecration of the British heritage that easily understood stories from the Gospels, such as the Parables of the Sower and the Prodigal Son, the account of the Wedding at Cana of

Galilee, the Acts of the Apostles and the incomparable beauty of St Paul's teaching on Faith, Hope and Charity, should be rewritten in words which add nothing to clarity and merely contrive to diminish their poetic impact. For great poetry is, after all, an expression of spiritual values and an aid to spiritual experience.

In a generation which has been stirred to conserve buildings, scenery and wildlife before they are crushed by the advancing tons of concrete, it is strange that the Church of England should be less than whole-hearted in conserving the treasures of English literature; and it is sad that rising generations of school-children are deprived of aids to their imagination, and to their experience of beauty without, in many cases, receiving the compensating advantage of clearer understanding. None but a pedant would argue that the famous 'No man can serve two masters' is improved by the new rendering 'No man can be the slave to two masters', unless it be held that twelve letters are to be preferred to five. 'Consider the lilies of the field, how they grow; they toil not neither do they spin. Yet I say unto you that even Solomon in all his glory was not arrayed like one of these'. No literate or semi-literate child fails to understand these words, and many remember them all their lives. The authors of the New English Bible presumed to improve. They achieved much the same success as a poor copyist who sets up his easel before a great masterpiece of which the colours, faded with age, none the less illuminate the eye and the mind of the beholder.

The Church of England has had the advantage over all other religious communities of owning cathedrals, abbeys and parish churches built in an age of faith, when they took precedence in the creative activities of mankind over all secular buildings. Mostly constructed between the 12th and the 16th centuries, they are in constant need of increasingly expensive repair; and some of the greatest, such as York Minster and Canterbury Cathedral, have been in actual danger of collapse. In almost any other country the preservation of these splendid national monuments would have been a burden readily shouldered by the State, a burden insignificant by comparison with the weights it carries in the fields of health, education, the Social Services and the living Arts. In the United Kingdom, the Treasury has shown no alacrity to volunteer assistance, and the Church Commissioners, using their well-administered investments to the full for the payment of the Clergy and the upkeep of their habitations, have had nothing to spare for the maintenance of historic churches.

In these recent years there has been a frequently repeated cry for financial rescue, and the heavily over-taxed citizens have been implored to heed it. Men and women of all creeds and denominations, and of none, have responded generously; so have Foundations and public companies; but there is only discredit for Parliament and Whitehall in their failure to assume responsibility for Church buildings which are among the richest inheritances of the country as a whole, and not just of those who continue to use them for the purposes for which they were built. The State's parsimony is a still greater disgrace in the late seventies than in days gone by; for the medieval buildings yearly need more money spent on them, and the rich patrons who once subscribed the requisite funds can no longer do so. Their subscriptions are now paid to the Inland Revenue instead.

The Church of Scotland has been no more conservative than the Church of England in the measures it has taken to come to terms with almost all the changing scenes of life. The dour, long-drawn-out services of the Kirk have been shortened. The uncompromising rejection of anything that might be considered sinfully cheerful or, worse still, conceivably linked with wicked episcopalian practices south of the border, has been itself rejected. Yet the Church of Scotland has retained its justifiable pride in a high standard of preaching, and if its God-fearing influence has scarcely penetrated the seething masses of Clydeside, its influence for sobriety of behaviour, and careful thought before action, is still strong in most Scottish burghs and in the glens.

The Jews in Britain are a closely-knit community of which, like the Christians, only a minority are now zealous in their religious observances. A visitor to a synagogue on the Day of Atonement might suppose that all Jews were synagogue-going and God-fearing, for that is the one occasion when all who profess Judaism join in corporate worship. A visitor on the Sabbath eve, or the Sabbath day itself, would see the Anglican experience of reduced church attendance mirrored in the synagogue. The mainstream of actively professing Jews are still the Orthodox, whose beliefs and liturgical observances have changed little, if at all, since 1952. To the 'right' of the Orthodox are sects of ultra-Orthodox Jews and to the 'left' are the Progressives, whose differences from the Orthodox are partly liturgical, the services being conducted mainly in English and much of the Orthodox ritual having been discarded. The Progressives have attracted some of the Orthodox to their ranks, and a female Rabbi has actually been inducted by the Union of Reformed and Liberal Synagogues.

Between Christians and Jews this quarter-century has seen a spirit of toleration and co-operation, fostered by the Council of Christians and Jews, and emphasised by occasions when Christian clergy have preached in a synagogue and Rabbis in a church. Marriage with a Christian or an agnostic, once regarded as a heinous offence, has become common and scarcely reprehensible. The schisms within Judaism itself have not been healed by any ecumenical spirit comparable to that which has grown in the Christian communion, though the emergence of the State of Israel in 1948 has healed the breach between Zionists and anti-Zionists. Most British Jews, while acknowledging full allegiance to the Queen, now also feel a sense of identity with Israel, so that in every synagogue on the Sabbath day there is a Prayer for Israel after those for the Queen, the royal family and the Ministers of the Crown.

Although the moral standards now accepted by the people, in so far as they admit to accepting moral standards at all, are further divorced from religious observances than was once the case, the part played by the Churches in forming and directing opinion should not be underestimated. Their active stimulation of social measures is long-established, as is that of the Jewish synagogues among their own people. Education was for centuries the responsibility of the Church of England. The Probation Service, itself the child of the London Police Court Mission, is of Anglican descent; and before the days of the Welfare State, care for the homeless, the widow and the orphan was almost entirely in the hands of the Churches, or of selfless Christian organisations such as the Salvation Army and the Church Army. Extensive governmental provision for social services has not discouraged the Churches from activities which they believe it is their duty to undertake, and the Church of England's Board of

Social Responsibility has been tireless in producing pamphlets providing information and advice. Drug addicts have been welcomed and helped in the crypt of St Martin-in-the-Fields and elsewhere. Christian Aid has been a projection of Overseas Missionary Work, and Oxfam has owed much to the Churches' encouragement and support.

The influence of the Established Church has been consistently on the liberal side. The days when the Bishops in the House of Lords saddened the deeply devout Wilberforce by opposing the abolition of the slave trade are long forgotten and, for the sake of their immortal souls, we may hope forgiven. The new Elizabethan Bishops have established themselves far over the other side of the fence. They have spoken almost unanimously in the cause of toleration. All but one (who took the logical view that a man in a condemned cell was more likely to repent than at any other time in his career) voted against capital punishment; and on such divisive issues as homosexuality, divorce reform, birth control and even abortion, it has been customary to find a majority of the episcopal bench, as well as the Synod, in support of liberal reform.

On the racial issues which became sharper as the reign progressed, the Church has preached tolerance and struggled to reduce the rising temperature. In every diocese where the problem is acute, the Bishop appoints two or three clergymen with the special task of reconciliation; and in July, 1976, the Archbishop of Canterbury, Dr Coggan, while calling for an upper limit to the number of new immigrants, reminded all Christians of their duty to their coloured neighbours, many of whom were by then second generation citizens of the United Kingdom. The Bishop of Stepney, Trevor Huddleston, has not rested in his endeavours to help and soothe the immigrants themselves and to give reality to the Archbishop of Canterbury's thesis that it is just as important, and nearly always more difficult, for a Christian to befriend an immigrant family as to contribute money to an overseas mission.

The Kingdom of Heaven is no easier of access in 1977 than it was in 1952, nor is its whereabouts easier to define, or the number in search of it greater. It can, however, be claimed that there is a closer and more Christian relationship between the different companies of the Church Militant than appeared conceivable twenty five years ago, and a determination not only to tolerate but to understand and co-operate with other religious bodies, whether they be, as the Good Friday prayer puts it, Jews, Turks or Infidels. This is a development to be welcomed with even greater joy than the wholly estimable resolve of the Established Church to set its own house in order.

CHAPTER 12

Moral Disarmament

Religion, as professed by the Christian Churches, has always claimed, though by no means always practised, a close relationship to morality; and although moral standards are no longer equated with religious belief by the majority of men and women, they are still, consciously or unconsciously, based on the teachings of Christianity and Judaism. The code of behaviour recommended to Russian school-children by their Marxist teachers is broadly that in which their grandparents were instructed by the Orthodox Church. The Ten Commandments, except for the first (exhorting men to recognise and not to desert the Lord their God), the third (forbidding men to take the name of the Lord their God in vain) and the fourth ('Remember that thou keep holy the Sabbath Day') are all valid precepts in the Soviet Union; and if Lenin's name be substituted for God's, even the first and third would apply, though the temporal penalty for taking Lenin's name in vain is much more severe than that for speaking ill or lightly about the Almighty has been for a great many years in Christian countries. Whether they admit it or not, humanists, agnostics and even atheists are profoundly affected by the teachings of the Bible; for it is impossible to escape the influence of more than five hundred generations.

This is true, to-day, of the law-abiding majority; but the fact that so many of them have outwardly rejected the religious basis of standards which in principle they still accept, and that this rejection is manifest in what the newspapers write, the television programmes present and the theatre proclaims, has deeply affected the moral attitudes of the community. Many of the conventions which used to be widely respected were indeed of social, rather than moral or religious significance. It is not therefore surprising that the outlook of the majority, whose ideas are only subconsciously moulded by the teachings of Christianity, has been conditioned by a far- and wide-reaching change in their way of life, and in particular, by two recent developments. The first is the reduction, amounting almost to abolition, of censorship. The other is the belief that tolerance, or as some might call it, appeasement, is the first of all the Cardinal Virtues. There are those for whom it is almost the only one that matters.

He who presumes to judge the morals of others, singly or collectively, runs a grave risk of falling into the trap to which the Sermon on the Mount draws attention, that of beholding the mote in his brother's eye and failing to consider the beam in his own (or 'the great plank', as the authors of the New English Bible, fearing that the word 'beam' may be incomprehensible, prefer to put it). It is none the less difficult to compare the moral standards of two generations without judging them.

In 1952 plays, films and books were sternly censored. In some newspapers references to sex were by no means taboo, although others, such as the *Daily Express*, achieved a vast circulation without finding the sexual stimulation of its readers essential to success. This may have been because Lord Beaverbrook was a son of the Presbyterian manse and was alarmed by the prospect of Hell Fire. In all cases, however, details of sexual habits and aberrations were considered unprintable and four-letter words were still the exclusive, and private, prerogative of male society. Glossy magazines published photographs of nude ladies, but few existed for that sole purpose, and the photographs were demure by subsequent standards. Shops selling more prurient literature were disguised as chemists or purveyors of 'surgical belts'. Films bordering on the 'blue' were only available to the *cognoscenti*, and the Lord Chamberlain was in duty bound to ensure that nothing offensive to the most old-fashioned maiden aunt was performed on the stage. Homosexuality was illegal and the great majority thought any kind of perversion socially demoralising. The word 'kinky' had not been coined. On the other hand, prostitutes still paraded the streets, flaunting their wares illegally but, on the whole, with impunity; and since this kind of vice is ineradicable, it pursued the uneven tenor of its way underground.

Two of the stoutest bastions of morality have always been example and fear. When divorce was socially unacceptable, a married couple hesitated long before they parted. Even in 1950, although the war-time disruption of family life had been a severe trial to conjugal fidelity, there were less than 30,000 divorces in Great Britain. By 1973 the number, having steadily increased year by year, reached 113,000 and in 1975 it was nearly 130,000; nor was there any sign either of a down-turn in numbers or of any social inclination to disapprove. Even the churches, remaining formally insistent on the virtues of monogamy, were tending to accept the breakdown of marriage as a regrettable but unavoidable fact of life. The number of broken homes, broken for many causes in addition to divorce, grew larger in all classes of the community as one barrier after another crashed. Things that had once been thought shameful, or at least deeply distressing, came to be looked upon as natural.

There were many other ways in which example ceased to carry weight. The fear of inhibiting the young, who had for the most part long ceased to be inhibited, became an obsession. Pomposity was often equated with conviction, and priggishness with the definition of right and wrong. Thrift became a forgotten word as prices rose and saving was seen to be at the mercy of inflation. Books, magazines and films which would, in 1952, have been regarded as unwholesome, were no longer banned. Heroes were declared to have feet of clay, motives were almost always considered suspect, the authority of parents, school-teachers and of the law itself was held up to ridicule. The age of 'debunking' not only the hypocritical but the sincere was inaugurated.

Fear diminished too. Sexual immorality, and in particular promiscuity, was formerly held in check by the threats of venereal disease, unwanted pregnancy and, even in 1952, by a residual instinct that it was wrong. Penicillin, as Lord Moran once said, made 'lust safe for democracy'. The Pill, which came into general use in the 1960s, diminished worries about pregnancy. The immoralities of the famous, recorded daily in the newspapers, combined with the growing belief that continence and chastity were unwholesome as well as unnecessary, removed moral doubts which had been inherited or instilled. None of this prevented a sharp rise in the incidence both of venereal disease and of unwanted pregnancies, presumably because as the risks declined the numbers prepared to take them increased.

As wealth became more widespread, and materialism grew with

it, indulgences which had formerly been prohibitively expensive to all but the few came within reach of the many. The improvement of living standards for the majority, desirable as this was, left a still under-privileged minority discontented with their lot and envious of those who seemed ostentatiously better off than themselves. It was even less tolerable to be deprived when there were millions who could afford to indulge, and the fact was widely disseminated by the Media, than when indulgence had been confined merely to thousands and the fact much less publicised. It was more of a temptation than ever before to seize by force what an unjust society or a perverse fate withheld, and this temptation grew steadily less resistible as the fear of punishment was reduced.

If the new way of life, the rise of affluent society and impatience with old-fashioned values, have had much to do with the changes that have taken place, the abolition of censorship, heralded by many as the dawn of liberal good sense, cannot be disregarded. It began in the late 1950s when a Court of Law upheld a claim by the publishers of the unexpurgated edition of *Lady Chatterley's Lover* by D. H. Lawrence, until then banned in the United Kingdom, that the book was not obscene. This was the Charter of Permissive Society. It became respectable to worship at the altar of eroticism. Pornographic books and magazines, frequently printed in Scandinavia but soon matched by British producers, were displayed for sale on the bookstalls. The Lord Chancellor, Lord Gardiner, lent his puissant support to an attack on the theatrical censorship exercised by the Lord Chamberlain, whose authority to give or withhold licences was removed by Act of Parliament in 1968. Plays and reviews in which the sexual act was mimed on the stage, if not actually performed, attracted large audiences. Sadistic instincts, regaled in the past by public hangings and whippings, but suppressed by the derided Victorians, were offered a new outlet in films and literature which specifically catered for them.

By the 1970s there was little that was unprintable. Homosexuals, relieved of harsh legal penalties by a compassionate bill which Lord Arran introduced in the House of Lords, have formed associations to further their activities, have made the words 'queer' and 'gay' all but obsolete in their true sense, and by 1976 were actively campaigning to reduce the age of consent to homosexual practices.

Most people have forgotten what it means to be shocked. Indeed it is widely thought ridiculous, or even discreditable, to admit to such an emotion at all. The problem for those determined not to be shocked, but none the less rendered uneasy by what they see and hear, has become one of distinguishing the positively unwholesome from breaches of old-established, excessively repressive conventions which, whatever their justification in the social conditions of yesterday, are out of date in the changed circumstances of to-day.

Tolerance has become so highly regarded that those who themselves lead blameless or even chaste lives have been gradually indoctrinated in the fashionable creed that to criticise the morals of others is itself immoral. There have been in these twenty five years crimes of a horror seldom exceeded: the 'Moors' murders of innocent children, the details of which were unbearable to policemen hardened by long experience; the explosion of Irish bombs in public houses, killing and maiming the luckless customers; the death, after torture, of both Protestants and Catholics by their adversaries in Northern Ireland; the strangulation of a girl, Leslie Whittle, in the gallery of a public sewer. The general public who, in 1952, would have reacted with nausea to any of these atrocities, had grown accustomed to them twenty five years later and, scarcely remembering one as a yet more dreadful example was reported, turned with escapist resignation to the television screen or the sports pages of the newspapers. As often as not an excuse is sought for the criminal, and the sufferings of the victim are overlooked. The police are excoriated if so much as a bruise is detected on the body of a captured criminal, but the shooting of a policeman, or the murder of a night-watchman, is merely an unfortunate incident. The virtue of forgiveness is applauded, provided the trespass has been committed against others, and there is a growing body who would have reproved Christ for intolerance in turning the money-lenders out of the Temple.

There is another side of the coin which gleams brighter as the years go by. It reflects compassion, not just for the criminal, who has often been given little chance in life, but for the deformed, the unfortunate, the mentally unbalanced and the under-privileged. This compassion is fed by ideals of service to the community, at home and abroad, encouraged by personal initiative and, more often than not, financed by the generosity of commercial and industrial companies. The tradition that an individual with more than sufficient for his wants should give money to charity has been largely destroyed by the weight of taxation; but many who can no longer afford to write cheques give their service instead, and this is of greater benefit to the giver as well as to the receiver than the old habit of salving conscience by annual subscriptions. The age of affluence has not choked idealism; on the contrary the naturally generous instincts of the young often react against materialism, so that even those who, losing their way in a bewildering world take to drugs or find consolation as 'hippies', can sometimes be perceived to be in search of something more satisfying to the soul than industrial society, however elusive that something may be.

For generations war, with all its horrors, brought out some of the finest instincts in man: loyalty, service, tireless devotion to duty and above all, self-sacrifice. Want, too, and physical insecurity, bred strength and satisfaction in many of those who conquered them; for a man who succeeded in bringing up his family well, without the help of the community and against all the odds of hunger, illness and inadequate shelter, felt that he had won a great victory. Moreover, the constant demands of either fighting the enemy or struggling to survive left little time for other worries. Whatever the personal virtues that war and want did sometimes bring forth in the individual – and they were, after all, of small account when set against the main vile consequences – both the instigators of those virtues had, in 1952, disappeared from the British scene. War, on anything but a local scale, had been rendered obsolete by the sheer terror of nuclear fission; and want had been greatly reduced, though not totally abolished, by the Welfare State. Thus, two deep-rooted instincts of humanity, to fight and to struggle for survival, have been deprived of their traditional outlets. The instincts themselves are still there, and it is by no means easy for a peaceful, prosperous generation to turn them to good purpose.

The craving for physical achievement and for adventure, with no war to feed it, found little satisfaction in National Service, which was in any case brought to an end in 1964. Strenuous efforts were made to find alternative consumptions for energy and substitutes for pugnacity. A lead was given by the Duke of Edinburgh, whose Award for adventurous achievement has been eagerly sought. Many organisations, including The Outward Bound Trust, the National Playing Fields Association, the Boys' Clubs and the Youth Clubs, and activities such as gliding, ballooning, sea-faring, hiking and hill-climbing were mobilised in an endeavour to soothe youthful restlessness, and to appease the hunger for excitement, in competition with television, easy sexual stimulation, drink, drugs, gambling and the other amenities of a materially rich society.

Ideals of service to the community have certainly prospered. Voluntary Service Overseas has no shortage of young people eager to go to under-developed countries for a year or more in order to teach and render whatever kind of assistance may be required. In the United Kingdom itself groups of boys and girls, sometimes spontaneously and sometimes encouraged by their schools, increasingly devote holidays and leisure hours to helping the old, the crippled and the mentally retarded. While the newspapers daily report mugging, larceny and rebellion by teenagers and those in their early twenties, they seldom print an account of the selfless devotion shown by a far greater number in offering social services of varying descriptions and of untold value. There is nothing new in this: it is exciting to read about vice and it is dull to read about virtue. The virtuous themselves provide no exception to this general rule and it is, of course, argued that unless the circulation of the newspapers be maintained by the provision of the news their readers enjoy, there will cease to be a free Press.

There has thus been some sunshine to compensate for the darkness of rising violence and falling integrity. The last twenty five years have, indeed, presented contrasting pictures of genuine compassion and vile brutality, of tolerance and hypocrisy. Capital punishment has been abolished; corporal punishment, even for school-children, is often regarded with disfavour. Prisons have become more humane and juvenile delinquency is increasingly regarded as misfortune rather than crime. Genuine horror has been felt at the inhuman excesses practised by foreign dictatorial régimes, and large sums have been subscribed to such organisations as Amnesty International. Even greater sympathy has gone to the starving millions of Asia and gifts have poured into the coffers of Oxfam.

On the other hand, there has been no decrease, and perhaps an actual increase, in the number of battered wives and battered babies; robbery with savage violence is a daily occurrence; rape is all the rage; and many otherwise kind citizens have forgotten the meaning of the word charity in their dealings with coloured immigrants who have come to these shores to seek refuge from starvation and unemployment.

Tolerance is shown in the willingness of all classes of society to find extra-marital relations socially acceptable, to treat unmarried couples on the same basis as those who are married, to discard the slur of illegitimacy, to regard abortion with indulgence and to consider fornication a normal and indeed almost a desirable occupation. Hypocrisy of a contemptible kind has been displayed whenever a leading politician has been discovered, or even suspected, to have indulged in an activity which would have been condoned, or at least quickly forgiven and forgotten, elsewhere in society. It would doubtless be false to suggest that hypocrisy is in any way peculiar to the neo-Elizabethan age, for there have always been double standards in private as well as in public life. What is new is the width of the gap in those double standards, for lip service has ceased to be paid to a code of morality which was formerly the stated aim of respectable members of society, however wide successive generations might sometimes be of the target. Yet men and women continue to be pilloried in public for sins which their accusers no longer pretend to deprecate in private.

In 1957 there was a Bank Rate Tribunal. Allegations that inside information had been used for private gain were shown to be false, but not before personal and political aspersions, unseemly as they were unfounded, had been cast. In 1963 the Profumo affair was shamelessly enlarged in a successful intrigue to embarrass the Government of the day. An honest and public-spirited Minister, who had certainly acted unwisely, was accused of breaches of national security of which he was totally innocent, and driven by organised persecution to tell a lie in the House of Commons. In this instance, hypocrisy was promoted to a status even higher than it normally occupies, in order to score a point in the game of party politics; and the hounds were incited to the chase regardless of the pain suffered by the accused and the death of two men whose names were dragged into the limelight during the subsequent manhunt.

A steady, unchecked growth of crime has been responsible for a slowing down of the administration of justice, which had formerly been more expeditious in Britain than anywhere else on Earth, and for a strain on the resources of the police forces, which were not increased in size sufficiently to meet the calls on their services. The endeavours of the hard-pressed Commissioners of Police and the Chief Constables to remedy the situation have seldom been assisted by the Exchequer. In 1976 the Department of Employment was endowed with £95 million to provide jobs for unemployed school-leavers, but at the same time, because police cadets were for some inscrutable reason categorised as civilians, the efficient Police College at Hendon, submerged by applications for places from girls as well as boys, was instructed to reduce its complement of 700 by 40%. The total of the police forces in the Kingdom had indeed reached 110,000, but the Metropolitan Police in London were far short of the numbers required to meet the demand for their multifarious services, even when Wardens were appointed to relieve them of traffic control. Throughout the country there was one Civil Servant to every ten inhabitants; but there was only one policeman to every five hundred.

The reasons for the increase in criminal activities cannot easily be diagnosed. It is indisputable that young people are the worst offenders. 65% of those arrested for robbery in London during 1975 were aged between 10 and 20. Perhaps the emphasis on crime in the cinema, television, the newspapers and the paperback novels is much to blame. Perhaps the loosening of parental and school discipline has played a part. Perhaps the human instincts of aggression, formerly satisfied by war and the battle for economic survival, now find their outlet in robbery and violence. Perhaps the influence of Christianity has waned and that of Permissive Society has waxed. Perhaps, too, the benefits of the Welfare State have had a maleficent by-product: the insidious induction of the belief that 'the world owes me a living' and a consequential determination to acquire that living at whatever cost and by whatever means. Young people have also discovered that conviction for crime no longer carries the social stigma, or indeed the punitive aftermath, of which previous generations have been acutely aware.

These may or may not have been the causes. The results are clear from the statistics. In 1952 the total of all indictable crimes known to the police was 513,339. In 1975 it was a little over four times as high at 2,105,631. Robbery with violence, or threat of violence, rose more than eleven-fold from 1,002 to 11,311. The least inflated figure was homicide, including manslaughter and the killing of infant children. Of these there were 379 in 1952 and a mere 36% increase to 515 in 1975. In the Metropolitan District of London there had been 17,400 crimes in 1921, a year of strikes and unemployment. In 1975 there were 452,000 comparable offences and the police force available to detect and correct the criminals had 400 less men than in 1921. Whether the abolition of the Cat-o-Nine-Tails has any relevance to the story we shall never know; but in 1921, when that savage implement was periodically in use, there were in the London area 56 robberies with violence, for which alone (apart from attacks on prison warders) the Cat might be applied in retribution. In 1975 there were 4,500 such robberies in London, and some of those who perpetrated them were punished by suspended prison sentences.

The prison population, which was 33,700 in 1967, reached 64,800 in 1974. There were by then open prisons, and there were experimental institutions, such as Grendon, for prisoners of high intelligence and apparent readiness to reform; but the majority of the prisons were still grim Victorian edifices built in days when retribution rather than reformation was normally the motive behind a prison sentence. The police saw many criminals whom they had laboriously tracked down, often in circumstances of physical danger to themselves, cautioned or given suspended sentences on grounds which seemed to them derisory. Juries, bewildered by complicated evidence or bewitched by a clever Counsel for the Defence, acquitted half the alleged criminals on whose cases they were required to pronounce. Between 1967 and 1974 there was a vast rise in summary offences, in respect of which the proportion granted bail rose from 66% to 85%. In the same years the story for the more serious, indictable offences was almost identical. In 1967, 11,400 of the accused were remanded in custody, but the remaining 66% were allowed bail; and in 1974 a mere 13,300 were held in custody while 51,500 went out on bail, representing 79% of those accused of serious crime. The Judges and the Magistrates were not entirely to blame, for the prisons were full. Every Government announced its intention to build more prisons and to modernise the existing ones; every Government failed to find the money to implement its admirable intention.

The opinion of the chorus of sentimental constables in *The Pirates of Penzance* that a policeman's job is not a happy one was based on the conviction that criminals are at heart endearing creatures, and that when the enterprising burglar's not a-burgling, he loves to lie a-basking in the sun. There are now many more burglars with whom this theory can be tested (there were 99,579 burglaries in 1975) and the majority are rich enough to enjoy a sunbathing holiday on the Costa Brava. The modern constable, however, may be forgiven for feeling less sentimental towards them than his Gilbertian predecessor, for they do tend to be armed and aggressive. This has not deterred the police force, whose efficiency in catching malefactors has improved each year. In 1975 the Flying Squad arrested 1,224 people in London for serious crime and they caught a further 865 in the first six months of 1976. In one period of three weeks five gangs of armed bank robbers were seized, two of them by unarmed policemen, and during 1975 £2.5 million of stolen property was recovered in London. This activity required physical courage and involved the ultimate risk of death; for the modern burglar, and still more the bank robber, is seldom amenable to sweet reason.

The outlook of Society has changed, for better or worse, since 1952 so that in 1977 the attitude towards such matters as abortion, bigamy, homosexuality and obscenity bears little relation to that generally held twenty five years ago. In keeping with the times, the Criminal Law has been modernised and codified and it is under constant scrutiny by Committees, Commissions and the Home Office, in a sustained effort to remove anomalies and eliminate administrative inefficiency. The police, too, have been required to keep abreast of the tide which has swept away so many cherished prejudices. They have naturally adopted the philosophy of their own generation as well as its technological amenities, such as the Computer. They are taught to use as little force as possible and to believe that the prevention of crime is more important than the apprehension of criminals. They are told that even if they can win by physical power in the short run, other and subtler methods are more likely to prevail in the long run.

There are two particularly uncongenial additions to the tasks which the police forces, all over the country, have to perform. The first is to conduct, control and whenever possible pacify mobs of demonstrators. Those who confront them, assault them and call them 'pigs' are a small minority; but they are also an unpleasant minority, of a kind which was neither seen nor heard in 1952. They are a vicious minority too, for during political demonstrations in the three years from 1972 onwards, 297 police officers were injured, as opposed to 76 of the combatant demonstrators, and as many as 3,000 policemen were assaulted each year in the performance of their duties.

Opponents of American policy in Vietnam, supporters of industrial action (who were often not the industrial workers themselves), Maoists, Trotskyites, hysterical students and International Socialists shouted and screamed, kicked, bit, threw stones and set off fireworks under police horses. However, the general public made their sympathies clear. A series of four public opinion polls in 1974 and 1975 showed that the police were more trusted and respected than any other organisation in the country. In all four they received a steady 70% of the favourable votes, with a short lead over the medical profession, while the Trade Unions with some 15%, and the Nationalised Industries with still less, were invariably at the foot of the column. It was, however, discouraging for the police that the Courts, fearing to be accused of political prejudice, exonerated those violent demonstrators who were arrested or fined them insignificant sums. In 1972 there were 230 proved cases of assault on the police or other crimes of violence by demonstrators. Of the 230 found guilty, only 12 were sent to prison and even the worst offenders received sentences of three months or less. In 1973 none were sent to prison at all. As Sir Robert Mark has said: 'Conduct that would provoke widespread condemnation in a football hooligan is condoned in a political demonstrator.'

From March, 1973, onwards, the police forces have had to face a new challenge: terror. It began with a few members of the Palestine

Liberation Organisation in pursuit of prominent supporters of Israel, and a small, transient body of anarchists who called themselves the Angry Brigade. They were quickly identified and deported or arrested; but their place was taken by the fanatical and much more formidable Irish Republican Army. In the three years from 1973 to 1976 there were no less than 263 terrorist attacks, or attempted attacks, in England, Scotland and Wales. Public Houses were demolished by bombs, regardless of the innocence of the customers within; explosive devices were placed in the Tower of London, in Army Camps, outside London tube stations and in crowded shopping areas. Murder and assassination, the least fruitful of political gestures, were used as a method of intimidation by young Irishmen who were heedless of the damage to their cause, not only in Britain but in their principal supply bases, Southern Ireland and the United States. The police addressed themselves vigorously to this unexpected emergency. Their explosive experts, with help from the Army but at great personal risk, defused many of the 302 lethal devices planted by the terrorists, and by the mid-summer of 1976 130 suspects had been arrested throughout the country. To search for criminals among the mass of law-abiding Irishmen resident in Great Britain was a daunting assignment, but the dangerous needles were extracted one by one from the haystack and by the autumn of 1976 68% of the miscreants responsible for the London bombing outrages had been arrested and convicted.

At the Coronation the Archbishop placed the Sceptre in the Queen's right hand, naming it 'the ensign of kingly power and justice'. He then handed her the Rod with the Dove, 'the Rod of Equity and Mercy'. He said: 'Be so merciful that you be not too remiss. Punish the wicked, protect and cherish the just, and lead your peoples in the way wherein they should go.'

The traditional answer to crime is punishment. There are some offenders who must be locked away for the protection of society and others who may be deflected from misdeeds by the fear or actual infliction of penalties. However, during these twenty five years the conviction has grown that detection is in itself the most potent defensive weapon against most wrong-doers. The police have accepted this doctrine, and while there are cases of arrested malefactors being handled roughly, it remains the pride of the

British police that they are not expected or allowed to resort to the strong-arm methods employed by police forces elsewhere. They have had their failings: for instance corruption on a disturbing scale had to be eradicated from the CID. But apart from isolated incidents the British police can justly claim that they do not consider punishment of offenders, or the extraction of evidence by violent methods, to be within their province.

In 1952 flogging had only recently been abolished under the Criminal Justice Act of 1948. The birching of youthful offenders, except in the Isle of Man and at Eton College, was also regarded with increasing disfavour, and even Eton substituted the cane in due course. The conception that punishment was a retribution for crime was dying fast, and the argument was between those who believed it to be valid as a deterrent and those who maintained that it could only be justified at all if its effect was reformative. It was generally agreed that corporal punishment, at any rate by judicial order, was not reformative, and the majority in the House of Commons and the Civil Service believed it was not a deterrent either. Alternative methods of dealing with violent criminals, especially the young ones, were advocated: therapeutic treatment, probation, suspended prison sentences and, for the apparently incorrigible, short spells in a Detention Centre or longer training in Borstals and, as they were then called, Approved Schools, where until the late 1960s children in need of care and protection were all too often mixed with young criminals. In 1969 Parliament passed a Children's and Young Persons' Act which went further: it removed from Juvenile Courts the power to deal with delinquents by custodial sentences. The intentions were admirable but, as the statistics inexorably proved, they met with no positive response. There were quite a lot of smiles on the faces of quite a lot of young tigers.

It would have helped the police in their struggle to compete with the rising tide of crime if they had at least been able to secure more convictions, however restricted the subsequent penalties might have been. They had, it is true, less cause for complaint than some of their American colleagues, for in 1971 the New York Police Department were pained to record that out of 94,071 charges of felony, only 552 were brought to trial. Nevertheless, it was galling to see leaders and organisers of crime, against whom evidence had finally been procured, acquitted because of ancient judicial formalities which had been properly and humanely erected as barriers against the prosecution in days when there were some 200 offences punishable by death. Several of the most notorious criminals were acquitted because of some technicality which gave free rein to their ingenious Counsel, so that the police, who had worked hard to rid society of the infection they were spreading, were obliged to start all over again.

If it was increasingly accepted that the right policy was to free society, by long sentences of imprisonment, from a minority of dangerous robbers and the still more dangerous organisers of crime, while dissuading the remainder by an increased probability of detection, the question of how to deal with cold blooded murder gave rise to much debate. By the time of the Queen's accession, and indeed for many years before it, executions were rare. The majority of death sentences were commuted to life imprisonment. However, there was a growing feeling among the better-educated, though almost certainly not among the people as a whole, that hanging, like flogging, was outmoded and barbaric. There were a number of post-war cases which lent force and credence to this movement. Evans was found guilty and hanged for a murder almost certainly committed by the psychopathic Christie; a girl called Ruth Elles was hanged for shooting her unfaithful lover in the street and, incongruously enough, a generation which was beginning to demand equality between the sexes was more deeply shocked by the hanging of a woman than of any number of men; when a 16 year old boy, too young to be executed, shot a policeman, his accomplice, Bentley, whose finger had been nowhere near the trigger, was hanged; and, finally, there were many who believed that Hanratty, executed for a murder on the A6 road, was innocent.

In 1965, after a free vote in both Houses of Parliament, even the modified law of 1957, whereby capital murder was only applicable to poisoners and the murderers of policemen, was suspended. Because there was a strong minority in Parliament, and certainly a majority in the country, in favour of retaining capital punishment for certain offences, this act of abolition was to be automatically repealed unless Parliament decided to the contrary in five years' time. Mr Harold Wilson, like Mr Edward Heath and the Liberal leader, Mr Jeremy Thorpe, was a strong opponent of the death penalty. He did not wait until the full five years had expired. In December, 1969, the emotive question was submitted to Parliament once again, and a majority in both Houses voted for final abolition. The number of killings has increased, but by no means on a scale comparable with other crimes, and in 1977 Britain remains one of the countries least addicted to homicide.

Indeed, alarming though the crime statistics be, the British Isles, apart from Ulster, contain a generally law-abiding community by comparison with most other countries, even though the emphasis of this statement must, alas, be on the word comparison. The Judges and the police remain free from political interference. The statistics prove that the numbers of armed bank raids have shown a gratifying fall in the 1970s, from 65 in 1972 to 27 in 1975. The theft of cars remains unshakeably high, but that of lorries loaded with saleable goods was reduced by police action from over 350 in 1973 to less than 100 in 1975. Meanwhile compensation, on a more generous scale than ever before, was paid to the victims of crime. Thus, for instance, £3 million was awarded to wronged citizens in 1972. Even burglars began to enjoy less cheerful prospects than of old, for by 1976 one in three was arrested in the provinces and one in five in London; and those who robbed openly, with menaces or with violence, stood an even chance of being caught, though they also stood an even chance of being acquitted by the sentimental purveyors of justice. Juvenile gangs of 'muggers', some drawn from the discontented immigrant community, were, in 1976, still an unresolved problem and a source of danger after dark to middle-aged pedestrians in a number of London suburbs; but the safety of the streets in Britain, and of the householder too, compared favourably with that available in the large cities of every other democratic state.

The people are, nevertheless, perplexed and disturbed by the growth of crime and violence; for, whatever the comparisons with other countries, still more gravely afflicted, there is no doubt that a spirit of lawlessness and defiance possesses too many of the rising generation, while their elders adopt a laxer code of financial integrity. An increase of population by some four million; discontent among young immigrants and among the unemployed, of whatever colour and origin; more successful methods of detection: all these have made some contribution to swelling the crime statistics, but they are not a full explanation of the problem. There are deeper causes, and pre-eminent among them is the change in moral outlook and in social behaviour.

It is difficult not to conclude that there has been a grave decline in standards of integrity. Parliament and the Civil Service have, with some rightly publicised lapses, sustained their reputation for general incorruptibility. In local government, and in political gerrymandering at constituency level, there has been a marked deterioration in honesty of all kinds. No doubt the majority of Town Halls and local government bodies are still as pure as driven snow, or very nearly so; but the urge to grow rich quickly, often by dubious short-cuts, has produced a crop of property-speculation inter-sown with bribery on a scale seldom exposed since the 18th century. This has ravaged the good name of local government, especially in the Midlands, some of the Scottish burghs and the north-east of England. It reflects a deterioration in a country which was still, in 1952, the most incorruptible in the world. Its cause is, in part, the heavy burden of taxation, and the inability of hard-working men of initiative to receive and retain a just reward for their labours, but it is due above all to the careless disdain with which a whole generation has decided to treat the hitherto accepted standards of right and wrong.

Example stands high among the remedies. The British public, contemplating the unsavoury affair of Watergate, which forced an American President to resign and caused profound distress in a whole nation, cannot fail to find satisfaction in the incorruptibility of the British Crown and to tighten their allegiance to a Queen who has never, for one moment, bent before the less edifying winds which have blown in the United Kingdom.

CHAPTER 13

Teaching and Healing

Opinion may be divided whether the quality of education has changed. There can be no doubt at all about the quantity. By 1952 Mr R. A. Butler's Education Act of 1944 had already gone far to modernise and rationalise an outdated educational system in which a high proportion of the children were taught in Church Schools, often in a poor state of repair and gravely affected by financial stringency. This great Act of Parliament made Secondary Education available to all. It envisaged the gradual lengthening of the educational years so that eventually all children might remain at school or college from 5 to 18; and until this could be achieved it proposed that young people should be released from industry for further part-time education. Nursery Schools were built for children under five and in 1947 the school-leaving age was raised from 14 to 15. In 1972 it was extended to 16.

Meanwhile, new universities appeared like mushrooms in an August meadow. In 1952 there were a number of university colleges, such as Hull and Exeter, offering London degrees, but only thirteen fully fledged English universities, of which the latest to open, four years previously, had been Nottingham. There were four in Scotland, the most recent dating from 1583; one in Wales and one in Ulster. In the next twenty five years, twenty new universities were founded in England, four in Scotland and one in Ulster. The University of Wales extended the scope and size of its several dispersed colleges, and so did the University of London.

The educational explosion outpaced the population explosion, for the 50.4 million inhabitants of the United Kingdom in 1952 had but grown to 55.6 million at the 1971 census and, with continuing immigration, to some 56 million in 1977. There has been, however, a disproportionate increase in the population under twenty so that a total of 7.4 million school-children in 1952 has become one of over 11 million twenty five years later, and the

70,000 students at universities in Great Britain nearly quadrupled. There are almost twice as many school-teachers, who are more than twice as discontented; there are thousands of new primary and secondary school-buildings; and the cost of education rose from £444 million in 1952 to over ten times as much, £4,864 million, in 1974. If due allowance be made for inflation, the increase in expenditure is still vast and represents more than twice as high a proportion of the Gross National Product.

This reform, innovation and expenditure should have resulted in a better educated nation; but there are few who would assert with conviction that it has, except at university level. It is difficult to decide whether the blame lies with the quality of the teaching, the steep climb in the Sixth Form population arising from Mr Butler's 1944 Act, the policy of the Department of Education and Science or the failure of successive Governments to make a firm, bi-partisan choice between a variety of educational theories. Those who demand that all children should be educated alike are confronted by opponents who believe that parents should have freedom of choice in their children's schooling. Some have thought it wrong that the apparently intelligent should be divided from the less patently gifted; others have felt with equal intensity that it is wicked to hold back the quick so as not to bruise the sensitivities of the slow. Nothing excites deeper antagonisms and stirs more cantankerous temper than education. Thus, whilst the theorists have done battle in Parliament and in the Local Educational Authorities, the children have suffered. Even in the Secondary Schools the average size of classes has remained high, and in many Primary Schools the teachers have so lost control that both learning and discipline have vanished. Juvenal's famous aphorism *Sed quis custodiet ipsos custodes*, (who shall be the custodian of the custodians themselves) was never more applicable to any body of men and women than to those responsible for British educational development in this generation.

The main argument, by no means always a well-reasoned one, has been between the supporters and opponents of the Comprehensive System. Those who look with antipathy at large schools teaching bright and dull children in the same class-rooms at the start of their Secondary Education, often forget that the better known Public Schools also bear a certain similarity to Comprehensive Schools, catering for various standards of intelligence, though the children have been allowed to wait till 13 rather than 11 before taking their entrance examinations and have had the advantage of such select and expensive teaching for the previous five years that only the real dunderhead fails to gain admission and reach at least 'O' Level standard. For him or her, if the parents can afford it, special independent schools, catering for the slow-developer or the slow-witted are available; but the State Comprehensive Schools must absorb, together with children of high or average ability, some whose Intelligence Quotient is exceptionally low. Nevertheless, it may be argued that Eton and Harrow were Comprehensive Schools before the State even contemplated such institutions; and Winchester, which demands a higher entrance standard than its competitors, has long been a more costly Manchester Grammar School for clever sons of the well-to-do.

Equally, those who believe that all State Secondary Education should be comprehensive, and saw their wishes met by a bill laid before Parliament in 1976, choose to be oblivious of the proved merits of the State-aided Grammar Schools. Instigated by a blind addiction to egalitarian ideology, they campaigned successfully for the conversion of schools with a long-established record of excellence, precisely at a time when good educational results were being scantily achieved in the State system. It was an act of iconoclasm comparable to Henry VIII's dissolution of the monasteries, though the motives were doubtless purer.

In 1961 only 5% of the children went to Comprehensive Schools. In 1970 the figure had risen to 32% and in September, 1976, to 70%. By then forty one of the ninety seven local educational authorities were already operating fully comprehensive systems, a further eighteen had submitted proposals, and only eight of the remaining thirty six had flatly refused. The eight, undaunted by the new Education bill, which would make it compulsory for them to abandon the selection of clever children for Grammar Schools at the age of eleven, while relegating the remainder to Secondary Modern Schools, were encouraged by events at Tameside in Lancashire. There the Judiciary overrode the decision of the Secretary of State to install a Comprehensive System against the express wish of the electorate. A new Minister, Mrs Shirley

Williams, nevertheless persisted with the demand for uniformity and ordered the eight recalcitrant authorities to comply.

Apart, however, from the folly of destroying the excellent, well-tried Grammar Schools in the unhallowed cause of total uniformity, the supporters of Comprehensive Education have had much in their favour. The aptitude, or lack of it, shown by a child of eleven is by no means a sure sign of ultimate ability; and it has been common experience that some apparently bright children subsequently become a drag on their Grammar School contemporaries while others, stigmatised as duller-witted but in reality late developers, have been unjustly handicapped. Comprehensive Schools have succeeded in postponing the decision about a child's academic future and have proved that, even if it be true that children of the highest intelligence would derive more benefit from a Grammar School, most children find their own level of capacity within a Comprehensive School, as they do in a Public School.

Whereas in the 1950s some 30% of the children educated by the State were sent to Grammar Schools and the remainder to Secondary Modern Schools, by the mid-1970s over two thirds were going to Comprehensive Schools and undoubtedly enjoying greater opportunities than so many of their predecessors who had been denied all possibility of access to Sixth Form education. The bitter grievance of the parents of children refused entrance to a Grammar School was removed; but at the same time the uneven quality of the Comprehensives has meant that, as has been the case in the United States, families tended to move away from areas where the Comprehensive School seemed, in their eyes, to be below the level they desired for their children. In many cases this move has been made on racial grounds, thus accentuating an already acute social problem.

Owing to the huge and rapid expansion of higher educational facilities in the 1960s, many who would have chosen to be Secondary School-teachers were lured away to the universities, polytechnics and colleges of further education where, for their professional purposes, better opportunities and higher prestige were to be found. This has been a serious loss to the schools, but the drain was partially halted by the Houghton pay award. Since teaching is, like nursing, a vocation, the number of first-rate teachers is in any case limited. The struggle to find suitable staff for the 38,000 schools in the

Kingdom has been hampered both by the inability of the Exchequer, faced by recurring economic crises, to raise the teachers'
pay to a level as attractive as it should be and by the occasional
eruption on to the scene of a minority of strange, wild and politically
motivated teachers in such a way as to excite critical attention by the
Press and a sense of outrage in the general public.

This abduction of teachers by the universities and polytechnics
is only one among the effects of the expansion of higher education,
which resulted, in large part, from the recommendations of the
Committee on Higher Education. This sat under the chairmanship
of Lord Robbins and presented its report in 1963. The Committee,
convinced that the availability of a university education to only
4% of the adolescent population was a national disgrace, proposed a
large and immediate expansion. Their deliberations began at a
time when a false but exceedingly bright dawn of prosperity was
illuminating the horizon and the economists were forecasting a
steady annual increase of 4% in the Gross National Product. The
Sixth Form population of the schools was bulging to bursting point
because of the post-war rise in the birth-rate, and a substantial new
outlet to the universities seemed to be an urgent necessity.

The universities, new and old, responded with alacrity. Between
the Queen's accession and the Robbins report, Southampton, Hull,
Exeter, Leicester, Sussex, Keele, East Anglia and York had opened
academic doors. Lancaster and Essex followed in the year after the
report was published, and there were another ten by the end of
1967. Between them they accepted even more students than the
Robbins Committee had recommended. They started post-graduate
courses of one kind and another, especially for those going into
industry. They welcomed students of both sexes. Even Oxford and
Cambridge, which were traditionally misogynist and had always
segregated such women as they felt obliged to admit, weakened to
the extent of allowing Trojan Fillies to be drawn within the walls
of some of their most renowned colleges. It was widely acknowledged that there was a shortage of trained engineers and practical
scientists, and when Mr Anthony Crosland, Secretary of State for
Education in 1965, announced the creation of thirty one polytechnics, one important objective was to produce technicians of
high quality. The polytechnics were, in the main, to be built on the

foundations of existing technical colleges, but to be populated by a greatly increased number of full-time students.

In consequence of these expansive and expensive decisions, the 4% of school-leavers gaining entry to a university when the Robbins Committee reported, had nearly doubled ten years later, and as many again found places at polytechnics, technical colleges, colleges of art and other establishments of a similar kind. In 1977 over 500,000 young men and women are receiving higher education in one form or another and it is intended that the figure should reach 600,000 by the end of the decade. The strain on available resources, both human and financial, has become almost too great to bear.

An exciting and imaginative innovation was the Open University, founded by Royal Charter in 1969, which began its courses in 1971. The inspiration came in large part from Jennie Lee, Aneurin Bevan's widow, who also served her country well by the encouragement which she gave, in her Ministerial capacity, to the Arts. The cost to students, a tenth of whom are given financial assistance, is only a quarter of that at a normal university, and degrees, requiring four years' study, are awarded in six faculties, although the courses are broad-based and there is no narrow specialisation. Tuition is mainly by correspondence course, but the experiment has been made of providing about one tenth of it by means of lectures on radio and television. The facilities offered by the Open University were received with enthusiasm, appealing in the main to mature students, as a spare-time occupation, rather than to the young. It was intended to be a university for the Workers; but in the event it has been used principally by the professional classes, and it is notable that a third of those seeking its degrees are school-teachers.

The resident universities and polytechnics have made their premises available for Open University Summer School courses, and there is provision for tutorial sessions at study-centres throughout the country. The proportion of students failing their examinations and deciding not to try again has been as low as 10%, with about the same number leaving before they completed their courses. In 1977 the Open University has 51,000 students, whereas London University, with its variegated, far-flung spread of colleges, specialist Schools and Institutes, has 37,000 internal students and 33,000 external students. Oxford registers 12,000 undergraduates and Cambridge 11,000. The number at both Manchester and Leeds is 10,000 and the other Universities are smaller still. The Open University is not so much the university of the Second Chance as of the Second Qualification; and as such it fills a gap and provides a service of value to the community.

Great as the increase in higher education has been in twenty five years, one of the important objectives of expansion has not been achieved. In the early 1950s leading industrialists were aware that there was an alarming shortage of young scientists and engineers, and that the universities were not producing graduates keen and suitable to swell the ranks of industrial or commercial management. Much enthusiasm was shown in an endeavour to remedy matters. The University Grants Committee spent great sums to finance the building of laboratories and workshops. Some of the largest companies, instigated by the chairman of Vickers, Lord Weeks, subscribed £1.5 million pounds to improve the scientific facilities available at the Public Schools. Sir Winston Churchill, immediately after his retirement from active politics, lent his name and energies to the foundation of Churchill College at Cambridge which would, he hoped, contribute to the provision of scientists and technologists of the highest quality. For a while these labours seemed to be bearing fruit and it was noted that graduates of ability, who in days gone by might have chosen the Civil Service as a career, were preferring industrial and commercial opportunities.

The trend was short-lived, although successive Governments did their best to encourage it. Mr Anthony Crosland's decision to establish thirty two polytechnics was inspired by a conviction that a vast increase in the output of qualified technologists was essential to the national economy. Ten years after his initiative, too many students in the polytechnics were studying the arts and the humanities, school-leavers were showing little interest in science or engineering, and the places available for chemists and physicists at the universities were being filled by grateful foreigners. Churchill College and other institutions of high scientific repute maintained and indeed improved their record; but young men and women of intelligence found dabbling in the mystique of sociology and other comparable Social Sciences more to their taste than the rigours of science and engineering.

Even those who did study the subjects so urgently needed in the practical interest of the national economy showed a marked preference for pure scientific research over the applied science required by industry. Rather than seek their fortunes in the rough, competitive but remunerative world of business they looked for openings in the calmer fields of academic life or the enclosed, and not particularly lush, pastures of local government; and Whitehall no longer needed to worry about recruits for the Civil Service.

Many people believe that the purpose of education should be to develop the mind, just as games and gymnastics develop the body. If this be so, utilitarian education, aiming to teach what will be of practical value to an adult, may in some respects scarcely be an education at all. Since most young people of the present generation are not content solely with the mental gymnastics which the long-accepted disciplines of mathematics and the Classics offer them, often preferring to explore less exacting subjects such as Sociology, it is arguable that the universities cater for the wrong age-group. It may be that school-leavers ought not to become undergraduates and that only after several years of practical experience in the world should they be admitted to universities, which would then, once again, revert to their medieval function of teaching wisdom, logic and philosophy. These are all, without question, in short supply to-day. Whether or not this be either practicable or desirable, it is certainly true that as the new Elizabethan age progresses, and the universities, polytechnics and colleges of further education multiply, many of their inmates are so concerned with the practical benefits they might obtain from their studies that they have neither the time nor the inclination to care for the wider values which higher educational institutions were once expected to teach and to propagate. Yet, all too many have sought those practical benefits in areas which are of little or no value to commerce, industry and the economy.

During these years the undergraduates at all the new Universities, and the majority even at Oxford and Cambridge, took to describing themselves as students, a word traditionally associated with foreign universities. In spite of their strong dislike of the United States during the Vietnam war, they even applied the American word *campus* to their own colleges and universities. This was of doubtful wisdom, because during the 1960s and early 70s, there was violence and indiscipline of so unbridled a nature in the European and American universities that the very word student acquired a distasteful sound in the ears of the adult population. The prejudice was in large measure unjustified since, although there were occasional student disorders in the United Kingdom and a number of 'sit-ins' and occupations of premises, especially at one or two of the new polytechnics and in the London School of Economics, the diligence of the great majority of students was undoubted and, by continental standards, the troubles were mild.

The reason for comparative calm in British universities is the lavishness of the facilities offered. The average ratio of staff to students in the establishments of higher education is as low as 1 to 8, and in subjects such as medicine and biology, 1 to 7. As a result, a far higher percentage of students win degrees than in universities abroad, and in the early 1970s only 14% were failing to do so. Thanks to consistently high expenditure by the University Grants Committee, there is none of the overcrowding such as that at the Sorbonne, where the cramped living conditions were a primary cause of the student violence in the streets of Paris in May, 1968; or at the University of Rome where 100,000 students are housed like the occupants of a giant ant-hill. Good facilities for sport are almost always available in Britain, and the Students' Unions receive a subsidy from the Government four times greater than that provided for the equivalent students bodies in Germany. Finally (though as inflation has driven the cost of living upwards, there are constant complaints of the inadequacy of student grants) 19 out of 20 British undergraduates are now subsidised by the tax- and rate-payers, and their individual grants were, for most of the period, more generous than those of their continental contemporaries. Such disturbances as occurred in Britain were seldom organised on ideological grounds, but were almost always in demand of higher grants or of lower rents for University accommodation.

Thus, the face of the British educational system has changed a great deal between 1952 and 1977. Whether the State or the universities were wise in electing to expand higher education so fast and so far; whether Industry in Britain will learn, as it has in America, to take advantage of opportunities for co-operation with the universities and polytechnics; whether school-leavers will decide, or be persuaded, to prefer for their further educational studies subjects of greater advantage to the national economy; whether the acute dissension in determining the form of Secondary Education will result in the emergence of that happy compromise by which the British believe their divergencies are invariably consummated; whether the problems of overcrowding, indiscipline and inadequate teaching in the Primary Schools will be solved, in spite of cuts in public expenditure, and the solution helped by the resort of so many Primary School-teachers to the facilities of the Open University: all these questions are posed by the changes that have taken place. The answers await the second quarter-century of the Queen's reign.

There can, however, be no doubt that some of the problems, and some of the opportunities also, arise from a radical change in the outlook and upbringing of the children themselves. The triumph of tolerance over negative discipline, the new environment of so many families, the influence of television and the speed of communication: these have contributed to a precocious sophistication and a greater freedom of juvenile choice, to which must be added earlier physical development due to better and more scientific feeding. They have also led to impatience and a decreasing willingness to accept either the conditions or the philosophy which an earlier generation would have believed to be ordained either by society or by God and therefore, in either case, to be indisputable.

Having educated the children, on a wider if not necessarily a better basis than ever before, it is an important function of the State to provide for their physical well-being.

In February, 1952, the National Health Service, conceived by Beveridge and delivered by Bevan, had been in existence for a little over three years. The first of its kind in the world, it not only provided free medical attention for the entire community, but performed the essential service of maintaining the hospitals, which could no longer have been financed and modernised by charitable gifts or Local Authority contributions as had been the case before the war. Aneurin Bevan had been an intelligent, enthusiastic and competent Minister of Health. He had established the Health Service on solid foundations and, after some hesitation on the part of the doctors, he had won their collaboration by agreeing to leave them independence and allow them to retain their private practice both in their own consulting rooms and in the private wings of the hospitals.

So it remained for the first twenty years of the Queen's reign; but there was a growing realisation in medical as well as Governmental circles that the country had been given a Hospital Service rather than a Health Service, for the emphasis was on treating illness rather than preventing it. There were indeed discoveries and developments of a scientific kind, such as Sir Peter Medawar's triumphant and Nobel Prize-winning advances in the field of immunology, and the constantly more successful early-warning treatment of cancer; but deaths from cancer increased from 98,000 in 1952 to 135,000 in 1973, and those from coronary diseases almost doubled in the period. The fact that, to all intents and purposes, tuberculosis was eliminated (deaths falling from 20,000 in 1952 to 1,600 in 1973) was not sufficient compensation. Primary care, preventive medicine and a better integration of those responsible for health at all the stages of medical attention were seen to be essential.

In 1973 Mr Heath's Government introduced a bill, the provisions of which became operative on 1st April, 1974. A radical change was made in the organisation of the Health Services and the direction of their activities. There had been a notable absence of co-ordination between the services offered to National Health patients by the General Practitioners, the hospitals to which they might be sent for treatment, and the Local Authorities responsible for much of the after-care required when the patient went home. The main objectives of the new Act were to bring these three stages of medical treatment closer together, ensuring that they were effectively under the same authority, and also to facilitate planning on a wider and more effective basis.

The old Regional Hospital Boards were replaced by fourteen Regional Health Authorities, with additional bodies for Scotland and Wales; and beneath them two additional tiers were established, the Area and the District Health Authorities. The principle was good, the intention was wise and, in general, the British National Health Service retained its reputation of being the best anywhere in the world. However, an element of rigidity was introduced by the new system, and the Health Authorities were burdened with too much bureaucratic control. Central command had certainly been desirable, but excessive centralisation, which is quite a different matter, was imported with it. Moreover, most of the old members of the Hospital Management Committees, and the Boards of Governors of the undergraduate teaching-hospitals, who had given their time and their energies on an entirely voluntary basis, retired from the scene. They were largely replaced by representatives of the Local Authorities whose interest in financial and administrative detail sometimes tended to be greater than their care for the quality of the hospital service. In spite of this, the famous teaching-hospitals, with their traditional concentration on excellence, struggled to maintain their high standing; but it was noticeable that the spirit of local pride and enthusiasm showed a tendency to wilt as the hospital lost its individuality and became part of an amorphous group.

In the 1970s there has been, for the first time, a head-on clash between the Medical Consultants and the Minister, Mrs Castle. The doctors are the only middle-class profession which, by threatening to withdraw labour, can face a Government with a challenge comparable to that of the miners, the electrical workers or the seamen. They were incensed by Mrs Castle's determination to close the private wards, or pay-beds, in hospitals, and the obvious desire of some Labour Ministers to abolish private practice altogether. There were many other considerations. In the case of the junior doctors, who also challenged Mrs Castle, it was largely a question of inadequate remuneration. In the case of their seniors, there was the unbearably high level of taxation, their professional dislike of Ministerial direction (combined, it must in many cases be admitted, with a personal antipathy to Mrs Castle herself), a feeling that their place in society was being undermined and, perhaps above all, a profound disquiet at the undermining of their clinical freedom – their right to devote effort to the quality of their service rather than be obliged to dilute and, as they thought, debase it. The battle was drawn, at least temporarily; and whatever their worries about the future, and the declared determination of some of the younger and more ambitious to emigrate, the doctors have left the Government in no doubt that they are a formidable body with whose interests and convictions liberties should not lightly be taken.

The nurses, underpaid and usually overworked, continue to provide Britain with a service unique in its quality and high vocational standards. The stresses and strains in the Health Service have grown no weaker as the years have gone by; and indeed Britain, the first nation ever to provide such a service for its citizens, and for foreign visitors as well, has ended by spending a smaller element of its national income on health than do most other Western countries. Nevertheless, British medicine as a whole remains as good as any to be found, and if, as is certainly true, there is no better country in which to suffer the misfortune of illness, much of the credit is due to the nurses whose selfless devotion is as evident in 1977 as it was in 1952.

CHAPTER 14

Moving with the Times

General de Gaulle, surveying the world of the 1960s with the Olympian detachment which was his hallmark, said that there was nothing startling about the changes that had taken place, for there had never been a generation in which there were no changes: what was new was the rate of acceleration of change. This has been notably true of physical communications, both in their speed and in their availability.

At the Queen's accession there were no motorways in the United Kingdom. There were woods and fields where the M-Routes, with their three-lane carriage-ways, now cut through the country-side. Motorists driving from London to Scotland drove wearily up the twisting, frequently narrow Great North Road, forcing their way through the leisurely local traffic of Stevenage and Stamford, Grantham, Newark and Doncaster until they became enmeshed in the apparently immovable jams of Darlington, Durham and Newcastle. Those heading westwards braved the hazards of Slough, and travellers aiming south-westwards found themselves locked for a whole hour in the main street of Staines. Battling north-westwards along Watling Street, the motorist was instructed to reduce his speed to an impossible 5 m.p.h. at Markyate and if, after a slow progress through the Five Towns, he reached the seething outskirts of Manchester or Liverpool fractionally less exhausted than those heading north or west, or struggling through Maidstone and Ashford to Folkestone, he owed his comparative comfort to the Romans who built Watling Street, like all their roads, straight.

Trains were a less tiring means of transport, but the smuts from the steam engines poured through open windows, and there was little difference between the time-tables of 1952 and those of 1900. It is true that by continental standards, British trains moved fast indeed, but it was only the exceptional and well-advertised long distance trains, like the *Flying Scotsman* and the *Cornish Riviera*

Express, which outdid their 19th century predecessors; and their improvement on the times of those running between the two world wars was negligible.

It was already possible to fly to Edinburgh, Glasgow or Belfast; but few had adjusted themselves to anything so dashing and dangerous. Those of Her Majesty's subjects who wished to go overseas could, and normally did, make use of the vast fleet of liners leaving weekly for New York, India, Cape Town and the Far East. The Blue Riband of the Atlantic was the undisputed possession of the two biggest ships in the world, the Cunard liners, *Queen Mary* and *Queen Elizabeth*. So popular and profitable were their five-day Atlantic crossings that new ships, like the *Caronia*, launched by Princess Elizabeth at the end of 1947, had been built to relieve the pressure on '*the Queens*'. The famous P & O liners all but monopolised the three-weeks' voyage through the Suez Canal to India and the Union Castle Line had successfully struggled to better their traditional fortnight's run to Cape Town. Those in a hurry could already fly to New York in the Boeing *Clippers*, but it was an eighteen-hour flight, with wearisome fuelling stops at Shannon and Gander during which the heavy-lidded passengers were mercilessly herded into inhospitable transit sheds and offered synthetic orangeade by way of compensation. Flights to Africa, entailing stops every few hundred miles, were slow and uncomfortable. Those who ventured to fly to Australia, taking a week or more in the process, were rightly acclaimed as heroes.

During the next twenty five years the developments were such that it seems as if not one generation but whole centuries have been spanned. Through the length and breadth of England concrete motorways, with their long succession of blue boards notifying the next exit or periodical service stations (including restaurants as aesthetically dissatisfying as they are gastronomically deplorable), have consumed countless acres of arable land but have enabled the motorist to reach his destination quickly, although it has been his fate to exchange the exasperation of traffic jams for the less painful, if not necessarily less dangerous, monotony of long, fast driving.

On the railways, speed and the cleanliness of diesel engines and electrified tracks are a change of revolutionary excellence qualified by an increase in the cost of fares which has dismayed the traveller and yet failed to balance the budget of the British Railways Board. In the air, the facilities offered to passengers in 1977 are unrecognisable by comparison with those of 1952. Internal flights, with shuttle services to such towns as Manchester and Glasgow, have become regularly accepted and much utilised. Every day at Heathrow and Gatwick, Luton, Manchester and Prestwick, jet-airliners, still in their prototype infancy when the reign began, lift thousands of passengers in a few hours to destinations which in 1952 were normally reached in days. The noble *Queens* have been dismantled and sold to foreign hoteliers, the *Queen Elizabeth* sinking to a fiery grave in Hong Kong. Her replacement, *The Queen Elizabeth II*, is employed in expensive cruises and those who choose to travel by sea to Cape Town do so for therapeutic reasons alone. Supersonic flight has been established and passengers in *Concorde* find themselves moving their watches back two hours on arrival in Washington. Man is on the way to the conquest not only of distance, but of time.

Telephone conversations were improved in speed and efficiency by the introduction of the STD system, enabling calls to be made direct to destinations at home and abroad; but there has been a marked deterioration in postal services, the reliability of which seem to fall in inverse proportion to the rise in cost. Thus, for instance, a letter from Cambridge to London in the 1880s was delivered eight hours after posting, bearing nothing more formidable than a penny stamp; by the 1930s, for a penny-halfpenny, a letter posted before 6.00 p.m. in London was sure to be delivered anywhere south of the Forth by the first post on the following morning; in 1952 the cost had risen to twopence-halfpenny, but there was no marked deterioration in delivery. Late in 1976 the Post Office was, in deference to the Government's appeal to assist in halting inflation, valiantly proposing to maintain the cost of first class postage stamps at 8½p, of which the equivalent in shillings and pence would be over 1s. 9d.; and now a writer may count himself fortunate if his letter, bearing such a costly tribute to the Exchequer, is received less than twenty four hours after its despatch.

The days of letter writing, apart from business letters and demands for contributions to charity, are evidently numbered. From the point of view of historians, the gradual demise of the long, manuscript letter written by eminent men and women to their friends, families and sweethearts will be a loss so grave that it is questionable whether biographers, dependent on film- and tape-recordings, will penetrate deeper than the surface or portray anything but the public face of their subject. Travelling has become easy and rapid, long telephone conversations are already an ingrained habit; and the greater the facilities of modern technology, the less time is found for the quiet reflection and undisturbed solitude which are essential to a well-conceived letter. It may be that a fall in the standards of literary composition will be among the by-products of the decline of the letter as a means of private communication; for the writing of letters is a valuable exercise in the imaginitive use of language.

Britain has taken little part in the space programme: the flights in orbit of the Earth, the landings on the Moon and on Mars, and the exploration of Venus, and even Jupiter, which have been the wonders of the world in the 1960s and 70s. Joddrel Bank, where Sir Bernard Lovell's Observatory was established, made a useful contribution by plotting signals, and the satellites *Skynet* and *Ariel* launched by the GEC-English Electric Company in 1974 were comparable in advanced technology to anything devised by the Americans or the Russians. This was widely acknowledged, but only the United States and the Soviet Union had the resources to conduct the expensive research, and implement the still more expensive programme of building and launching the rockets and satellites. The wealth of the United States, as constantly replenished as the Widow's Cruse, bore the strain with apparent ease: the Russian Government restricted their people's consumption (already held at a level not easily distinguishable from austerity to pay the cost of an expanding army, navy and air force) in order to take an active part in the costly discoveries and to avoid the risk of being deemed inferior to their American rivals. Britain, which in 1952 would have been loth to admit any substantial inferiority either to the United States or to the Soviet Union, has by 1977 renounced all lingering pretence to an equal strength and, in common with the other independent European nations, has stood back from the contest, admiring the results and profiting at least to the extent that she was among the first to launch *Telstar* communications satellites and to utilise the opportunities they provide for improved wireless and telephonic communications.

The dissemination of news and opinions has been affected by the infiltration of television into almost every home. It has become the most powerful influence on the thought and habits of the people in the present reign. It has helped to mould their views, improve their knowledge, determine their choice of goods and services and make or mar their political leaders. It has introduced new opportunities and also new dangers. The opportunities include broadcasts in schools, the Open University lectures and access to information on a variety of subjects, well presented and illustrated, about which most people would have had no incentive to read. One of the less obvious dangers is that, however impartial the debate, viewers are often presented with conclusions as packaged, ready-made and synthetic as as the food they buy in the supermarkets. Those who read a a serious book may retain in their memory a summary of its conclusions. Those who read a summary retain nothing but an indistinct impression: and the serious programmes on television are all too often summaries.

The revolution in the scope and speed of physical communication and the arrival of television were not the only important changes. Advances in technology, the increasing size of business organisations, the complexity of social and fiscal innovations, the speed of travel and the improvement of telephone and telex services: all these, instead of simplifying the life of the individual, have added to the number of his preoccupations, widened the field of his activities and complicated the nature of his work. Computers and calculating machines save the time of clerks and remove the need for much pencil and paperwork, as well as reducing the training in mental agility which arithmetic provides; but those who had spent hours adding and subtracting, filling in ledgers and writing up books, have been pitch-forked into new fields of activity. In many cases these have put a heavier strain on their capacity and deprived them of the slow, but often satisfying, sense of achievement that a day's routine, like an afternoon's relentless weeding of the flowerbeds, offers to the unambitious who are, after all, in the majority. In addition, a new and formidable obstacle has begun to be apparent: the capacity of the language to convey meaning and the ability of men and women to make the best use of it.

It was ironical that precisely when British political influence was declining, and the country's industrial and commercial power was at least temporarily in eclipse, the English language became firmly established as that of first importance in the world. The countries with the largest territories and populations, China and the Soviet Union, closed their frontiers and were more concerned with the export of their ideologies than of their language. The Indian subcontinent and the greater part of Africa, confronted by a hotchpotch of mutually incomprehensible dialects, adopted English for the purpose of internal communication. Countries such as Nigeria, with some four hundred distinct languages, had no alternative, repugnant though it might be to the more dedicated nationalists, to continue using the speech of the former Colonial rulers. Kenya announced that Swaheli was the national tongue, but it was scarcely the language for modern commerce or for international negotiation. The Irish continued to assert the validity of Erse, but in practice confined its application to street names and the less important official documents. The South Africans intensified the use of their late 19th century invention, Afrikaans, to the annoyance of half the country's white population and all its black inhabitants. The French, conscious that their beautiful language had been for hundreds of years the mark of an educated man, whatever his native tongue, and the instrument of civilised intercourse between the nations, fought an offensive delaying action worthy of Napoleon himself; but neither the pleas of President Pompidou to the European Community nor the 'anti-franglais' decrees of Valérie Giscard d'Estaing could halt the advance of the English language. After a struggle lasting a hundred and fifty years, the British have had to admit defeat by Buonaparte in the battle of Decimalisation and not much better than a drawn battle over Metrication. Tons are being replaced by tonnes, and pounds, whether Troy or *Avoir du Poids*, are at their last gasp; but the decision of Waterloo has not been wholly reversed, for airports throughout the world announce in English the arrival and departure of flights, whether or not they carry British or American passengers, and it could be claimed that the Old Guard had finally surrendered when Air-France took to making announcements in English on flights between Paris and Madrid.

Since the English language has a far larger vocabulary than

French, German or Spanish, it should be the best choice for a world in which increasingly complicated processes, as well as increasingly diffuse thoughts, have to be explained. That it falls far short of perfection in this respect is partly because this is an age of specialists, and it is difficult for the specialist, in whatever tongue he speaks, to explain a complicated formula in words which are comprehensible to a layman. Thus, specialised sections of the community have sought refuge, as the mysteries of their trade become deeper, in the invention of a jargon which none but the initiates can translate, and they have been tempted to disdain the discipline of lucid expression, however expertly lucid they may be in their own esoteric thought. The Americans have been the main pioneers of this retrogressive habit, so that British bankers may soon need interpreters when negotiating with American bankers; although since the tendency to appeasement has gained much ground in recent years, the solution of adopting the American specialist dialect is widely favoured. What is true of bankers is scarcely less true of diplomats, economists, traders, soldiers and oilmen; but the proposed solution is only local and temporary, for as the years pass new specialist words must be invented and it is already difficult enough for bankers, whether British or American, to understand their own diplomats, and for economists to remember the jargon of town planners, mining engineers and computer programmers. A new Tower of Babel is being built by people who were all brought up to speak the same language.

The complexity of modern technology is not the sole barrier to linguistic communication. There can be little doubt that the majority of neo-Elizabethans have fared ill at the hands of those entrusted with the task of teaching them to speak and write English nor, because of the many distractions presented to them, have they sought to improve matters by their own efforts. Many of those with the advantage of a higher education specialised too soon in the solitary subject of their choice. They discarded the dead languages, Latin and Greek, which are well attuned to teach the values of clear, unambiguous expression as well as to instil an appreciation of the structure of a sentence. Brevity is a stylistic virtue that feeds on a classical education and it is not least among the casualties of the modern system. The length and obscurity which now characterise the writings of Civil Servants and business executives weary the reader and are the fertile parents of ambiguity. Few children are any longer required to learn poetry by heart, thus renouncing, together with much else, one tried method of discovering the value of a word or a phrase used in an apt and imaginative context. Reading the Bible, not only, as the Moderator of the Church of Scotland told the Queen, 'the most valuable thing that the world affords', but also the best manual of the English language, has ceased to be a daily, or even a normal practice, and those who do read it may well do so under scholastic duress.

The widening of State education, and the huge sums of money devoted to it, should at least have spread literacy over a broader section of the community; but if they be honest, the most dedicated supporters of the educational changes of the last twenty five years can find little satisfaction in the results of the experiment. Whether the classes be too large, the subjects ill-chosen, the methods of teaching ill-conceived or the children discouraged from learning by heedless families and excessive diversions, it is a fact that the total of illiterates is estimated at two million, and the ability of the rising generation to communicate their thoughts and their experience is no greater than that of their predecessors. Since those thoughts and that experience are by the very nature of social and industrial development less straightforward than in years gone by, it is reasonable to assume that the general capacity to express and explain grows weaker year by year.

The acceleration of the rate of change, of which General de Gaulle spoke, has been so rapid and so recent that it is only possible to guess its ultimate effects on the individual, on the British nation, and indeed on the human race as a whole; for this is not, of course, an experience confined to the British Commonwealth or to the United States. They are but few in number whose duties and initiative lead them to fly frequently and far, travelling in pressurised cabins, covering in hours distances that twenty five years ago required days, and challenging the versatility of their digestions and their sleeping habits as they traverse the longitudes; but they include the Queen and her family, Ministers of the Crown, Members of Parliament, Civil Servants, bankers, industrialists and professional men; in fact most of those who conduct the affairs of the nation. The millions who stay at home are none the less affected, in a different way, by the new speed of life. It is rare to find a community sheltered from rapid movement, from the insistent ringing of the telephone, from the contact with effervescent humanity offered, if not forced upon them, by radio and television, and from all the other noise and clatter of the modern world. The factory worker leaves his conveyor belt, the white-collared worker his desk, the miner ascends from the deep shaft, the child returns from school, not to a quiet, secluded home, but to the sound of canned music and to the bustle of an increasingly restless community.

Man, said Aristotle, is a social animal. Unless he chooses to be a hermit (and even then he would assuredly be pursued by the Department of Health and Social Security) he cannot contract out of a social system tightened every year by more efficient communication and by the remorseless growth of computerised information. He may kick against the pricks; he may, as many young people did in the 1960s and 70s, seek escape in a variety of rebellious ways; but neither rebellion nor even revolution, nor anything except the triumph of the human spirit over material considerations, will free him from slavery to an environment which grows steadily more uniform in design, and which shrinks in size as the communications between man and man improve, and as Alice's Red Queen shouts 'Faster, Faster,' with the conscious satisfaction of knowing she is being obeyed.

The revolution which has taken place in every form and method of communication is a triumph of technology, if indeed it turns out to have been a triumph at all. It has been accompanied by quieter, though assuredly no less significant, advances in the scientific laboratories. There, in the last twenty five years, British genius has flourished with that distinction which has seldom been found wanting in any generation since the days of Isaac Newton.

It is difficult to establish an accurate gauge of national ability in any field, for ability is not always equated with success. It is, for instance, scarcely credible that East Germany, whose success in the 1976 Olympic Games was so noteworthy, contains potentially better athletes than any other country with a well-fed population; but assiduous training and years of concentration by the selected athletes to the exclusion of all else, at unstinted Government expense, produces more gold medals than amateur enthusiasm. This reflects credit on the generosity and imagination of the East German Government and on their method of selecting athletes: it does not prove that East Germans are naturally more athletic than Kurds, Croats or Peloponnesians. However, in so far as any record of success is an accurate gauge of ability, the Nobel Prizes for original scientific discovery may be thought to be such a gauge; for they represent a judgement of excellence without national bias.

In this select field of merit, Britain led the field by many lengths between 1952 and 1975 in proportion to the size of her population. She won 26 Nobel Prizes for Physics, Chemistry and Physiology or Medicine. Germany won 10, Russia 7 and France 5. The United States, with a population nearly four times as large as Britain, won 62. Almost half of Britain's Nobel Prizes were for Chemistry. They reflect a progress in one scientific development which is of an importance to the future of the human race that cannot yet be measured in full.

In fact the two most important scientific discoveries in this century were both the results of research by British scientists within the walls of the Cavendish Laboratory at Cambridge University. The first, during the reign of the Queen's grandfather, came when Sir J. J. Thompson discovered the electron and Lord Rutherford split the atom, thus facing humanity with the revolutionary effects, actual and potential, of nuclear fission. If the world's inhabitants resist the temptation to destroy themselves which arises from this neo-Georgian enterprise, they must now come to terms with the second, neo-Elizabethan miracle of DNA.

The discovery and analysis of this substance solved the mystery of reproduction, by revealing how chromosomes renewed themselves. It explained what was thought to be inexplicable, the basis of life itself. It owed much to Francis Crick, who received a Nobel award in 1962. Two other British Nobel Prize-winners in chemistry, Max Perutz and Sir John Kendrew, are generally acknowledged to have made the first breakthrough in this vital area of the X-Ray crystallography of large biological molecules.

These great scientists, reviving in the Second Elizabethan age the Age of Discovery associated with the First, achieved their success by pursuing and perfecting the methods developed at Cambridge and the Royal Institution by Sir William Bragg and his son, Lawrence. The resultant advances in molecular biology place the control and artificial manipulation of genes within the grasp of human beings, so that they may not only change the quality of the plants they grow, but may even be able to determine the physical and mental characteristics of their own descendants. Man will, it seems, soon be left with no uncertainties apart from those relating to his immortal soul and his chances of surviving nuclear fission.

This brief account of recent scientific achievement makes no pretence to include a full or even a balanced account of scientific and technological progress as a whole; but it is reasonable to lay stress on the identification of DNA, for it may well turn out to have been the most significant development of any kind since 1952, not only in Britain but in the whole world. It brings in its train some ancillary discoveries such, for instance, as the fact that a virus (which seems to the innocent observer to be much less amenable than the old-fashioned germ) is essentially a package of DNA. This will, it may be hoped, lead to beneficial advances in the conquest of the virus, and no doubt to other medical triumphs. It may also contribute to the diminution, perhaps even the elimination, of mental deficiency.

There is at least one other field, in addition to molecular biology, in which Britain has outshone all rivals: that of radio-astronomy. In 1974, Nobel Prizes were awarded to Sir Martin Ryle and Professor Antony Hewish for discoveries of profound significance to man's understanding of the universe. They included the identification of the hitherto unknown and unsuspected pulsars. Thus, although Britain could not afford to take part in the gigantic space programme inaugurated, partly for competitive reasons, by the Americans and the Russians (a programme which is in essence more a brilliant achievement of engineering than of scientific skills), her contribution to the exploration of outer space, which no humanly-devised spacecraft seems likely to penetrate, has been of marked value.

Britain has also held her place in the field of technology. The most useful inventions during these twenty five years include floatglass, created by Sir Alastair Pilkington, and the 'Emiscan' medical X-Ray apparatus, developed for EMI by Mr Hounsfield and capable of

taking X-Ray photographs in three dimensions.
It seems to be in these stories of success that a failure of communication can be detected. The people, worried by industrial discontents, constantly faced by predictions of economic disaster, harassed by bureaucratic excesses and unhappily aware that Britain had abdicated her place among the leading nations, might have been cheered by the knowledge of their country's eminence in other fields. Yet, how many are even aware of Britain's scientific and technological achievements? What is the use of being able to fly round the world in a few days, watch men walking on the Moon, and converse clearly by telephone with Australia, if methods of communication are inadequate to convey the most important information at home? Yet, perhaps it is not, after all, a failure of communication. Perhaps the simple truth is that whatever the rate in the acceleration of change and whatever the brilliance of scientific discoveries, the human brain cannot be increased in size or capacity. In the final analysis, that is what counts.

CHAPTER 15

The Arts

In the realm of scientific discovery, money, physical resources and expensive equipment cannot be foregone; but although little could be achieved without them, it is on the genius of the individual, and his or her capacity to work with a group of other scientists that results depend. In the arts, talent is, of course, also a basic requirement, but a distinction must be made between the great artists – painters, musicians, sculptors and designers – whose individual renown brings credit and justifiable pride to their fellow-countrymen, and the facilities for enjoyment and practice of the arts available to the people. To both, but particularly to the artistic service of the Community, the provision of money is, if possible, of still more vital importance than to the scientists, comparatively secure in a University fastness.

The days of the private patron are over. The Court, the Nobility and the rich merchants who once financed a striving artist, and as often as not gave him opportunities without which his natural gifts would never have had the chance to bear fruit, are now impotent to help. The place of Maecenas, of Charles I and George IV, of the Dukes of Buckingham, Devonshire and Bridgewater, of Sarah Marlborough and Horace Walpole, and of countless 18th and 19th century grandees who were also art lovers, has been taken by the charitable foundations, by the Local and Regional Authorities, and above all by the State. It is to opportunities for the many to learn, practise and enjoy, rather than to give the talented few the means to develop their genius, that this new patronage is directed. In considering the artistic attainments of the reign, it would be presumptuous to do more than mention some of the great performers, for none but an artist dare criticise them. It is no less important, and certainly less contentious, to describe the new opportunities available to the community.

The Arts Council, established shortly after the war, and to a great extent the brain-child of Professor J. M. Keynes, thought itself fortunate in 1952 to receive £675,000 with which to support and encourage the arts. In 1976 it was granted £37 million, and this, allowing for inflation, is six or seven times greater in value. Credit is due to two Ministers, one Labour and one Conservative. Jennie Lee at one time, strongly supported by Sir Harold Wilson, and Lord Eccles at another, spared no pains to promote the interests of the arts and to soften the flinty hearts of successive Chancellors of the Exchequer. They succeeded where so many Ministers, representing other Departments, failed in their importunities. It is tempting to conclude that the Treasury Knights, being cultivated men, felt a sympathy for the arts and that this induced them to unloosen their tight purse strings for the Arts Council, however anguished might be the cries of competitive beggars from the Social Services and Defence Ministries. It has not only been Ministers and Treasury Knights who have shown this enlightenment. Lord Feather, General Secretary of the Trades Union Congress at a critical time in its rise to power, was a Fellow of the Royal Society of Arts, and in the summer of 1976 a TUC working-party recommended that the Government should double its contribution to the Arts, including a handsome rise in subsidies to museums and galleries. This was no extravagant proposal for, despite the acceptance by the State and Local Authorities of a new measure of responsibility for the arts, less than £100 million has been spent each year on the encouragement of Art in all its forms, while the receipts from foreign tourists, much attracted to the British Isles for cultural reasons, exceeded this amount by far; and the total of £100 million can be compared with some £5,000 million spent on education.

In spite of this praiseworthy attitude, common to all politica parties, the unbearable weight of death duties and taxation has forced the owners of private collections formed by their ancestors to sell pictures and other treasures. Many of these had been on loan to public galleries or were shown to visitors in the great country houses, almost all of which were opened to public view in the 1960s and 70s. Lord Harewood sold a splendid Titian, which had been on loan to the National Gallery, and Lord Radnor a magnificent Velasquez; Lady Crawford was obliged to dispose of one of the few Duccios in the country; the Duke of Sutherland, whose most famous pictures are lent to the National Gallery of Scotland, was forced to sell a Van Dyck on loan to the Fitzwilliam Museum at Cambridge and other valuable pictures and drawings which he had lent elsewhere. This tendency is discouraging to the generally under-endowed municipal Art Galleries precisely when they are doing their utmost to improve the quality of both their acquisitions and their display. At one time poems and plays of Byron and Sheridan seemed likely to swell that substantial element of the British heritage which has crossed the Atlantic. However, many treasures were saved when, in 1954 a Review Committee for the export of works of Art was set up, first under Lord Waverley and then with Lord Robens as Chairman. It was given the right to postpone the export of objects of national importance until it could be ascertained whether the cost of retaining them might be raised by subscription within the Kingdom; but with taxation established at a penal rate, it has become clear that unless the State itself steps in as the buyer, many irreplaceable works of art and historic possessions will continue to vanish overseas.

London has remained the indisputable centre of the world's art market. The supremacy of Sotheby's and Christie's as auctioneers is unchallenged and they have opened branches in many foreign capitals. Pictures and furniture, silver, books and porcelain, and every kind of *objet d'art* arrives from abroad for sale in Bond Street or King Street. As the pound has sunk in value against the leading foreign currencies, sterling prices have soared and the newly-rich from Japan and other distant countries have ranged themselves alongside the North and South Americans to fill the collectors' places which had once been occupied by the British themselves. The art market has become one of Britain's most thriving enterprises so that the Exchequer makes high profits from the foreign exchange earnings and capital gains taxes which it generates. But though much comes to London to be sold, still more is extracted from the greatest of all surviving treasure houses, the British private collections. Even the parish churches, with crumbling 14th century towers and decaying medieval roofs, are obliged to sell their Elizabethan and Jacobean plate to pay for repairs which in most European countries would be considered an obligation of the State.

This threatened disintegration of the nation's artistic inheritance is to some extent compensated by a renaissance of British modern art. The centre of artistic quality has moved from France to Britain and the United States, although there are individual schools of painting, such as the Catalan, which produce pictures of high merit. When the Queen came to the throne the names of Henry Moore and Barbara Hepworth, of Graham Sutherland, John Piper, Matthew Smith and Ben Nicholson were already famous. They have continued to produce works of international repute. Others, also now famous, such as Francis Bacon, Bridget Riley, David Hockney and the sculptor, Anthony Caro, joined their illustrious ranks. The Institute of Contemporary Art, supporting artists with advanced and original ideas, made a note-worthy contribution; while in 1968 the Hayward Gallery was opened. It is owned by the Greater London Council and managed by the Arts Council. It mounts challenging exhibitions on the south bank of the Thames and has established an international reputation. In 1970 it was followed by the Serpentine Gallery in Kensington Gardens devoted to the work of modern artists, especially those who are young and whose reputation remains to be established. This has not been a period of monolithic style, as was the case in 18th century England and France, but one of diversity, in which individual talent of striking variety has emerged.

The number of artists has been swollen by the flourishing growth of art education, much assisted by instructive and popular television programmes. Art schools are established in provincial cities and in schools and colleges throughout the length and breadth of the land. They are visited by painters and sculptors whose names are already famous, but who often dedicate time to teaching, lecturing and demonstrating for the younger generation. The Arts occupy a large place in the syllabus of all schools, both State and Independent. Local Authorities have made their contribution by financing art establishments. These have decreased in number, as the smaller were amalgamated and the new polytechnics absorbed others, but the total of full-time art students has grown larger. In no other country has art education been so sedulously fostered, and there must therefore be wide expectations that in the last quarter of the 20th century Britain will continue to hold the distinguished, and perhaps pre-eminent, place in modern painting and sculpture which she now occupies.

Modern English silversmiths have established a claim to international acknowledgment, and there is much well-designed china which has won an export market of substantial size. The Design Council, founded at the end of the war, exists to improve the quality of the products of industry, especially in the field of engineering, and even if artistic embellishment is not first on its list of priorities, it is permissible to claim that the high standard it promotes in industrial design does not only have a utilitarian value; for the outward appearance of engineering structures is but second in importance to their strength and performance.

The praise that can with all sincerity be lavished on modern British painting, sculpture, silver and china, is less easily bestowed on furniture which, with rare exceptions, has been lacking in taste and unsuccessfully straining for original effect. It can hardly be bestowed at all on modern British architecture, even if there be one or two architects with claims to individual merit such as Sir Denys Lasdun, designer of the National Theatre, and James Stirling whose university buildings are widely esteemed. City centres have been desecrated by glass and concrete buildings, built to the specification of developers for whom maximum occupancy was the prime consideration, and sometimes resembling a child's efforts at geometry, sometimes self-consciously eccentric in their design. There have been some unexceptionable school-buildings, a few modern churches of charm, if seldom of distinction, some New Towns and Garden Cities more notable for their gardens than their houses, and a rash of high tower-blocks, disagreeable to inhabit and destructive to the landscape. Those who wish to see modern architecture which is endowed with inspiration must travel to Europe or the United States. Far from being a great epoch for British architecture, almost all but the architects themselves agree that this has been a disastrous one.

The decline in the total number of play-houses in London is no yard-stick of the virility of the theatre as a whole. There are fewer light and popular performances in the West End of London, because costs are high and large casts are prohibitively expensive; but all over the country there has been a constantly rising interest in serious theatrical production, as well as a growth of provincial repertory companies and Amateur Dramatic Societies. Deliberately sponsored decentralisation has resulted in a move from the centre to the regions. Repertory companies of quality, performing more adventurous plays for longer runs than ever before, are established in such towns as Bristol, Birmingham and Nottingham. The Arts Council and the Local Authorities support them financially, and the number has steadily grown, from 22 in 1956 to 48 in 1974. Meanwhile new theatres, financed by the Arts Council's Housing-the-Arts Fund, have sprung up in numerous provincial towns.

'Fringe Theatre's, lunch-time theatres, informal studio theatres and experimental theatres of one kind or another play to selective audiences in settings which range from a public house in Shepherd's Bush to a converted synagogue in Whitechapel. They provide a stage for young actors and an opportunity for new playwrights. The Arts Council has begun to extend support to itinerant theatre companies which tour the countryside, offering performances in school-buildings and community halls. No less important has been the development in the late 1960s and early 70s of 'Theatre-in-Education' by the repertory or regional theatres, which provide small teams of actors to visit schools and, as often as not, include the children themselves in the performances they offer.

The great light-hearted 'Spectaculars', such as *South Pacific The King and I* and *My Fair Lady* were still drawing packed audiences in the first ten years of the reign; but they have all but ceased for the sad, economic reason that even if Drury Lane be filled night after night, the costs of production and of paying a cast of fifty or more cannot be met. The West End theatres of London still offer a wide choice of light entertainment, though many have closed or been converted to other uses; but serious theatrical audiences have multiplied, and just as those who now go to church go because they care, and not because it is the thing to do, so in a different context the modern theatre-goer is more often a devotee of drama than a searcher for carefree amusement. In consequence plays have tended to be more political in their intent. The two playwrights whose works are most widely-known at home and abroad, John Osborne and Harold Pinter, both represent the critics of society once associated with Bloomsbury and now resident in

Hampstead. The political or socially conscious content of a play soon dates. Bernard Shaw, who raised conservative hackles seventy years ago, is now enshrined in the classical Pantheon and his audiences fail to perceive anything revolutionary in his words. The same distinguished fate is already overtaking Osborne and Pinter who will, because of the quality of their work, doubtless be included in the long list of famous British playwrights.

By opening a London branch at the Aldwych, the Royal Shakespeare Company of Stratford on Avon has made some compensation to the metropolis for the general decentralisation of dramatic interest and performance, and the English Stage Company has established a firm reputation at the Royal Court; but the most memorable theatrical event of the reign has been the opening, after a full ninety years of planning and dreaming, of the National Theatre in a fine building, specifically made to measure, on the south bank of the Thames. Until the summer of 1976, when the National Theatre took possession of its Promised Land, it had been wandering, like the Children of Israel, in the desert; although for the previous twenty five years that desert had been the famous, if not wholly adequate, Old Vic. The National Theatre Company's final establishment in the new building is an important milestone in English theatrical history. It is in part indebted to the Greater London Council and in still greater part to the indirect support provided by the Central Government through the Arts Council. It can be cited as the prime example of the encouragement given to the Arts by governmental authorities, whether central or local, both in London and in the regions.

Without such encouragement, and the expenditure of the tax- and rate-payers' money which it involves, British art could not have reached the high peak of achievement on which it stands to-day. In 1973, when there was a survey of foreign tourists to enquire why they had come to Britain, more than half replied that one of their main incentives was to go to the London theatres; and it is believed that the money spent by foreign visitors in patronising the arts in one form or another is greater than the entire sum spent by the State and the Local Authorities in supporting them. The main instrument of success in the field of drama, as in the arts generally, has been the imaginitive, effective and annually better-endowed Arts Council.

The story of British films, which were once second to none in quality and international appeal, is less stimulating. The irresistible invasion of television has meant that cinema audiences throughout the Western world have contracted. In Britain some 25 million people went to the cinema each week in 1952, but by 1976 the number had fallen to 3 million. Commercial film production faltered and cinemas closed in thousands. Nevertheless the cinema, with its wide-screen and stereophonic sound, offers qualities with which the television screen cannot compete, and films provide educational and artistic opportunities of a high order. Therefore in 1965 the British Film Institute, mainly financed by the Department of Education and Science, sought to improve the availability of serious films by sponsoring regional film theatres, of which there are nearly fifty in existence in 1977, showing ordinary commercial films when they are not pursuing their primary objective.

Music can never have had so many lovers. There are poets, there are clubs and circles in which modern verse is read and discussed, and there are those who still aspire to express their thoughts and beliefs in poetic form; but poetry, once the rival of music in popular sentiment and in lovers' dreams, seems to have lost its hold on all but a select few. Perhaps its popular decline dates from the end of the First World War, despite the efforts of Auden, Spender, T. S. Eliot and a few others to give it the kiss of life. However that may be, there are no recognised great poets of the Second Elizabethan Age, popular, agreeable and sometimes inspired as the verse of the Poet Laureate, Sir John Betjeman, undoubtedly is. There are, however, many music composers and performers and countless music lovers.

It is appropriate to write first of pop music, which has risen straight and naturally from the heart, if not the very bowels, of the people. There is no modern historical parallel. Perhaps the Negro Spirituals, the Spanish Flamencos and the West Indian Calypsos are the closest analogy, but even they do not represent the same all-embracing and, in a sense, spiritual, appeal to the whole youth of a country. The upsurge began with the Beatles in the early 1960s, and their virtuosity was soon equalled by the Rolling Stones, while hundreds of other groups sang and twanged their way to the hearts of ecstatic and frequently hysterical teenagers. It is a genuine folk movement and even if people over forty may be partially deaf to its message, none would deny the wistful beauty of the best pop songs, nor would many dispute the quality of the music or the skill of the performance. It has brought to its impresarios wealth hitherto reserved for the oil magnates, Greek shipowners, Rand gold exploiters and the descendants of American railway pioneers. Thus, the more successful pop groups almost invariably emigrate to milder tax climates. The art has also become associated in the public mind with drugs and hippies, because some pop stars have had an illicit predilection for Cannabis Resin, and because they are inclined to appear in weird clothes and to attract still weirder disciples. Nevertheless, the music they have produced and the pleasure they have given are justly praised, and whatever their intrinsic merits relative to DNA and pulsars, Henry Moore and Francis Bacon, Osborne and Pinter, there can be no doubt at all that pop stars and pop music are the most widely-known British export in the world to-day.

The general addiction to music is proved by the popularity of Joseph Cooper's television programme 'Face the Music' and the generous ration given to music of all kinds, including new works, by radio and television. For those who stir beyond their television sets there are five full orchestras in London and a number of famous regional symphony orchestras elsewhere in England and Scotland. There are, in addition, many smaller chamber orchestras and the Purcell Hall provides a setting for the production of little-known works by minor composers. London now possesses seven large concert halls and opera houses, which are consistently filled, and since young people show a growing musical enthusiasm, their interest is reflected in youth orchestras established in almost every large city. The National Youth Orchestra, created in the 1950s and supported by the Arts Council, was the first of its kind in the world. It owed its survival to enthusiastic sponsorship by the *Daily Mirror* and there is now fierce competition to be included among its two hundred players.

Organisations such as 'Youth and Music' founded by Sir Robert and Lady Mayer, have enabled groups of young people under 25 to attend concerts, opera and ballet at reduced prices, to visit musical centres abroad and to receive young foreign musicians in Britain. They have no lack either of youthful subscribers or of financial supporters. A Pianoforte Competition, held in Leeds every third year, also deserves a special reference. It is open to young pianists from all countries, and is so highly regarded that the successful performers are guaranteed an entry to Concert Halls wherever they choose to go. Leeds, already renowned for its musical festival, has thus become still further recognised as an international centre of proficiency.

In the schools music has priority over all the arts, and perhaps for this reason there has been a change in taste and a rise in the demand for music of good and varied quality. Thus, not only are the standards of performance better, but musically sophisticated audiences have listened with pleasure and approval to the works of composers such as Mahler and Bruckner whose very names were known to few but the initiates when the reign began. The sale of records has risen to a high level. Their quality improved, as much as the performances they reproduced, when 'LP' gave way to 'stereo'. Now 'stereo' in turn prepares to yield to 'quadrophonic'. The effect of these large sales of new recordings has been a well-heeded demand to increase the orchestral repertory and to expand its content.

At the end of the 19th century, and early in the 20th, music was unmistakably national. Wagner could have been nothing but German and Dvorak was a true son of Bohemia. Vaughan Williams and Elgar, like their successors, Britten, Walton and Tippett, were no less recognisably English. Just as modern painters have been individual in their inspiration, so the new British composers, such as Rodney Bennett, Maxwell Davies and Goehr have no clearly-defined national style and their audience is not confined within these shores. However, their stage works have been applauded at Covent Garden, at the Coliseum, where the former Sadler's Wells Company, now called the English National Opera, has found a home, and at performances by the new and strikingly successful Scottish and Welsh National Opera Companies. Devolution is already a reality in the world of opera, for Scotland and Wales have produced Companies which do not only play in their own cities and regions. They tour in England and abroad, and have been acclaimed as peers of the English National Opera.

Glyndebourne is not a neo-Elizabethan innovation, but while all else now depends on the Arts Council or the Local Authorities for survival, Glyndebourne is almost the sole remaining example of private patronage in modern Britain. There are, however, other enterprising companies, such as the Kent Opera, and the Arts Council has itself sponsored the 'Opera for All Group', enabling it to tour England and provide performances, with nothing but piano accompaniment, in remote towns and villages.

The rise of Covent Garden to an international fame which has caused even the Scala in Milan and the Bolshoi Ballet in Moscow to look critically at their long-established laurels, is a triumph of will, talent and initiative backed by a constantly packed theatre, much corporate support and munificent subsidies. The cost of maintaining its high standard rises every year, but while the London County Council, and its successor the GLC, was devoting its energies and opening its purse to build the Festival Hall and the Queen Elizabeth Hall on the south bank of the Thames, (thus, with strong support from the Arts Council, enabling seats for concerts to be offered at reasonable prices, and both composers and performers to receive opportunities which only lavish subsidy could provide), the Arts Council also extended to the Royal Opera House at Covent Garden the financial help without which it could scarcely have survived.

Before the war, the lease of Covent Garden was held by Mecca Ltd and apart from two months of opera in the London Season, financed by such musically enthusiastic companies and individuals as Courtaulds and Hambro's, Lady Cunard and Mr Philip Hill, the Opera House was a *palais de danse*. During the war it was only a *palais de danse*: there was no opera season at all. John Maynard Keynes, whose wife, Lydia Lopokova, had been a Russian dancer, aided by Sir Kenneth Clark and other pillars of the Arts, devoted himself to raising financial support and restoring the Royal Opera House to its proper use as a permanent home for opera and ballet. He was so successful that the Treasury made an initial grant of £50,000, and in 1946 a ballet season was inaugurated under the auspices of Ninette de Valois from Sadler's Wells. With this small initial subsidy Covent Garden rose from the ashes. For opera, however, an entirely new Company had to be started from scratch.

There were few British singers or conductors with operatic experience and many difficulties and strong criticism had to be faced during the early years when the general policy was to give all performances in English.

When Keynes died, Lord Waverley, a former Chancellor of the Exchequer whose wife was fond of opera, succeeded him. He persuaded the new Socialist Chancellor, Dr Dalton, to increase the grant to £150,000 and to bind future Chancellors to support the company provided it justified their confidence. Lord Drogheda, who had been connected with the Royal Opera House since 1951, succeeded Waverley as Chairman in 1958. He retained that office till 1974, and combining passionate enthusiasm with an ability to charm yet higher grants from the Arts Council and reluctant Chancellors of the Exchequer, he was as instrumental as any single man in raising Covent Garden to its present eminence. The original £50,000 of 1946 has risen steadily to £4.4 million thirty years later, but this large increase has been, of course, deeply eroded by the galloping inflation of the 1970s, and if Covent Garden is to maintain its exceptional position it is bound to continue soliciting still more generous subsidies.

The Coronation was celebrated by, amongst other things, a full-dress gala performance at the Royal Opera House of Benjamin Britten's *Gloriana*, written specially for the occasion. It is now recognised as a work of merit, but it was an inept choice for the occasion because it presented to the young Queen Elizabeth II a portrait of Queen Elizabeth I, old and raddled, removing her wig to display an almost bald head and every other sign of decay. The audience were more interested in inspecting their own dazzling dresses, jewels and uniforms than in looking at the stage. Fortunately, this was a false dawn to an increasingly bright morning.

In 1959 an Australian opera singer, Joan Sutherland, established an instant and world-wide reputation by singing *Lucia di Lammermoor* at Covent Garden in Italian under Tullio Serafin. The following year it was agreed, with a struggle, that after a gradual process of transition, operas should be sung in their original language, rather than in English; for some of the best foreign singers who were attracted to Covent Garden from abroad were unwilling, if not unable, to sing in an English translation. The quality of the performances improved, and it was left to the Sadlers Wells Company to sing opera in the vernacular. This they achieved admirably and in the early 1970s they succeeded in producing the whole of Wagner's *Ring* in English. The magnificent productions of Visconti at Covent Garden were followed by those of the equally brilliant Zeffirelli. George Solti served for a period of ten years and his work resulted in still better performances. The chorus and orchestra attained a far higher standard. The repertory was increased to twenty five operas and as many ballets.

Thus, Covent Garden soon achieved world-wide renown. The warmth of its audience delighted distinguished foreign singers, its glittering performances and productions enhanced its international fame year by year, the places in its boxes, stalls and galleries were eagerly booked weeks ahead, while its players were reassured by the conviction that even if their contracts were only renewed annually, singing in opera or playing in the Covent Garden orchestra was now an assured career. The visitors to London, by 1976 the cheapest capital in the Western world, grew to vast proportions; thousands of them had the same, usually unfulfilled, ambition to go to Covent Garden as tourists to Moscow have to get tickets for the Bolshoi.

The Sadler's Wells Ballet, driven from its home in Rosebery Avenue during the war in order to make room for bombed-out Londoners, moved undaunted to the New Theatre and also toured the country. Its dancers included Margot Fonteyn and Robert Helpmann, and its success was such that after meeting, for its impoverished parent company, the cost of the rent, rates and upkeep of Sadler's Wells itself, the profit which the Ballet earned during the war years was £50,000; and that, in 1945, was a large sum of money.

The fact that it was able to maintain its activities during the war and to be seen throughout the country, meant that the return to a peace-time régime was a somewhat less exacting trial than for many organisations which had been disrupted by six years of national emergency. It had the peculiar additional advantages of an inspired and inspiring Director, Ninette de Valois, who had founded the Ballet in 1931, and a group of exceptionally gifted dancers. In 1946, the Sadlers Wells Ballet was installed on the larger stage of Covent Garden where the first performance was given in February with a company numbering less than fifty in all.

Meanwhile the Sadler's Wells Trust gave back to the Ballet half the profit it had made in the war. With this a house was bought and a School founded at Barons Court by Ninette de Valois. Frederick Ashton and Michael Somes, both pre-war members, rejoined the company when they were demobilised, and so popular were the performances that in 1955 it was financially possible to acquire, from the Crown, White Lodge in Richmond Park. This quiet and elegant house, which had been Queen Mary's childhood home, was furnished as a junior school to train both boys and girls as ballet dancers, in addition to providing a thorough education in the ordinary school subjects.

After its move to Covent Garden, the Sadler's Wells Ballet grew in size as well as in reputation. In 1976 there were 135 dancers and they could be justly proud that although ballet in England is less than fifty years old, whereas the Danes, the French and the Italians have been dancing for two centuries or more, and the Russians for well over a hundred years, the ballet at Covent Garden yielded pride of place to none of them. There may well be no ballet school in the world to rival the Bolshoi in Moscow; but the Western world has had the advantage of more imaginative choreography; for the Russians, in their hermetically-sealed society, denied the opportunity to receive new ideas and experiment with modern techniques, have been consistently conservative in their choreographic initiatives. Their dancers are matchless and their physique magnificent; but those such as Nureyev, who succeeded in breaking through the Iron Curtain, improved their technique and versatility when they were also given an opportunity to pull aside the musty, brocade curtains of 19th century convention.

The Sadler's Wells Ballet, or the Royal Ballet as it has now become, was not only singularly fortunate in its first director and presiding genius, Ninette de Valois, but it has danced under the inspiration of exceptional choreographers. The first, when it moved to Covent Garden, was Frederick Ashton. John Cranko, a brilliant Sadler's Wells pupil went on to found and train the ballet at Stuttgart. Then came Kenneth Macmillan who combines the role of Director and Choreographer. Great dancers are a joy to behold, but great choreographers, all of whom must have once been dancers of quality, are a rarer breed. 'You can,' says Dame Ninette de Valois, 'expect to produce one great choreographer to fifty great dancers.'

In addition to Dame Ninette de Valois herself, the Royal Ballet has been taught by a long series of guest teachers from abroad, for although Covent Garden itself is now capable of producing teachers of experience and ability, the very youth of the Company and of its Schools has necessitated help from maturer sources. They have given of their best and they have trained pupils to a standard which sometimes exceeds in quality that of the ballets from which they originate.

So it is that in 1977 the Royal Ballet, with its 135 members, provides three distinct companies. First there is the 'Big Company' to be seen regularly at Covent Garden. It has crossed the Atlantic every other year since the war for a season in the United States. Then, there is the 'Touring Company', which gives performances throughout the United Kingdom and sometimes abroad. Lastly there is the enterprising 'Ballet for All', comprising five young dancers, two actors from the Big Company and one pianist, which plays its repertory in the smaller towns. With these three elements, the Ballet gives at least fifteen performances a week and sometimes the total rises to twenty two. It would be difficult to match so great an achievement in so short a span of years, but honourable mention must also be made of the longer established Ballet Rambert, and the newer comers such as the Festival Ballet and the Modern Dance Theatre, all of which produced more polished performances and grew in reputation during the period.

It is no less difficult to draw a well-balanced sketch of recent artistic landmarks than of the monuments to scientific progress; and if greater emphasis be laid on Opera and Ballet, which present more foreign than British works, it is because their improved performance and international reputation have been such an outstanding triumph for Britain in these twenty five years.

It has indeed been a golden epoch for the Arts, one in which economic decline, whether it be temporary or permanent, has been compensated by another kind of growth that is already acknowledged far beyond the British Isles and will leave its stamp on the national heritage. The English school of modern painting will have no mere transitory appeal; English music of the 1960s and 70s may well be played for centuries to come; and perhaps future generations will look nostalgically back to Ninette de Valois' Ballet and to Covent Garden Opera as people to-day look back to the Globe Theatre of the First Elizabethan age. There are no Shakespeares, Spensers or Marlowes, for words seem to have lost their music in the 20th century. There are highly-talented individuals among the painters, the composers, the pianists and the instrumentalists; but it is preeminently an age of combined effort, and among the memories of these twenty five years will be the teams who worked in harmony: not only the scientists and the doctors, but the opera companies, the ballet dancers and, almost certainly, the pop groups.

CHAPTER 16

The Way We Live Now

This is the title of one of Anthony Trollope's lesser-known novels, which describes the habits of the newly-rich in mid-Victorian times, illustrating a materialist attitude to life which was strange, and in most respects shocking, to Trollope, but which sets a lot of bells ringing in more than one class of the new Elizabethan society. There are now many more newly-rich; and there are also many newly-poor, at least by the standards to which they were formerly accustomed. In the best tradition of the Magnificat, the mighty have been put down from their seat; and a lot who were not mighty have been exalted, although it may be questioned whether they have remained humble and meek.

In the 1950s and 60s the nation grew poorer by comparison with its competitors, but paradoxically there was an increase of wealth for almost all the people on a scale never previously known. Earlier periods of great prosperity, following the Dissolution of the Monasteries, the expansion of colonial trade and the Industrial Revolution, had enriched the ruling classes and the merchants alone. This time the people as a whole became part of what was generally called 'The Affluent Society'.

For some fifteen years the purchasing power of the pound fell but slowly, while wages and salaries trebled and quadrupled, helped by a shortage of labour in almost every industry and by a rising profit trend. Those whom narrow circumstances had always obliged to be thrifty enjoyed the new experience of finding within their means consumer goods and domestic appliances they had never dreamed of possessing. Private consumption, which was £212 per head throughout the country in 1952, was £1,227 in 1975. Cars, washing-machines, refrigerators and television sets became more the rule than the exception in working-class homes. The second family car, and even the second television set were no longer unusual. The formidable Mrs Braddock, a massive Labour Member of Parliament, was reported as saying that the fear of the modern working-class family in case of a depression would no longer be 'the dole', but the arrival of a Hire Purchase official to remove the refrigerator. 'You have,' said Mr Harold Macmillan, 'never had it so good' - a statement to which some objected but none could plausibly contradict.

Elated by this unaccustomed wealth, families who might formerly, in a prosperous year, have thought themselves fortunate if they could afford to venture as far as Blackpool, Margate or Minehead for a week's holiday in the summer, set off by air to the Costa Brava, and still further afield. The day of the Package Tour arrived, with numerous mushroom-growth agencies, sometimes disastrously over-extended in their financial resources, advertising a fortnight's holiday at a distant resort with all arrangements made and all expenses paid in advance. For the first time in history the Islanders crossed the sea in vast numbers, bent on pleasure instead of on war.

Whatever their station in life, the way people now conduct their affairs differs, voluntarily or involuntarily, in both opportunity and amenity from what was customary twenty five years ago. They feed and dress differently, they talk, live and spend their leisure differently; and they do so partly by choice and partly by force of circumstances.

The era of tinned food began in England before the Second World War but dependence on frozen food is a trans-Atlantic habit which gripped the British Isles in the present reign. The refrigerator is an institution of comparatively ancient antecedents, albeit mainly the prerogative of the well-to-do until the fifties; but the deep-freeze is an upstart. Its convenience, whether in the home or the Supermarket, is undoubted, but the sternly immutable law of compensation has decreed that something must pay the penalty; and that something has been the human taste bud. Good bread, made and sold by the small baker, may still be found; but the search is long and arduous. Kippers, coated in a yellow substance, are bought in plastic packets instead of reposing, wide-spread and seductive, on the fish-mongers' slab. Fish fingers, their piscine origin undisclosed, replace the fresh herring, the cod and even the humble hake. The tasteless broiler emerges from its polythene bag pretending to lineal descent from the old-fashioned chicken which formerly pecked its way to succulence when it contrived to avoid being flattened by a passing motor-car. The sausage has become a hybrid of unknown ancestry; the egg, pale of yolk, is laid by an imprisoned hen in a battery; and the age of a pat of butter is as indeterminate as its origins. Yet English cooking, as opposed to the Scottish which always had a distinction of its own, has been revolutionised. In 1952 there was no country in the world where the food was more justly censured by foreigners. Many of them even avoided the United Kingdom for culinary reasons. An influx of foreign chefs into London restaurants helped, but the British themselves began to take an interest in cooking and in sauces. The day of tepid, over-done mutton and two mushy vegetables has all but ended. British food can, at long last, stand comparison with almost all but that of the invincible French and their runners-up, the Italians.

For several critical years it seemed that one of the country's proudest and most ancient products, ale, might go the way of the chicken, the kipper and the sausage. Britain is only surpassed by the United States and West Germany as a beer producer, though she ranks but ninth in the world as a consumer. In 1952 there were even more large- or medium-sized brewers than there were Trade Unions, and most of them brewed mild or bitter draught beer with a distinctive flavour. The economics of production and distribution induced mergers and rationalisation. The end-product suffered gravely, but even the giant breweries could not defeat 'the man in the pub', and the outcry was such that 'draught' reasserted its superiority to 'keg', and the diversity of brews with a genuine resemblance to beer was victoriously re-established. Meanwhile, a wider section of the public than ever before took to drinking wine, and English vineyards, planted in the 1950s and 60s, started to produce small but excellent vintages of white wine. Port, a fortified wine invented for the English Whig market in days when Scots and Tories stuck obstinately to claret, lost its hold on the man or woman in the pub. Vintage ports were still favoured by the rich, but the barrels of Tawny and Ruby were redirected to such new light-port drinkers as the French and the Norwegians.

Women's clothes changed but little, except for a determined effort, regarded with some masculine disfavour, to hide the beauty of their legs beneath trousers, thus accentuating posteriors which would often have been better hidden by a voluminous skirt. Hems moved up and down and there was, in the sixties, a brief dedication to the mini-skirt which was much to be admired on the very young with very good legs. The majority stopped wearing hats altogether, except on special occasions. The true sartorial revolution has been masculine. Young men have discarded, except in their offices, the uniform suits, collars and ties which have long borne some responsibility for the male human, alone among animals, birds and even lizards, being less magnificent than the female. They abandoned drab colours and adorned themselves in every imaginable hue. They found comfort in the T-Shirt, often inscribed with some witty message or aphorism; they found economy in jeans, all too often patched and creased; and they found liberation in long hair and beards. Having grown their hair, only a minority took the same trouble as women to have it well dressed, so that the streets were not, as might have been hoped, filled with young men as dashing and debonair in appearance as the Cavaliers of Charles I. It became smart to be casual in dress, as well as in speech and living.

Much time and money was spent on sport, though less in participation than in watching and in gambling on the results. In the event, the British, whose love of sport is traditional and who were the inventors of cricket, football, golf, lawn-tennis and squash-rackets, have been miserable exponents of these favoured diversions throughout the whole twenty five years. They rejoiced in one or two moments of glory, winning the World Football Cup in 1966, the European Cup in 1967 and 1968, and shining in the equestrian events at the Olympic Games of 1972 and 1976. But their professional golfers were erratic, their cricketers were outmatched by the Australians and West Indians, and their tennis players were undistinguished at Wimbledon. From time to time they produced an Olympic medallist in swimming, they skied, skated and danced with grace, and on occasions they found some long-distance runners with a fine turn of speed; but although all the race-horses in the world descend from English bloodstock, the neo-Elizabethan horses seldom ran fast enough to beat their foreign competitors, and even in their natural element, the sea, the British were left far behind when it came to international yacht racing. It was a source of pride that the Queen's daughter, Princess Anne, qualified for inclusion in the team which contested the Olympic equestrian events at Montreal in 1976, and that she acquitted herself with courage and distinction; but sporting prowess does not stand high in Britain's list of achievements.

A disturbing element in a country which has always taken pride in its sportsmanship has been the vandalism and destructive rampages of the crowds who throng to watch the football matches. This is more an indication of the licence which is a hallmark of the times than an indictment of sporting events, but it has afflicted society to a greater extent in the seventies than in the previous decades. It is accompanied by a steady increase in gambling and the crimes associated with it. Countless millions of pounds are spent each week in football pools, on which no political party dare impose anything but the lightest of taxes; and betting on dogs and horses, on and off the tracks and race-courses, has swelled to vast proportions. With all this has come a thriving trade in 'protection money', blackmail, gang-warfare and the other by-products of a gambling society.

Social life has fundamentally changed. The rich are affected by a great diminution of domestic servants, compensated to some extent by new labour-saving devices upstairs as well as downstairs. The professional middle-classes have moved from the cities and formed an army of commuters. They are relieved of the necessity of travelling to work on Saturday mornings, for the British decided to improve on the arrangement originally made by the Almighty, and to rest on the sixth day of the week as well as on the seventh. In this most of the European countries were quick to imitate them. Since the artificers, such as plumbers, carpenters, painters and electricians, who used to relieve the middle-classes of domestic exertions in their hours of leisure, have grown both rare and expensive, men and women who had always earned their living by mental endeavour, or subsisted on their investments, have accustomed themselves to manual labour too. The practice of 'do it yourself' has become almost universal, encouraged by ingenious new tools and methods specifically designed for the amateur.

In 1952 there was no country in Europe with greater landowners or more inherited wealth. Over the years death duties made inroads, but there were still men and women who owned several hundred thousand acres, and many whose estates were measured in tens of thousands. Taxation was already high, but until 1962 there was no Capital Gains Tax, and as Stock Markets, in spite of occasional set-backs, maintained a steady upward trend, those with money free to invest maintained their standard of living with the help of tax-free capital gains. In the sixties, too, the price of land soared and some landowners were enabled, by the sale of a few acres on which planning permission had been given for development, to pay the heavy cost of maintaining and developing the rest.

The poor, or at any rate the less well-to-do, tended to leave the long, sombre streets of mid-Victorian town centres and move into three-room flats in high-rise buildings or pleasanter Council Houses, often with a garden. They acquired modern domestic appliances, bought motor-cars, watched television, gambled at Bingo and on 'the pools', went to football matches and became interested in rare, exotic shrubs in addition to tomatoes, wall-flowers and chrysanthemums. A sufficient supply of new housing remained a problem throughout the period, but great and continuous improvements were made. Mr Harold Macmillan, in the 1951 Government, triumphantly fulfilled the Tory promise, much derided when it was made, to build 300,000 new houses in a year. In 1969 Mr Harold Wilson announced, with an equally loud fanfare, that his Government had built two million homes in five years. There are still slums in Glasgow, Liverpool and elsewhere, but they have been reduced in both extent and in horror by the combined efforts of the Central Government and Local Authorities. The New Towns, garden cities rather than urban centres, were extended and multiplied as commerce and light industry moved into their industrial areas.

The old city centres were vacated by their original inhabitants and colonised by immigrant families. Danger signals began to flash a warning that a new version of Disraeli's Two Englands, and indeed Two Scotlands, was in process of creation. There was a fundamental change in society, yet more relevant to the future than to the present or immediate past, when the impact of immigration began to be felt by the mass of the people.

The scene is extensively altered in 1977. Taxes, amounting almost to confiscation, have been imposed on unearned income. There is a severe Capital Gains Tax, Stock Markets have fallen from the skies and have not fully recovered, Development Levies on land values have been enacted and a Capital Transfer Tax, more devastating than death duties, has penalised the heirs to whom landowners, anxious to keep their property intact, wish to hand over what they possess. Stringent economies have had to be made. Houses have been closed or sold, farms have been alienated and estates commercialised. Grouse and pheasants now fall to the guns of Americans, Frenchmen and Germans, who find in Britain magnificent sporting opportunities which they lack at home. Deer forests, grouse moors, salmon rivers and famous pheasant shoots are not, indeed, at the disposal of the militant minority who, while not in the least desirous of shooting birds, catching salmon, or stalking stags, nevertheless regard with envious indignation those who are. With an ironic turn of the wheel, these sporting rights contribute to the Invisible Exports boom by earning for the foreign exchange reserves large sums of dollars, francs and deutschmarks willingly paid by gratified foreign sportsmen.

A more serious result of the break-up of the great estates, which is clearly foreshadowed in 1977, is the effect on the countryside and the villages. The community life of agricultural England, of the glens of Scotland and of those Welsh valleys which are still green, has existed for centuries, more often than not under the protective banner of the local squire or large landowner. There have always been bad, careless or personally extravagant landlords, but the majority were conscientious both by upbringing and by inclination. In bad times tenant farmers have looked to the land-owner for support; in good times they received valuable services, and benefited from capital investments provided by the Estate to which the freehold of their farm belonged. The large Estates themselves employed workers, manual and white-collared, of all kinds; and these, together with the tenant farmers, the parson, the schoolmaster and the shop-keeper, formed a village community which was tight-knit and, on the whole, both prosperous and content. They were, too, an essential feature of the countryside which they thought it their duty to guard and conserve. Despite the growing importance of agriculture to the economy, the profitability of those engaged in it, and the indisputable efficiency of the existing system, in which the village communities play a vital part, the bell for their interment began to toll when the Capital Transfer Tax became law.

A new and variegated breed of rich men emerged. They were, for the most part, unencumbered by the responsibilities, social, local and often national, which fell to the landowning class, and as they made their own fortunes, and did not inherit them, they were uninhibited as to how they used them and, quite often, as to where they placed them. Their fortunes were sometimes honourably made by the sale on the Stock Exchange of shares in a successful business they had founded and developed; sometimes they were made by the stripping and sale of assets from companies acquired at a low price; sometimes by astute property deals. The latter, arising from the soaring boom in land prices between 1969 and 1973, were, for the most part, socially undesirable, and a far uglier and less acceptable form of capitalism than many of the other examples held up to public obloquy in the period. There were other men who earned their fortunes by individual talent and enterprise, rather than by financial machinations. They included the vastly rich pop stars, only a few of whom elected to remain in the United Kingdom and pay their taxes; and there were the organisers of gambling in every form whose tax liabilities, or at any rate, payments, were minimal.

The managers who worked hard to make profits for industry and commerce were not in this category, for however successful their labours and however high their salaries, the tax they paid left them no scope to build up capital. Should their grateful Board of Directors offer them share-options in the enterprise, this was decreed to be a reward taxable at the full rate. In 1976, Parliament decided that even the few fringe benefits, such as a company car, by which they had been accustomed to augment their greatly reduced net earnings, should be assessed against them. It became clear that those who were determined to keep a reasonable share of the remuneration they earned by steady, hard work, must either resort to tax evasion or take up residence abroad. This is one consequence of the Social Contract between the Government and the Trade Unions, which included a new political philosophy with the central belief that incentive and initiative are inimical to fair shares. There has certainly arisen in Britain a conviction that a fairer and juster society must be created, and it is a conviction by no means exclusive to the Trade Unions and the Labour Party; but it is doubted by many, indeed certainly by the great majority, whether this end can be attained by dampening the ardour of men with ability and refusing them a reward commensurate with the success of their endeavours.

The proud boast of Britain that, like Rome nearly two thousand years ago, her frontiers were open to all the subjects and citizens of her Empire, was heard no more from the mid-1960s onwards; for it seemed that an unending stream of settlers from the West Indies and the Indian sub-continent was liable to swamp the island. It was a new phenomenon, first visible in the late 1940s, which made an indelible mark on the social face of England and, to a later and much lesser extent, on that of Scotland, by the time the first limitations on entry had to be imposed.

After the war the overcrowding and impoverishment of Jamaica and the Barbados were matched by a demand in the British Isles for workers willing and able to fill jobs for which the British themselves had neither the inclination nor the manpower. The jobs were mainly lowly-paid, in transport, the construction industry or municipal works; but the newcomers, unemployed and often undernourished at home, accepted them thankfully. Those from the West Indies were soon joined by thousands from the endemically poor and over-populated Indian sub-continent. In 1952, there were 82,000 immigrants, in 1965 219,000 (with a larger proportion arriving from India and Pakistan than from the West Indies), and in 1975 189,000. These high immigrant figures were only partly composed of coloured people, and in all these years the total emigrating from the United Kingdom exceeded those coming in. The leavers tended to be young white people, seeking their fortune in Australia, Canada and other countries where the tax burden and the prospects of advancement seemed better than at home. By contrast, at the beginning of 1977 40% of the coloured people in Britain have been born here and have as much right, though often less disposition, to regard the country as their home as any fair-skinned Anglo-Saxon or dark-haired Celt. The total of the black and brown population is approaching two million. It has doubled since 1965 as much by natural reproduction as by immigration.

With their truly British disdain for logic, the white majority have seen every advantage in having their buses, underground railways, hospitals, sports grounds and municipal rubbish dumps efficiently serviced by smiling natives of the West Indies, and are not the least averse to Pakistani railway clerks or Indian shop-keepers; but at the same time they object to their children sharing educational facilities, or their wives maternity wards, with the immigrant community. Many consider that black families living in the same street lower the tone of the neighbourhood. They also shake their heads over the number of young black people said to be addicted to robbery, with or without violence, of which they read constant accounts in the newspapers; for whereas crimes by white men are deplored as an indication of the regrettable breakdown of law and order, and a lack of discipline in the schools, assaults by young immigrants are seen as an indictment of the whole policy of immigration. There were serious riots by the coloured inhabitants of Notting Hill, and their visiting friends from other London Boroughs, in 1958. These were repeated, with no fatal casualties but with much ill-will, in the late summer of 1976 during a carnival in North Kensington.

The Asian immigrants seldom mix with those of African descent who come from the West Indies. As events in Kenya and Uganda have shown, and as the old antipathy of the Indians and the Zulus in Natal has long demonstrated, the Bantu races regard the Indian peoples with suspicion and dislike, the suspicion arising from the astute trading skill of the Indians. Indians and Pakistanis (less hostile to each other in Britain than at home) have built their communities far and wide, in London, the Midlands and the West Riding of Yorkshire, equipping their own places of worship and establishing separate communal societies. The West Indians and a few Africans settled in London boroughs, forming large colonies in Lambeth, Wandsworth, Brent and Ealing, as well as in Wolverhampton, Birmingham and other Midland cities, where they have done their best to segregate themselves, not only from the white population, but from Asian communities. It is not yet a situation comparable to that in the United States. There are no Harlems, no demands for separate buses for school-children, nor areas from which the white man is virtually excluded. On the other hand, there are no coloured Members of the House of Commons and there has been only one

West Indian Mayor. There are a sprinkling of coloured Councillors and Aldermen, and a few black soldiers and policemen. Occasional Black Power Salutes are publicised in the Press, but there is neither the co-operation between Asian and African, nor the economic resources necessary to make the demands of nearly two million of Her Majesty's coloured subjects and residents politically disturbing to the more united and much richer white majority.

All the same, the white population has shown anxiety and some hostility. In the autumn Election of 1964, the Labour Foreign Secretary elect, Mr Gordon Walker, was defeated at Smethwick by the Conservative candidate who had expressed opposition to continued immigration. Mr Harold Wilson was deeply incensed and labelled the successful Conservative 'a parliamentary leper', suggesting that he be held untouchable by other Members of Parliament. It was, nevertheless, undoubted that the electors of Smethwick had deliberately made their choice on racial grounds and when, a few weeks later, an elderly Socialist was ennobled so as to provide Mr Gordon Walker with a safe seat at Leyton, the unhappy Foreign Secretary was again defeated. The implication seemed to be that the Leyton electors shared some of the feelings expressed in the ballot boxes of Smethwick, though the successful Conservative had been careful to avoid the racial issue.

In 1965 Sir Frank Soskice, the Labour Home Secretary, introduced in the House of Commons a bill which forbade racial discrimination. It sought at the same time to stop the evasion of controls by would-be immigrants, to tighten the regulations and to reduce the opportunities for entry with a faked passport. In the following year the Government established, under the Chairmanship of Mr Mark Bonham-Carter, a Race Relations Board with the object both of devising methods to alleviate racial tensions and of dealing with complaints of discrimination. It is, as most of Queen Elizabeth's Governments have failed to realise, impossible to change social, moral or, for that matter, immoral attitudes by law, and almost as difficult to regulate social behaviour. Racial discrimination continued, whatever Parliament or the Race Relations Board might say and the unhappy antagonism to the immigrants continued to grow.

1967 and 1968 were the peak years of immigration. In April,

1968, Mr Enoch Powell made a speech which stirred the country. In an undeniably effective attack on coloured immigration, he prophesied that rivers of blood would flow unless there was an immediate halt to it. To the horror of Mr Wilson, and of many Conservatives and Liberals too, the London dockers temporarily abandoned their favourite hobby of striking and marched to the House of Commons in support of Mr Powell. In the following year the Government tried once again to solve the problem by legislation: they brought in another still more stringent, but scarcely more effective, Race Relations bill. In 1976, still convinced, against all the evidence, that legal penalties would oblige the recalcitrant to conform, they made a third attempt. They introduced a new Race Relations bill with stronger sanctions attached.

Efforts to contain the situation were hampered, as far as the Asians were concerned, by a legal obligation to receive in the United Kingdom a large body of Indians who, having refused Kenyan citizenship, were driven penniless from their homes after Kenya became independent in 1963. They had been born in a British Colony and were British subjects. In 1974 the egregious General Amin drove thousands of Asians out of Uganda, and since India and Pakistan refused to welcome them back in their ancestral homes, Britain was the only refuge open to them. The Red Cross and other voluntary organisations had to beg and buy food, blankets and clothing to receive the wretched exiles, robbed of their possessions by Amin's gangster police, and flown in an emergency airlift to face the hazards of an English winter. Temporary accommodation was provided and as many of the refugees were both skilled and industrious, they gradually found employment.

As if the arrival of Asians from Kenya and Uganda, over and above the quota of immigrants which the Government had established, was not sufficient to distort the current policy, others arrived from India, and particularly from Pakistan, by clandestine and illegal means. They were smuggled ashore from ships hired for the purpose in Antwerp. A few came pretending kinship with families already in Britain, for it was considered humane to allow in those who already had parents or close relations in the country. These abuses were much publicised and added fuel to the existing flames of prejudice. Nevertheless, the arrivals of coloured immigrants notably decreased after the inrush years of 1967 and 1968. In 1971 there were 30,000 arrivals from the Indian sub-continent, the West Indies and Africa, and there were 14,000 departures. In 1972 the incomers were 27,000 and the outgoers 16,000; and in 1973 the figures were 14,600 arriving while 9,300 departed, giving a net coloured immigration of only 5,300.

Anxious though the immigrants were to reach Britain, whether they came from east or west, they were often disappointed by what they found. They stayed because the alternative in their own countries was so bleak, and because if they found no job the resources of Social Security or Unemployment Benefit were available; and these, by Pakistani or Jamaican standards, were wealth indeed. Yet many were not content, for they did not seem to belong to the community, and although some formed friendships with white families, others were made to feel they were not wanted. This was especially the case with young coloured men during the economic recession of the early 1970s. They found jobs scarce and their white contemporaries were usually preferred for those that were available. It was difficult in Brixton to recreate the easy-going, if penurious, communal gaiety of the West Indies. Facilities for recreation were restricted and, except among school-children, the companionship of white people was likely to be more the exception than the rule.

Yet it is wrong to be despondent, grave though the anxieties are and socially divisive though the results of further large-scale immigration would be. A call for tolerance, good manners and active co-operation with immigrant families has been made by all political parties and, more firmly still, by the leaders of the Christian churches. There are certainly not enough men and women of good-will who devote themselves to the improvement of community relations, but they are increasing in number. There are also thousands of immigrants who are not embittered, who have accepted Britain as their home and who do not share the restlessness of some of their young compatriots. There are, too, hopeful signs of a readiness to mix, and a lack of colour-consciousness among children in the schools. The problem did, after all, only arise in the first twenty five years of the Queen's reign and it is in war-time alone that the British are quick to adjust themselves to new situations. No doubt they will do so, though perhaps not without tears, animosity and frustration, in the years ahead; for most of the immigrants are in Britain to stay and, sooner or later, the British must accept the reality of a mixed society. In the long run they normally face facts, but while they are open to persuasion they resent constraint. The cause of racial peace and understanding may be retarded rather than advanced by a series of Statutes which, like so many other Acts of Parliament in the present reign, have encouraged normally respectable citizens to hold the law of the land in contempt.

As the years went by family life centred increasingly round the television set in the evenings, so that the younger generation became more widely informed than their parents, though they found little time for reading anything but the set books of their school studies. The combination of easily accessible news and the violence of the times meant that atrocities were a daily diet. A murder was formerly a sufficiently rare event to excite general horror and fill the newspapers for days. A rape or a homosexual assault was almost too indecent to mention. These barriers were already beginning to crumble in 1952, and in 1977 there are no barriers at all. Murders, and even assassinations in Northern Ireland, rate no more than a short paragraph in the Press and the briefest mention on radio or television. Mugging, hi-jacks and kidnaps are daily fare on the news, though neither of the last two has infected the United Kingdom. Restless young men, happily deprived of war as an outlet for aggressive instincts, found a substitute in gang-warfare, sometimes converging on sea-side resorts with their motor-cycles, leather jackets and home-made weapons. Others found demonstrations a relief for their emotions. 'Aggros' and 'Demos' became a popular diversion, if not for the majority, at least on a sufficient scale to try the temper of the police force and disturb the community as a whole. Demonstrations were by no means restricted to the young or to left- and right-wing militants: they took place at airports to protest against noise and at public hearings to oppose new motorways.

People grow up quicker. The result of better feeding and more scientific child-care is that the race has become taller and healthier, and children are physically mature at a younger age than ever before. Accordingly they marry early and, all too often, impetuously. So it was that in 1972 nearly forty five thousand divorces, which was well over a third of the total, were of boys and girls under twenty. A new law in 1971 endeavoured to simplify and rationalise the process of divorce without encouraging hasty decisions. It was to a great extent successful, but as the figures mounted so did the number of remarriages. They were soon a quarter of the total. A distressing feature of this social change is that divorcing couples are seen to be increasingly careless of the distress to their children, either putting their immediate self-interest first or convincing themselves that the damage arising from broken homes is grossly exaggerated. School-teachers and others responsible for juvenile flotsam and jetsam sometimes have a different tale to tell.

The stresses and strains of life, due to the speed of communication, to the ceaseless noise of modern civilisation, and the paradox that better facilities and greater leisure leave less time for thought, repose, reading and contemplation, take their toll in a variety of ways. Alcoholism, at last recognised as a disease and not just a pernicious habit, has become more prevalent, especially among women. Smoking, declared to be dangerous to heart and lungs, has decreased among the duly alarmed middle-aged, while the young pay little attention to the warnings. Sexual perversions and in-versions, long discouraged both by law and social convention, are publicly advertised and widely condoned. In consequence some who might once have been induced to suppress unnatural instincts by the force of social disapproval see little reason to continue doing so. The most distressing of all the reprehensible tendencies is drug addiction, which at one stage in the late 1960s and early 70s seemed likely to cause incalculable damage in schools and universities. There were attempts, firmly resisted by the Government, to make the possession of Cannabis Resin legal. Its defenders, with no convincing weight of medical support, spread the rumour among young people that to smoke 'pot' was no more damaging than to drink a whisky and soda. Stringent fines and imprisonment con-tributed to abate the menace. By the end of 1976 there were indications that the peak of the infection had passed; and there were equally encouraging signs that addiction to heroin, LSD and the other mortally dangerous hard drugs was gradually declining.

Hero worship is endemic, but there are new types of hero. Partly, no doubt, in reaction to the war and to the stories, films and books to which the rising generation were subjected, those who held the stage and the public interest in 1952 – Churchill and Attlee, Alexander, Montgomery, Mountbatten and Slim, the great Air Marshals and the famous war heroes – were gently relegated to the pages of history books without, however, suffering the merciless and largely unjust posthumous persecution which was the lot of Lloyd George, Haig, Jellicoe and other leaders of World War I. Leadership itself was scarcely a recognisable factor in the later years, for in peace-time it is seldom acknowledged or accepted, and it is a quality particularly hard to assert in a world where the television screen encourages familiarity to breed contempt.

For the Queen's first two years Sir Winston Churchill, more a Prophet in the Old Testament sense than a political leader, retained the spell which he had cast on Britain ten years previously. Sir Harold Wilson, a convert, at least publicly, to the creed of government by consensus, found little consensus in his Cabinet and his Party. Mr Edward Heath had the capacity to impress and the strength to dominate, but both his Country and his Party rejected him. The sole political leader of stature in these years was Mr Harold Macmillan, who did control his Government and his Party by a combination of humour, patience, determination, political experience and clever public relations. On to the heroic plinths and pedestals, left vacant by Statesmen and Generals, the British public hoisted a motley group of pop stars, footballers, Trade Union leaders, tycoons, actresses and television personalities. In the 1970s, the generation gap has been widened by the entirely different attributes of heroism that were deemed appropriate by those who were over forty and by those who were not.

'Some people,' said Mrs Gamp, 'may be Rooshans and others may be Prooshans. They are born so and will please themselves. Them which is of other nations thinks different.' The British disdain for foreigners is not quite as close to the surface in 1977 as when Charles Dickens wrote *Martin Chuzzlewit*, and in some circles it has long been thought indecent to display any traces of patriotism at all. One undoubted factor in public life has been the grudging acceptance by the British of the irreversible internationalism which late 20th century requirements present. There is, it is true, contempt for the futilities of the United Nations, despite the fact that, whatever its faults, it is the only world organisation in existence; there is little popular enthusiasm for the Commonwealth, despite its historic origins and widespread, if largely unreported, advantages; and there is still a deep antagonism, on both the extreme right and the extreme left, to Britain's firm commitment to the Common Market. All these are surviving manifestations of an insularity which, however persistent, has been slowly weakening as travel becomes easier and foreign lands more familiar. It is already a trifle less deeply-rooted in 1977 than it was a generation ago.

There has been a gradual Americanisation of the language and of behaviour. Habits, many of them excellent, which are trans-Atlantic in origin and inspiration, have winged their way to the British Isles in films, in magazines and on television. Old forms of English, such as 'gotten', used in the United States but long discarded in Britain, have not yet returned. The British do, indeed, now find things 'proven', an archaic word formerly reserved for the law courts north of the border; but for that the Scots, and not the Americans, are to blame. It is increasingly common to *have* something done instead of *getting* it done, and to meet *with* people instead of meeting them. American stresses, such as résearch instead of reséarch, and dístribute or cóntribute instead of distríbute and contríbute have also crept into speech; and the British have copied the Americans by *listing* their Shares on the Stock Exchange instead of *quoting* them. They have adopted adverbial habits originating with German immigrants into the United States, so that they do things *hopefully*, *currently* or *presently*, using grammatical structures which would have outraged the pedagogues twenty five years ago and still distress a diminishing band of purists. Insularity is thus all but extinct in linguistic matters, occasionally (but by no means always) to the greater glory of the English language.

In 1975 the Conservative Party chose Mrs Denis Thatcher as their Leader and therefore as a potential Prime Minister. This was the first time that any woman, other than a Queen, had been placed in a position of high political authority in Britain, although there had been several female Cabinet Ministers. It was in many respects apposite; for the status of women has changed a great deal in these years. It may be doubted whether the Women's Liberation Movement or the Equal Opportunities Commission made any serious impact on the mass of the people, but it was generally agreed that women doing the same work as men should receive equal pay, and aided by the Equal Pay Act of 1970 they were admitted, at first grudgingly, into professions which had hitherto been male preserves. In 1976 the Head of the Commonwealth was a woman, the Prime Ministers of two important Commonwealth countries were women, the American Ambassador in London was a woman and it was well on the cards that the next British Prime Minister would also be a woman. A Lady Chancellor and an Archbishopress of Canterbury are no longer unthinkable, but the doors of many male clubs, whether in St James's Street or in working-class districts are still firmly closed to the ladies.

The changes in morals, habits and appearances, and in the way of life generally, have been accompanied by officious governmental interference in the private lives of the citizens. There seems to be no limit to its growth. Occasionally a brave or eccentric individual protests by declining to obey some edict he thinks unreasonable, but even if the public are unimpressed by the paternalism of their rulers, too often expressed in mealy-mouthed terms at which their ancestors would have rebelled, they suffer it with a detachment new to the British character.

In the early 1950s, the servants of the State were even expected to be quiet. The raucous klaxons of police cars would have been resented as a deplorable continental or American innovation, and King George VI's fire engines used nothing but inoffensive bells. Nobody had any right to disturb the peace of the law-abiding citizen. Without any doubt at all, intrusions into private houses by officers of the State would have been furiously resisted. This is scarcely true any longer. Perhaps it is because so many worse things have befallen; perhaps because regulations have become too complicated to be comprehensible; or perhaps the encroachments of the Community have destroyed the spirit of the individual. Whatever the reason, the British who, regardless of their social status, were always loudly insistent on their rights, and critical of the smallest threat to their privacy, have developed a new, apathetic instinct to shrug their shoulders and acquiesce in official encroachment on their time, on their peace of mind and, as is now threatened, on their private premises.

Official forms, annually more numerous, have become so long and involved that ordinarily endowed members of the public are unable to understand them. The few who do succeed in penetrating the arcane mysteries of modern official jargon often discover that they are required to sign solemn undertakings which, if they were strictly honest, they could not possibly give. It is found less wearisome to accept them. Thus, for instance, a Director of a company applying for a licence under the Consumer Credit Act of 1974 might be required to declare that no lineal ancestor had ever committed a fraud or been pronounced bankrupt. Since ancestors increase by geometric progression, such a declaration assumes the signatory to have an accurate knowledge of what several hundred thousand ancestors may or may not have been doing in the 13th and 14th centuries. If this was not the intention of the Act, Parliament, which was in all probability allowed no time to consider the details of the bill, certainly failed to make any sensible correction. Again, a senior executive of an Insurance Company, accepting an invitation to dinner from some relation who happened some years ago to take out a mortgage from the company at a rate of interest lower than that prevailing at the time of the dinner party, may in accordance with the Finance Act of 1976 find himself personally liable to pay the difference between the rate at which his relation borrowed and the current market rate. There are countless such examples of folly arising from the new paternalist legislation: the age of the *Reductio ad Absurdum* is statutorily established.

The Department of Social Security took advantage of the 1975 Finance Act to exact multiple deductions from the salaries of men and women with more than one employment, to retain these forced loans without payment of interest and to delay their ultimate refund as long as possible. Their legally endorsed oppressions are, however, as nothing to those forced on the Inland Revenue, who were given the invidious task not only of extorting taxes at confiscatory rates, but also of enforcing regulations which grow more opaque with each succeeding Finance Act. Almost everybody with income from more than one source has been obliged, unless he be himself a Chartered Accountant or a Solicitor by training, to employ an expensive tax expert to unravel the tangled skein of his affairs. Advice on tax avoidance has become a profession in itself, occupying fine brains which might usefully be directed to more productive activities. Anxiety has grown as parliamentary authority is sought to give officials the right to force an entry into private houses in order to verify a suspicion that a small trader, dumbfounded by the compound complications of Value Added Tax, may have made an inaccurate return. The foreboding expressed in Churchill's Gestapo Speech of 1945, of Civil Servants no longer Servants and no longer Civil, has begun to have an uncomfortably prophetic sound.

Yet it would be unjust not to recognise the positive benefits that, despite the irritations, interferences and anomalies, well-intentioned and, indeed, imaginative legislation has conferred on the poor, the old and the unemployed. Britain has built a broadly-based edifice of welfare services which are, perhaps, more than the country can afford, but are in the main an object of pardonable pride. National Insurance payments, increasingly weighted at the expense of the employer rather than the employee, have been raised at ever shorter intervals in an effort to outpace inflation; maternity benefits, children's allowances and widows' pensions do more to strengthen the weaker sex than the Equal Opportunities Commission; Social Security benefits alleviate the misery of the unemployed on a generous scale. It is difficult to delimit the frontier between a scale of unemployment benefits so large that they encourage idleness and one so low that they leave the families of unemployed workers close to destitution. Reasonably wide discretion has been left to those who administrate relief, and if officials sometimes err on the lavish side, paying for hire purchase instalments and television licences, at least the State can claim to have disowned Ebenezer Scrooge.

All political parties have been genuinely conscious of the nation's obligations to its poorer citizens, but the Labour Party can justly claim special recognition of the consistent, if sometimes exuberant, enthusiasm and thoughtful care with which they have pressed for the expansion and improvement of the Welfare State. Mr Richard Crossman's Grand Design for an all-embracing National Pension Scheme foundered on the exigencies of retrenchment. Reform, however, has been an unending preoccupation. In 1977 the State is closer than in 1952 to caring for all its citizens from the cradle to the grave (though perhaps those closest to both are the least regarded) and apart from a certain self-conscious egalitarianism, nourished less by experience than by ideology, there is but one pernicious and persistent fly contaminating the ointment: cost.

In most periods of history people at least had an illusion that they knew where they were going. They were often wrong; they were often unpleasantly surprised; but except in times of physical ordeal, such as War, Revolution or Pestilence, the immediate future has seldom been more obscure than in the closing days of this quarter-century. It is not just that the economic problems have failed. again and again, to respond to treatment, that so much lawlessness goes unchecked or at least unpunished, and that divided Governments, without real popular support, mistakenly believe that increasing legislation is the right prescription for uncertainty. It is that the British Isles are in the painful process of adapting themselves to a new world in which, whether the inhabitants like it or not, they are destined to undergo political, social, economic and environmental experiences which are no longer their own unfettered choice. Yet the ultimate pattern of future developments may already be dimly discernible.

EPILOGUE

Epilogue

Those who, like Tennyson in his poem *Locksley Hall*, have dipped into the future to see 'the visions of the world and all the wonders that would be', risk their reputation with posterity. Some, like Harold Nicolson, writing of a nuclear bomb and a Churchill coalition many years before either event, lived to see their prophecies come largely true (though Nicolson did go awry when he linked the name of Churchill with Sir Oswald Mosley as joint leaders of the Coalition). Others, like the Early Christians, expecting the Second Coming in their own life-time, and Lenin, proclaiming the immediacy of a World Proletarian Revolution, were less accurate in their predictions. It is wise to tread warily when forecasting the shape of things to come; but the revolution, middle-class rather than proletarian, which has been in progress for a generation has reached a stage at which dipping into the future may require less imaginative skill than it did in 1832, the year Tennyson wrote *Locksley Hall* with such uncanny premonition of aerial bombardment. Tendencies that are scarcely reversible can already be distinguished above a not-so-distant horizon.

Nationalism remains a strong and dangerous force in 1977, but the day of the self-sufficient nation is drawing to its close. The United States, Russia and China will keep their independent armed forces and nuclear weapons for many years to come. Other nations will be obliged to rely on joint military forces as weapons grow more complex and expensive. This is equally true of national economies, for even the countries which are self-sufficient in food demand much more than subsistence. The European Economic Community has had a disturbed childhood, and it will have to surmount many disappointments during its adolescence. It will draw back, perhaps again and again, from the brink of dissolution before it is firmly and permanently established. It represents, all the same, a pattern which will be copied in Africa, South East Asia, Central America and the

Spanish-speaking countries of South America. It is, however, legitimate to doubt whether Tennyson's most splendid vision, 'the Parliament of Man, the Federation of the World', will be within sight of fulfilment during the reign of Elizabeth II.

Just as closer international co-operation is essential to a world in which neither space nor time are any longer of great account, so the lesson of unprofitable division at home, and barren, competing ideologies, will sooner rather than later alert the British peoples to the fact that economic survival and their very freedom depend on unity of purpose. The foundations of such unity are there: common sentiment, the absence of deep-rooted bitterness (except among Irishmen and a handful of political extremists) and the success of such an organisation as the National Economic Development Council, at which Ministers, Employers and Trade Unionists discuss matters of national interest with a cool detachment that few dare display in the presence of their own political myrmidons.

There will be electoral reform. There will be constitutional changes too; for a system built on precedent and tradition which served the country well in the 19th century, now serves it so ill that Parliament has become little more than a stamping machine, existing to endorse the decisions of the Executive. The House of Lords cannot last many years on its present semi-hereditary basis, and an elected Second Chamber, doubtless containing some or all of Britain's representatives in the European Parliament, as well as regional representatives, will replace it. The Crown will remain the repository of British self-respect and its wearer will continue to play an active part in maintaining national unity and encouraging the peoples of the Commonwealth to pool their skills and their influence. When Scotland and Wales have attained their devolutionary goals, the importance of the Queen, whether she remains Queen of the United Kingdom or adds to her other titles Queen of Scots, will be greater still; for her Crown will form the supreme link holding the regions of the British Isles together. It may even be that the Honours of Scotland, carried before the Queen on velvet cushions when she attended a service in St Giles Cathedral, Edinburgh, in 1953, will be promoted to be the Crown Jewels of Scotland at the Coronation of King Charles III. In the meanwhile, when devolution is established further south, neither the title nor the functions of the Prince of Wales are likely to be disregarded.

The greater unity of purpose and ideals which Britain so urgently needs does not demand stronger centralisation. On the contrary, insistence on devolution is the blast on the trumpet which will demolish the walls of a bureaucracy that has become too deeply entrenched in this last quarter-century. England, as well as Scotland and Wales, will grow impatient with dictation from Whitehall, and one by one the English regions, North, West and East, South-East and South-West, will demand a wider measure of local autonomy. The British in all the regions will at last decide what they mean by democracy, a word more misused and misapplied in the 20th century than any other in the language. There will be a delicate political problem to resolve; for British Parliamentary Government was successful in the past precisely because the majority took it for granted, only expressing an interest at election times. This resulted in the abdication by the masses of their responsibilities for local government, constituency organisations and, above all, Trade Union affairs. It gradually led to the assumption of authority by unrepresentative minorities. The exercise by the people of the choices which are theirs by right, law and custom, will be encouraged by greater local self-government, but when those who formerly slept awake to their obligations, it may be that clashes and confrontations previously confined to a minority will become a preoccupation of the majority.

Privilege will not disappear, for those in power, whatever their origins, will create it; but the privileges of class, based on the ownership of land and on superior educational opportunities, are being eroded in the 1970s. The process will continue and accelerate. However, since equality is abhorrent to the acquisitive, and it is the acquisitive who rise to power, new forms of inequality will emerge. They will be more resented than those that were hallowed by the centuries. This is the law of secular society, which the profession of Christianity has failed to modify in two thousand years and which the Soviet Union and its Marxist satellites have faithfully obeyed. In 1534 the Anabaptists of Münster did, for a brief period, establish a truly egalitarian, Christian society; but a year later the Holy Roman Emperor put them all to the sword. The Kremlin would have approved.

Epilogue

An antidote to the corruption which tarnished local government and even, it was alleged, the House of Commons in the sixties and seventies will be fiscal reform, allowing more generous retentions of earnings and returns on savings. The re-establishment of discarded moral precepts and a socially accepted code of right and wrong, based on belief in eternal truths, will come when reliance on material values is seen to bring no lasting reward or personal satisfaction. Only then will the rise in crime and violence be halted, for late 20th century crime is inspired by greed rather than destitution, and modern violence is, in the main, a perverted form of self-expression.

The restoration of 'plenty and prosperity' for which a prayer was offered at the Coronation, depends on the willingness of managers and workers to move with the times, welcome new developments and adapt themselves to competitive conditions in world trade. Their failure to do so brought Britain to the verge of bankruptcy in 1976 and administered a shock which had a therapeutic effect. The 'assistance of God's infinite goodness' and 'the vigilant care of his anointed Servant, our Gracious Sovereign' have not been withheld from these Islands; but neither has as yet been directed towards ridding the economy of that heavy mill-stone, the Sterling Balances. However, since the International Monetary Fund and the European Economic Community do not wish to support the country's faltering gait indefinitely, it was already clear by the autumn of 1976 that concerted measures would be taken to remove this burden. When that has been done, Britain will be obliged to ensure her own economic survival, for it is one thing for the nations to take steps to prevent a world reserve currency from crashing and another to continue bolstering the finances of a nation which they have already relieved of far-reaching and insupportable commitments.

It may be rash to have dipped into the future thus far: it would be foolhardy to dip further. The immediate past, confusing though its strange vicissitudes have been, can be more fruitfully assessed; but it is all too easy, when writing of current events and recent history, to be infected by emotions prevalent at the time. In the winter of 1976/77 pessimism is in the ascendant and it is therefore tempting to draw a depressing picture of the years gone by, matching it with one of the future painted in dark foreboding colours. There is an Italian proverb: *Il pessimista é colui che é stato socio di un ottimista,* which may be translated 'a pessimist is one who has been associated with an optimist'. This proverb can be inverted. When pessimists abound, it is pardonable to feel well-disposed to optimists, and it is appropriate to sum up this account of the changes in the first twenty five years of the present reign with a brief repetition of the cheerful tendencies and developments.

Britain yields to none in the arts, whether in creation, performance or marketing. She has produced, and is producing, painters and musicians, actors and writers, whose names circumnavigate the globe almost as famously as did Sir Francis Drake. Her pop stars enjoy a renown different from that of the Francis Bacons of either Elizabethan reign; but they are genuine artistic innovators acclaimed by young people in all the lands, yet successfully imitated nowhere outside the British Isles. Nor have the scientists anything to fear from foreign comparisons, for they have shown a creative ability which cannot fail to affect the future of mankind and is in direct succession to a long line of British inventors and innovators.

Whatever the vexations of industry, the sufferings of the pound sterling, the misjudgements in aircraft production and nuclear strategy, Britain has contrived to strengthen her position as a financial metropolis. When Sir Harold Wilson, appointed to examine the mechanisms of the City of London in order to appease the left-wing of his party (who are for ever spotting a gnome under the bed) produces his report, he cannot fail to draw attention to the consistent rise in Invisible Exports, the unchallenged position of Lloyds in the world of insurance and the skill of the banks in both creating and managing the Eurodollar markets. Nor can he overlook the reputation of British Chartered Accountants in the Western world and the integrity with which the country's commercial law has been interpreted and applied.

The successes of British agriculture, against all the odds in a country which considers itself first and foremost industrial, have been greater in these years than in any since the days of Coke of Norfolk and Jethro Tull. They have also been a tribute to private enterprise, supported and encouraged by the State with model co-operation between the public and private sectors. Conservation of land and water resources, important to agriculture and to the community as a whole, has been studied with care and judiciously pursued. In measures to clean the air, the rivers, the areas of industrial waste, the slag-heaps and even the sea, Britain leads the international field, so that foreign delegations, instructed to propose measures to purify their own polluted cities and rivers, come to Britain to listen and to learn.

As the Silver Jubilee approached, unemployment stood at a figure higher than any since the early 1930s, inflation was still rampant, industrial investment was sluggish, and interest rates were set at startling heights to reduce the demand for money. The people had lost faith in the politicians to an even greater extent than the politicians deserved. These were prominent among the reasons why an anxious melancholy oppressed men's spirits and obsessed their minds. Yet, the silver linings to the clouds are growing broader. When at last a recovery in world trade takes place, Britain will have capacity to expand her industrial productivity without the over-heating of the economy to which a long succession of Stops, after spasmodic Go's, had been due. There is the competitive challenge, not by any means divorced from protective coverings, which the Common Market offers, and which Britain, if she takes advantage of her opportunities, may use to emulate the successes of France and Germany. There are the riches of North Sea Oil and Gas, piped ashore in fast-growing quantity after a conquest of technological difficulties, and a willingness to face hardship and exposure in cold, rough and inhospitable conditions, which should allow none to assert that the British have become a decadent race, devoted to nothing but comfort and the pursuit of pleasure. The soldiers, in mortal danger as they patrol the streets of Belfast or Londonderry and the borders of Ulster, have an even more telling riposte to those who level charges of degeneracy and decline.

There are some general considerations which arm the optimist against his associate, the pessimist. The economic wheel has in some respects come round full circle. When the Queen came to the throne, the outlook was black indeed. There was a heavy deficit, a serious balance of payments crisis and no shortage of Jeremiahs. In the intervening quarter-century, the lights have alternately gleamed and faded. Some commentators have declared they were going out altogether, just as in 1914 Sir Edward Grey believed the lights of Europe would not be lit again in his time. They have not gone out and short of some total calamity, such as an improbable nuclear war, they will not do so. The British, in these mercurial times, have remained commendably calm. Perhaps a little more impatience would have been to their advantage. However that may be, there is no sign in 1977 that the inveterate good sense of the people has deserted them, facing though they do the challenges of inflation, immigration and constant interference by the State in their private affairs.

Some of the old legacies have fructified; others have not. On the one hand the Empire has been peacefully translated into a Commonwealth which, with all its strains and imperfections, is still an influence for good in a divided world and a source of pride and strength to most of its members. On the other hand, sterling, long the most prominent of international currencies, has become an incubus, mainly on account of the unstable balances held by foreign depositors.

There is one legacy which, as this book has tried to show, provides the framework of the solid stability in which the country still rejoices. It sets Britain apart from all other nations, whatever their constitutional arrangements, and ensures her an honourable, indeed an envied, place in the international sun. It is the British Monarchy, its glamour crystallised by the personal example of good sense, good manners and good morals which the Queen has set.

As the fireworks explode to celebrate the Silver Jubilee, there may be some who reason that in 1977 a hereditary Monarchy is an anachronism. They should reflect that while new miracles of science are revealed each year, new heights of technical ingenuity scaled, and the very chemistry of Man and the Universe exposed to view, the values and virtues of humanity itself remain constant. The cleverest physicists, the ablest computer programmers, the shrewdest experts in electronics have no better brains than did Socrates 2,500 years ago, and certainly no greater wisdom. Nor is the modern individual as self-supporting as circumstances obliged his ancestors to be. The capacity of men and women has been far outpaced by the intricacies of the tools they have constructed. Yet their requirements, whether physical or emotional, remain simple. They look, as much as they ever did, for a comforting and familiar gauge of the permanence which, at heart, all men desire. They look, too, for an emblem of their faith and temporal loyalty, an institution they can admire because it is above dispute and untarnished by corruption.

This is the true mystique of the Crown: not belief in Divine Right, not traditional reverence for an ancient symbol. It is not rash to prophesy that when, in 2002 AD, Queen Elizabeth celebrates her Golden Jubilee, the applauding crowds will be as great, and the cheers as loud as in 1977, and the people will sing, as fervently as they did at the Coronation and do to-day, God Save The Queen.

Index

Acheson, Dean 30
Alexander of Tunis, F. M. Earl 19
Allen, Sir Douglas 91
Amery, Rt. Hon. Julian 38, 183
Amin, President Idi 25, 59-60, 295
Anne, Princess 287
Anne, Queen 15, 78
Armstrong of Sanderstead, Lord 91
Arran, Earl of 229
Ashby, Lord 196
Ashton, Sir Frederick 281
Astor of Hever, 1st Lord 113-14
Attlee, 1st Earl 13, 19, 43-4, 62, 76, 81, 87, 89
Avon, Earl of see Eden
Aylestone, Lord 108-9
Ayub Khan, President 34
Azikwe, President 34, 48

Bacon, Francis 271, 276
Baird, John Logie 106
Balewa, Sir Abubakar 47-8
Balogh, Lord 96
Beatles, the 274-5
Beaver, Sir Hugh 195
Beaverbrook, Lord 111, 114, 227
Beeching, Lord 102
Benn, Rt. Hon. A. Wedgwood 82, 148
Berrill, Sir Kenneth 98
Betjeman, Sir John 275
Bevan, Rt. Hon. Aneurin 62, 118, 252
Beveridge, Lord 89, 252
Bevin, Rt. Hon. Ernest 76, 118
Birmingham, E. W. Barnes, Bishop of 216
Blake, Lord 176
Bonham-Carter, Hon. Mark 294
Bowden, Rt. Hon. Herbert see Aylestone
Braddock, Mrs. Bessie 284
Bragg, Sir Laurence 266

Bragg, Sir William 265
Bridges, 1st Lord 19, 90
Britten, Lord (Benjamin) 277, 279
Brook, Sir Norman 28, 90, 147
Butler of Saffron Walden, Lord 19, 29, 77, 146, 150, 187, 188, 243
Byrne, John 116-17

Cadogan, Sir Alexander 103
Callaghan, Rt. Hon. James 33, 58, 78, 97, 130, 152-3, 187
Cannon, Leslie 117
Canterbury, Donald Coggan, Archbishop of 224
Canterbury, Geoffrey Fisher, Archbishop of 15, 42, 102-3, 212-13, 214
Canterbury, Hewlett Johnson, Dean of 216
Canterbury, Michael Ramsay, Archbishop of 212, 215
Cardigan, 7th Earl of 153
Caro, Anthony 271
Carr of Hadley, Lord 121, 126
Castle, Rt. Hon. Barbara: Secretary of State for Employment, 118-21, 126, 187; for Social Services, 254
Chadwick, Rev. Owen 214-15
Chandos, 1st Viscount 77
Chapple, Frank 117
Chataway, Rt. Hon. Christopher 106
Cherwell, Lord 96, 98
Chichester, Sir Francis 16
Christie, J. 240
Churchill, Sir Winston: as Prime minister, 76-7, 86-7, 89, 115-16, 144-6, 299; on death of George VI, 13-15; foreign policy of, 22-3; on the monarchy, 75; and selection of bishops, 216; mentioned, 26, 27, 43, 67, 83, 96, 98, 103, 104, 107, 148, 249, 303, 307

315

Index

Index

Index

Index